Ghost Ranch

Lesley Poling-Kempes

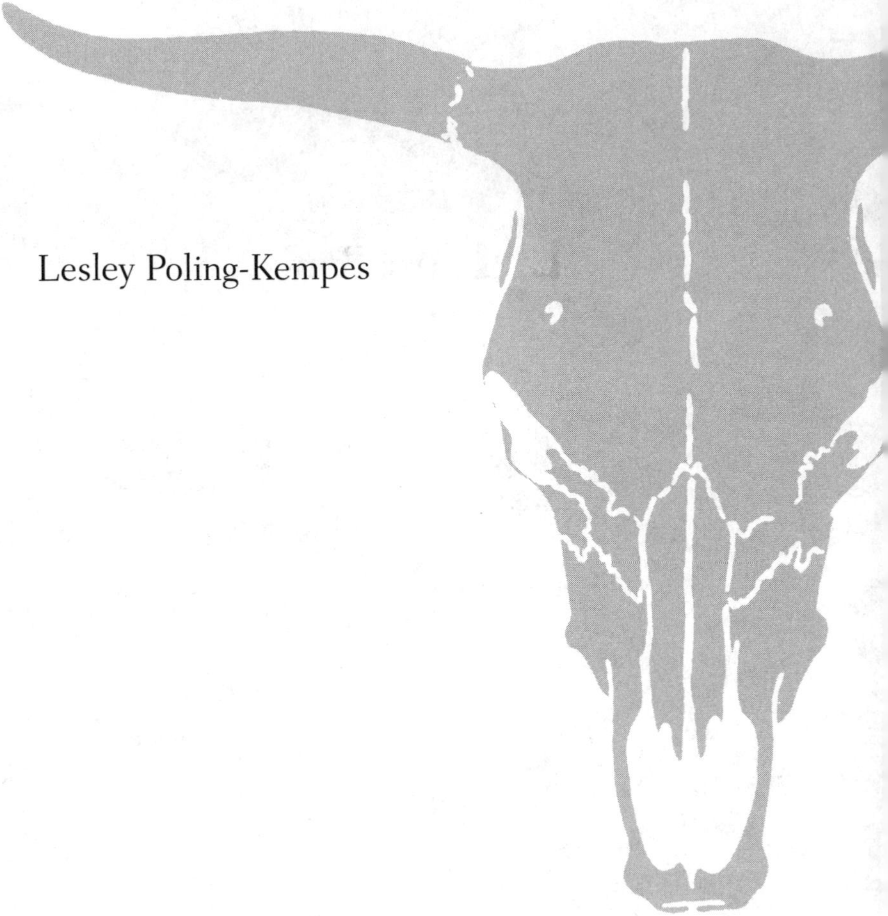

Ghost Ranch

The University of Arizona Press *Tucson*

The University of Arizona Press
www.uapress.arizona.edu

Printed in the United States of America

ISBN-13: 978-0-8165-2346-7 (cloth)
ISBN-13: 978-0-8165-2347-4 (paper)

Cover illustration: Cliffs above the dinosaur quarry at Ghost Ranch, by Jack Parsons.

Library of Congress Cataloging-in-Publication Data
Poling-Kempes, Lesley.
Ghost Ranch / Lesley Poling-Kempes.
p. cm.
Includes bibliographical references and index.
ISBN-13: 978-0-8165-2346-7 (alk. paper)
ISBN-10: 0-8165-2346-0 (alk. paper)
ISBN-13: 978-0-8165-2347-4 (pbk. : alk. paper)
ISBN-10: 0-8165-2347-9 (pbk. : alk. paper)
1. Ghost Ranch (Abiquiu, N.M.)—History. 2. Ghost Ranch (Abiquiu, N.M.)—Biography. 3. Abiquiu Region (N.M.)—History—20th century. 4. Abiquiu Region (N.M.)—Biography. 5. Abiquiu Region (N.M.)—Social life and customs—20th century. 6. Community life—New Mexico—Abiquiu Region—History—20th century. I. Title.
F804.A23P647 2005
978.9'952053—dc22 2005005824

∞ This paper meets the requirements of ANSI/NISO Z39.48-1992 (Permanence of Paper).

This book is dedicated to Arthur and Phoebe Pack,
whose gift opened wide the gate,
and to Jim and Ruth Hall,
who blazed the trail home.

Contents

Illustrations

Preface

In the early 1990s I researched and wrote a book, *Valley of Shining Stone: The Story of Abiquiu*, that wove together the historic events and personal narratives of the region of the Piedra Lumbre (Shining Stone) proper basin and the Chama River Valley near Abiquiú. Although the story of Ghost Ranch—a place that once lay claim to more than thirty thousand acres of the Piedra Lumbre land grant, and that today maintains almost twenty-three thousand acres of that high desert paradise—was told in *Valley of Shining Stone*, that book focused on the wider narrative of the region that the ranch and the Piedra Lumbre have been connected to historically; many stories personal to the place called Ghost Ranch were compressed or simply omitted.

Following publication of *Valley of Shining Stone* it became important to me that the complete story of Ghost Ranch be told. This book is the result of several more years of interviews and research that expanded and enhanced the story begun in *Valley of Shining Stone*. Some stories are retold in this volume, often with information and insight not available when the first book was written: the biography of Juan de Dios Gallegos has been enhanced and definitively corrected with generous input from his daughter, Anna Maria Gallegos Houser, and his grandson, Robert Haozous. And the Johnson & Johnson family's years at Ghost Ranch are herein recounted with personal reminiscences from family members. The memories of David H. McAlpin Jr. shed light on the pre-Ghost Ranch Princeton community of friends that included the Packs, the Johnsons, the Rockefellers, and the McAlpins, helping to explain how and why each of these families ended up as summer neighbors on the high desert of New Mexico. The stories of several personalities—Carol Bishop Stanley, Arthur Newton Pack, Edwin H. Colbert, and others—will be familiar to readers of the first book. But it was my intention and hope that characters and events introduced in

Valley of Shining Stone would be fleshed out and understood in more detail and depth in this volume. And deservedly so: Ghost Ranch has attracted people of enormous energy and creativity for more than a century, and in this book they are given their due.

This book stands on its own, and it is not necessary for readers to have read *Valley of Shining Stone*. However, if the reader wants to understand Ghost Ranch and the Piedra Lumbre's historic and geographic relationship to the wider region of northern New Mexico, I heartily recommend a reading of the previous volume.

Acknowledgments

The biography of Ghost Ranch comprises the stories, memories, myths, and legends lived, recounted, remembered, and shared by the following individuals: Tomás Atencio, Carolyn Barford, Richard Barr, Edward H. Bennett Jr., Janet Biddle, Karl Bode, Derek Bok, Chad and Joan Boliek, Martha Cox Boyle, Dale Brubaker, Cirrelda Snider Bryant, Maria Chabot, Mark Chalom, Kathy Chilton, Betty Colbert, Edwin H. Colbert, Margaret Mathew Colbert, Kathy Conner, Helen Crofford, Jimmy Crofford, John Crosby, John Dancy, Joe Dempsey, Tom Dozier, Florence Hawley Ellis, John Fife, Jessie Fitzgerald, Joe Fitzgibbon, Dorthy Burnham Fredericks, Toby Gallegos, Carl Glock, Sara Haber, James Wallace Hall, James William Hall, Jon F. Hall, Ruth Hall, Tim Hall, Jane Hanna, Jane Harris, Will T. Harris, John Hayden, Diedre Hessel, Eleanor Brown Hibben, Frank C. Hibben, Thad Holcombe, Pomona Hollenbeck, Vic Jameson, Janet Johnson, Larry Johnson, Peter Johnson, Seward Johnson III, Robert H. Kempes, Father Robert Kirsh, Yvonne H. Kyle, John LeVan, Dean Lewis, Eleanor Pack Liddell, Anne Morrow Lindbergh, Bill Mackey, Carol Mackey, Debbie Manzanares, Irene B. Martinez, Molly Martinez, Rebecca Martinez, David McAlpin II, Sally McAlpin, Henry McKinley, Peggy Pack McKinley, Wayne McKinley, Dave and Kathy Morrison, Carol Neely, Anne B. Noss, Ronald P. Olowin, Aubrey Owen, Phoebe Pack, Vernon Pack, Earl B. Parker, Henry Peabody, Willie Picaro, David and Ann Poling, John Purdy, Mary Purdy, Robert Radnitz, Vadis Woolsey Robshaw, Janet Russek, Teresa Archuleta Sagel, Gary B. Salazar, Joe I. Salazar, David Scheinbaum, Elizabeth Bartlett Seals, Jim and Judy Shibley, Dave Sholin, Carl Soderberg, Peggy Terrell, Jim Thorpe, Floyd Trujillo, Rosie Trujillo, Virgil Trujillo, Uvaldo Velasquez, Maria Varella, Linda Watts, Samuel Welles, Richard Wells, Ann Breese White, Roger White, Quentin Wilson, and Elaine Johnson Wolde.

Henry Peabody brought to light Carol Bishop Stanley's account book and guest notebook, and in doing so, opened doors to Stanley's story that had been closed for decades. Thank you to Henry, and to Troy and Marilyn Peabody.

The Pack family story could not have been written with such candid detail had it not been for the enthusiasm and attention given the project over many years by Arthur's children, Peggy, Norrie, and Vernon; and by Henry and Wayne McKinley.

The story of Edwin H. Colbert and the importance of the Coelophysis quarry at Ghost Ranch were greatly enhanced by interviews with David Gillette, Museum of Northern Arizona; Adrian Hunt, New Mexico Museum of Natural History; and Robert M. Hunt, University of Nebraska, Lincoln. Alex Downs, curator of the Ruth Hall Museum of Paleontology, was invaluable to my understanding of the fossil story of the Piedra Lumbre and shared with me the field notes of Dr. Charles Camp, held at U. C. Berkeley, which contained a rich deposit of Ghost Ranch stories. A decade ago, I corresponded with Sam Welles, who sent me a copy of his Piedra Lumbre field notes from the early 1930s, further enriching my understanding of those wondrous early days of fossil digging at Ghost Ranch.

Cheryl Muceus, director and curator of the Florence Hawley Museum of Anthropology, gave immeasurable help in my research and understanding of the story of the early archaeology programs of Ghost Ranch and placed these efforts into the greater story of Southwestern archaeology. Mary Purdy described with vivid detail what those first archaeology digs were like from the ground up.

Edgar W. Davy, Ghost Ranch librarian, once again cheerfully endured the temporary but lengthy disappearance of dozens of often-rare books from his fine library collection for the duration of this project. Every author should have such a trusting and patient librarian!

Barbara Buhler Lynes, curator of the Georgia O'Keeffe Museum, and Eumie Imm-Stroukoff, librarian and archives manager of the Georgia O'Keeffe Museum Research Center, offered invaluable research guidance, scholarly advice, and contextual information about O'Keeffe's life at Ghost Ranch. A thousand thanks for their generous help over several years! And Abiquiú neighbor Judy Lopez, of the Georgia O'Keeffe Foundation, has always kept me on the right track. Thank you, Pita!

Carl Schafer and Mac Schafer introduced me to members of the Seward Johnson family, who added a dimension to the Ghost Ranch–Johnson story that has too long been absent. Many thanks to Seward Johnson Jr. and his sister Elaine Wolde for sharing their family's personal reminiscences.

Anna Maria Gallegos Houser and her son, Bob Haozous, shared their memories of Juan de Dios Gallegos and helped to correct the record, or lack thereof, of her father and his grandfather! Many thanks!

Susan E. Perry, senior library assistant at the Ryerson and Burnham Libraries of the Art Institute of Chicago, located pertinent diaries of Edward H. Bennett held in the Edward H. Bennett Collection and graciously sent copies for my perusal.

Al Bredenberg generously shared his research about Natalie Curtis Burlin and Carol Bishop Stanley and introduced me to important historical connections for both women.

The New England Conservatory of Music lent valuable help in locating Carol Bishop Stanley in photographs and school records. And Dona Bolding knocked on library and historical society doors in Boston searching for clues and information about Stanley and her family's Massachusetts roots.

Publication usage of the photographs by Ansel Adams of Georgia O'Keeffe and Ghost Ranch were generously donated by the Ansel Adams Trust.

Fred Lynes shared his photographs of Cary Grant and Georgia O'Keeffe from his visit to Ghost Ranch in 1952. And Janet Jepson Biddle pulled out her photo album from the 1930s and copied and shared numerous, wonderful pictures of her summer at Ghost Ranch. Thanks to both of you!

Kent Bowser spent dozens of hours in the darkroom reprinting old photographs and untold hours out in the field capturing new photographs of the ranch landscape. You're the real thing, Kent!

Mi amigo David Manzanares granted me access to his insider's collection of photographs from various movie shoots at Ghost Ranch. You make it look easy, David!

Rebecca Collinsworth, archivist, and her staff at the Los Alamos Historical Museum assisted me in my search for clues and facts about Carol Bishop Stanley Pfaffle Miller in the Peggy Pond Church Collection. Those dusty boxes held a historical gold mine!

Leatrice Armstrong, of the Wheelwright Museum of the American Indian, unearthed pertinent legal and financial documents from the 1920s that gave me a better understanding of the demise of San Gabriel Ranch; and my thanks to everyone at the Wheelwright Museum of the American Indian for their generosity and helpfulness over many years.

The oral histories that became the foundation for much of this book were collected for more than a decade. The Ghost Ranch History Project was initiated in 1988 by Ghost Ranch Conference Center director Dr. James W. Hall; the project continued under Hall's successor, the Reverend Joseph Keesecker, in the early 1990s. The history project was revived again in 2002 as the 50th Anniversary History Project, with support and endorsement from Ghost Ranch executive director Reverend Rob Craig and the Ghost Ranch Governance Board. I am indebted to the directors of Ghost Ranch for their encouragement and enthusiasm for the history project that culminated in this book.

Thanks to my project consultation committee—Joan Boliek, Rob Craig, Jan Doak, Cheryl Muceus, Jean Richardson, and Barbara Schmidtzinsky.

Members of the National Ghost Ranch Foundation (NGRF) offered continued support and encouragement for this project. And Mary Martinez, NGRF coordinator, cheerfully lent a hand, tracking down addresses and phone numbers of individuals associated with Ghost Ranch.

Generous contributions to the 50th Anniversary History Project at Ghost Ranch made the oral history collection, the photo collection, and the writing of this book possible. I am forever grateful to the support given by Richard Barr, Chad and Joan Boliek, Howard and Marian Bonebrake, Pat Brandenburg, Donald and Margaret Brown, Dale Brubaker, Mary Ann Bumgarner, Helen and Jim Crawford, Edgar Davy, Joseph Dempsey, Michelle Francis, Robert S. Gee, Jane Hanna, Diedre Hessel, Jan and Ted Koeberle, Henry and Peggy McKinley, H. Clayton Neel, Vernon Pack, David and Ann Poling, John C. and Mary Purdy, John L. Rust, Lindell Sawyers, Lloyd Smith, and Carolyn and Fred Swearingen.

Sizable financial support was given to the project by Presbyterian Health Care Services, Albuquerque, New Mexico; from Kerry Rice and the Volunteers in Mission Office of the Presbyterian Church,

Louisville, Kentucky; and from the Jim and Ruth Hall Humanities Fund. *Muchas gracias* to each of these organizations!

Barbara Schmidtzinsky, the Ghost Ranch archivist, became my partner in research and shared with me the starts and stops involved with tracking down and uncovering the stories of the past. Her knowledge of Ghost Ranch's history is remarkable, and her passion for preservation contagious. Barbara, may all your folders be acid-free, and may your tireless, humble, and often solitary effort to create a professional, user-friendly Ghost Ranch archive receive the recognition and praise it and you so richly deserve!

My friend Terry Evans embodies the perfection of the morning in her creative endeavors and reminds me to continually aspire to do the same with my own work. My parents have cheered me on through years of often overwhelming work. And my home- and heart-mates Jim, Chris, and Mari Kempes live the high desert wonder with me each day. I love you all.

The skull motif used in this book is based on a drawing by Georgia O'Keeffe given to Arthur N. Pack by the artist in the mid-1930s. In 1971, with O'Keeffe's blessing, this skull was officially adopted as the symbol of the Ghost Ranch Conference Center. It is used here with the generous permission of Ghost Ranch, Abiquiú, New Mexico.

Ghost Ranch

Introduction

I began to see, in the place of emptiness, presence. I began to see not only the visible landscape but the invisible one, a landscape in which history, unrecorded and unremembered as it is, had transmuted itself into an always present spiritual dimension. —SHARON BUTALA[1]

This is the story of a place called Ghost Ranch. The physical boundaries of the place encompass about twenty-two thousand acres of the high desert of the Piedra Lumbre basin of northern New Mexico. The ethereal space of Ghost Ranch is larger, and higher, and includes the boundless, wordless world that exists above, below, and within this place. It is a place of great emptiness, a place that is "more sky than earth," a place of vivid color, voluptuous proportion, and vast distances.[2]

Within the sky and earth of Ghost Ranch the world of humans is given its proper perspective in the scheme of the universe. But even as the land diminishes people, within the landscape of Ghost Ranch people also find a connection to the infinite in ways that profoundly and permanently change their sense of interior and exterior scale, of the present and the past, the before and the hereafter.

The name, Ghost Ranch, acknowledges both the brightest and the darkest threads of the place's real and imagined history. Over a century, the place at Yeso Canyon underwent transformation from el Rancho de los Brujos, the Ranch of the Witches, a stone and sand-land hideout associated with legendary evildoers, to Ghost Ranch, a spirited, magical sanctuary where the veil between the realms of heaven and earth seems to be so thin as to be transparent.

But what is a *place* and how does one qualify to become one? According to Wallace Stegner, a place becomes a *place* when it meets two criteria: "First, things that have happened upon it are remembered in history, ballads, yarns, legends, or monuments; and second, it has had that human attention that at its highest reach we call poetry."[3]

The land itself is a monument to the earth's natural beauty and needs nothing more to assure its inclusion among legendary places. In the last hundred or so years, things began to happen upon this land as a good deal of living by sometimes spectacular overachievers has happened at Ghost Ranch. There have been numerous yarns told and a handful of ballads sung about the place over the years. And plenty of poetry both marginal and memorable has been written about Ghost Ranch. As for human attention at its highest reach, the place was the love of artist Georgia O'Keeffe's life, and her passion for this landscape, rendered with paint on canvas over half a century, catapulted Ghost Ranch into international recognition as a Great Place.

Ghost Ranch and the Piedra Lumbre basin, which the ranch claims one-third of, surely qualify as an Intimate Immensity—Gaston Bachelard's name for those bright edges of the natural world that merge within their landscape a sense of shelter and exposure, enclosure and expansion. Places of Intimate Immensity are high places of extraordinary beauty, but they are also landscapes of paradox: universal and personal, dangerous and comforting, temporal and transcendent.

The Four Corners region of the American Southwest is rich with these deeply wild, untouched places. Most are inaccessible or pose so many obstacles that people never come to know them. Herein is one of Ghost Ranch's rare qualities: at least in modern times, it is an Intimate Immensity within reach of common folks. People of all physical abilities, ages, and experience levels can step into the ranch's immense desert, canyon, and cliff country and know, intimately, the magic that exists in a pristine landscape.

Ghost Ranch is a place that cannot be understood in a glance. Distance is deceptive here, near and far difficult to ascertain. It is a raw, exposed country with sparse vegetation, where the contours of the land are still and always in erosive transformation. One senses an ancient story here, in the ground and the sky, and a long history held in the sand and stones about those who have known this land before.

If George Sibley is correct, and "geography only becomes a place when some set of humans becomes all bound up with it in some way," then the story of Ghost Ranch is inevitably tangled up with the story of the people who have become all bound up with it.[4] O'Keeffe was not the first, but she is inarguably the most famous. She called the high desert under the Cliffs of Shining Stone the Faraway, and from her adobe house on the vast, wide badlands of Ghost Ranch, proclaimed Cerro Pedernal, the narrow-shouldered, flat-topped, indigo blue mountain that lives across the basin to the south, her private mountain.

When O'Keeffe fell in love with the mountain, it already had a long history of relationships, especially with women of power: Changing Woman of the Navajo, myth remembers, was found wrapped in colored lights on Pedernal's knife-thin summit; and when Spider Woman of the Jicarilla Apaches emerged onto the earth, she looked out across the creation landscape at Pedernal's enigmatic profile.

The Piedra Lumbre is the gateway, literally and figuratively, to the great Colorado Plateau. The landscape of northern New Mexico takes a dramatic geologic shift as it moves north and west away from the Indio-Hispanic village of Abiquiú. Five miles up the Chama River from the mesa-top pueblo, the surface of the earth lifts five hundred feet into the sky and opens onto the one-hundred-square-mile basin of the Piedra Lumbre. The land sheds the characteristics of the Rio Grande Rift and takes on the rugged, dramatic, oversized qualities of the Colorado Plateau. Everything that is to come to the west and north in the Four Corners country is found on the Piedra Lumbre on a smaller scale: deep eroded canyons; wind- and rain-chiseled buttes and spires; multihued sand lands; sheer, variegated cliffs; and a sky that dwarfs it all. Even the light changes on the plateau—perhaps it is the altitude and the transparency of the thin air; or maybe it is the intensity of the heat and the sudden proximity of the sun and the universe hovering above in the clouds. Whatever *it* is, it gives a mythic sense to the physical and a tangible sense to the transcendent.

The land of Ghost Ranch encompasses the northern third of the Piedra Lumbre Land Grant, its southern boundary along what was once the course of the Chama River, now inundated by the reservoir behind Abiquiú Dam, and its northern boundary following the rim of the great cliffs of stone that shine at sundown. The land is the first story. Who has come, and what they have and have not done here, has been shaped, always, by the topography of the Piedra Lumbre. Historic and prehistoric Native Americans—Tewa, Navajo, Ute, Apache—set up hunting camps under these cliffs on the northern edge of the basin because there was a perennial source of water. But their time on this arid plateau was always seasonal. The first Spanish family to maintain a permanent home on what became Ghost Ranch—the Gallegos at their Arroyo Seco Ranch—survived for several decades in the early 1800s on the year-round trickle from the Rito del Yeso that irrigated crops and a kitchen garden.

Life on the Piedra Lumbre hovers around water. Beyond the narrow, glistening wet bed of the Yeso stream unfolds an enormous sand land, badland country, beautiful but unforgiving. Only the strongest desert dwellers survive here—cholla, yucca, and prickly pear cactus, juniper and pinion, scruffy grasses that come and go with the cycles of drought and rain. Rain is a rare event—the Piedra Lumbre receives ten inches in a very good year—and when it comes, it can be in a torrential, destructive fashion, sweeping away whatever is in its path.

Until the 1930s, the place under the northern edge of the Piedra Lumbre basin was a natural beauty to be experienced only in passing. Living here for any length of time was a hardship until modern conveniences like electrical generators and automobiles, refrigeration and airplanes made the extreme isolation on the high desert less life threatening. The story of people here had an ominous beginning and literally gave the place a bad name. And the ensuing relationship between Ghost Ranch and its various owners became adversarial for a few decades.

This book is about a place and its people: the story of the land is as old as the earth here, but the story of the people is relatively new. This narrative focuses on those who made the cliff country of Ghost Ranch into a beloved, almost otherworldly home—the people who came to Ghost Ranch from the late 1800s until the late 1900s. In the early years, when the ranch was a dude ranch, there were only a few who called Ghost Ranch home. After 1955, and Arthur Pack's gift of the ranch to the Presbyterian Church, Ghost Ranch became, if not the year-round home, the spiritual and emotional home for hundreds, if not thousands, of people. Beginning in 1955, a community of people sprung up upon the land of Ghost Ranch. Many are Presbyterians; just as many are not. This is a community bound not by religious affiliation or denomination, but by land—by a common understanding that Ghost

Ranch is a special, if not sacred, place in their lives and in the life of the earth.

This book focuses on the individuals who created modern Ghost Ranch, and whose lives and choices made the place at Yeso Canyon into the community on the desert that it is today. The central character is Ghost Ranch itself. Ghost Ranch, like all large, undeveloped, undivided, pristine swatches of glorious land, is an endangered species worthy of continual protection and watchfulness. It has been blessed thus far with watchful, even remarkable, owners. Perhaps knowledge of the place's history will reinforce future owners' defense of Ghost Ranch as an owned but honored wilderness.

In 1955, when Ghost Ranch was reinvented as an educational center of the Presbyterian Church, its story went public. Thousands of people discovered Ghost Ranch. Fortunately, the immensity of the place, and the care given to protect its land and its character, have preserved the land's sense of intimacy. In the twenty-first century, people are still awestruck by the silence, the clarity, and size of the Ghost Ranch landscape. In a world running at a high-tech pace, where the connection between humans and the earth is all but severed by the noise and bustle endemic to urban living, people find a part of themselves, of their spirit, is reawakened and given voice in the monumental stillness under the Piedra Lumbre cliffs. People are changed by Ghost Ranch.

The desert has always provoked and invited personal reflection and spiritual contemplation, and the landscape of Ghost Ranch offers these transforming opportunities in an almost biblical proportion.

"It's difficult to talk about Ghost Ranch in a few words," a magazine editor once said. "You end up sounding like an advertisement for God and New Mexico. But then, maybe that's what Ghost Ranch really is."[5]

One The Road to Ghost Ranch

Led by the exigencies of my profession, by feminine curiosity, or merely by the determination not to be left at home, I have been shaken, thrown, bitten, sunburned, rained on, shot at, stone bruised, frozen, broiled and scared with monotonous regularity. —MARY ROBERTS RINEHART[1]

The high desert corner embraced on three sides by the variegated cliffs on the northern edge of the Piedra Lumbre basin was known as Yeso Canyon by the 1800s. Named for el Rito del Yeso, the spring-fed perennial stream that cuts a deep course in a sliver-thin canyon, the Little River of the Gypsum emerges from the stone walls of a box canyon hidden at the southern foot of the Canjilon—Deer Horn—Mountains. The rito seeps out of fifty-foot-high walls and trickles across the floor of a secret, damp, shadowed place called T'ibuhu'u by the Tewa people of San Juan Pueblo. When broken into its ancient etymological parts—T'i, a winter dance; bu'u, in a large, low, roundish place; hu'u, of a large groove or arroyo—the native place-name gives clues to Box Canyon's ceremonial persona.[2]

The stream meanders away from its stone birthplace down a slender gorge edged by hundred-foot-high ledges where eagles and peregrine falcons nest. From the mesa country above the cliffs, the glistening three-sided canyon and its liquid treasure are invisible until they are directly underfoot. In winter, the walls of the box change from stone to ice, from dark to light. The bottom of the canyon carved by the Rito del Yeso is a lush, moist microcosm in the otherwise arid high desert plateau of the Piedra Lumbre: thick grass, ponderosas, deciduous trees, and wildflowers have thrived along its course for centuries, and the hidden canyon and cliff country are home to deer, bear, raccoons, bobcats, hawks, coyotes, turkeys, rattlesnakes, and mountain lions.

The Rito del Yeso reaches the wide-open space of the Piedra Lumbre five miles across the plateau from the Chama River. Unless it swells with spring snowmelt, or floods in a summer thunderstorm, the Yeso stream rarely reaches the Chama: it trickles across sandbars and down through smooth boulder chutes, through cottonwood and elm groves, finally out into the badlands, where it disappears in the heat of summer, its precious water sucked up by the cedar and pinion trees, the cactus and spindly grasses, or pilfered by the sky through evaporation into the thin, parched air.

The Rito del Yeso is why we are here. Only a perpetual, unfailing, drought-resistant source of water could bring people to live on this sand land under the cliffs. Without the spring, this corner of the New Mexican high desert would not have included humans in its story.

People came here to stay in the late 1800s, when the flat, sage-covered lands at the mouth of Yeso Canyon were claimed by two Archuleta brothers. They built two jacal dwellings—primitive structures with walls made of cedar poles set stockade style and filled with adobe mud and straw mortar—at the foot of a mesa enclosed by the cliffs on three sides. The homestead was virtually invisible from the wagon road that crossed the basin east to west. The nearest village of any size or authority was Abiquiú, a fifteen-mile ride over rugged terrain that included several precipitous miles on the cliff-hugging road through the Chama Canyon. The Archuletas' nearest neighbors were in Cañones, a hamlet nestled in a spring-fed canyon at the foot of Cerro Pedernal, ten miles across the river to the south.

The Rito del Yeso homestead had everything industrious *pobladores* needed to build a successful farm or ranch. However, the Archuletas were not looking to be successful pioneers. The *hermanos* were aspiring cattle rustlers, and in the natural corral formed by the Piedra Lumbre cliffs at Yeso Canyon they saw the perfect location in which to develop their rustling empire. With little or no fencing, cattle could be persuaded to remain hidden under the cliffs, tucked away in the canyon where there was water and shade. There was only one entrance to their hideout—from the llanos to the south and west. Approaching riders, uninvited intruders all, could be seen coming in from the badlands by their dust trail or by their profile against the horizon.

The brothers and the ruffians who rode with them scouted for herds on the vast, lonely, far-from-town ranges of northern New Mexico and

An aerial photograph of the Ghost Ranch cliffs taken by Ted Bennett in 1935.

southern Colorado. They stole cattle by subterfuge and/or confrontation and then moved them through the outback to their Yeso Canyon holding pen. Buyers were not difficult to find, and, after payment in gold coin was obtained, the herd was moved by night from the Piedra Lumbre to its new home.

It did not take long for the local ranchers to become suspicious about the brothers' cattle operation, especially given the way the home herd was moved in and out in the middle of the night. But New Mexico was a wild, mostly lawless territory in the late 1800s, and people in the Chama Valley left the Archuletas to themselves. They were unfriendly and gruff, ill mannered and defensive. The brothers were soon called Los Animales, the animals, by their neighbors, and even the members of their extended family rode a wide berth around the Archuletas of the Rito del Yeso homestead.

The persona of Yeso Canyon might have been burdened throughout history with nothing worse than the slightly romantic stigma attached to all places once claimed by thieves, robbers, and socially upsetting ne'er-do-wells—a Hispanic New Mexican equivalent of Wyoming's Hole in the Wall—except that the Archuletas' plan for invisibility failed, and they were forced to become murderers to protect their investment.

A few travelers passing through the valley, newcomers uninformed about the place's sinister reputation, stopped in at the dwellings under the cliffs for water, shelter, and frontier hospitality. They were never seen among the living again. However, their saddles and bridles, boots, rifles, and chaps *were* seen among the living, adorning the men and horses of the Archuleta gang. Stories began to circulate in the local communities about missing persons, about bodies being thrown down into a well, about cries and whispers echoing into the night from the cliffs near Yeso Canyon, spooking shepherds camped along the Chama River. And thus, the beautiful, spacious Rito del Yeso country was transformed in a few short years into an evil shadow land inhabited by murderers and thieves, and by the disgruntled ghosts of the murdered that haunted them. The place at Yeso Canyon was soon renamed el Rancho de los Brujos—the Ranch of the Witches.

Stories of Los Animales's heinous deeds and bloody dealings were told and retold by northern New Mexican ranchers and villagers in the 1890s. Everyone from Abiquiú to Coyote, south to Española and north to Tierra Amarilla believed the brothers were getting away with murder, but no one wanted to confront them and their gang up in their cursed canyon.

One of the Archuletas had a wife and daughter living with him in his jacal cabin. The wife's people were from San Juan Pueblo, but she was rarely allowed to leave the homestead to visit them. The daughter, who returned years later to visit the canyon and to tell this story, although raised in the bright landscape below Cerro Pedernal, lived in a world darkened by the superstition and fear encouraged and perpetuated by her uncle and her father.

The wife and daughter were prisoners of both the brothers and the spirits of the country. The daughter was told by her father and uncle to be watchful of the "earth babies"—six-foot-long, humanlike beasts covered with red hair—that emerged from the sand under the cliffs and howled like abandoned babies in the dark. There was also a resident witch that had taken the form of a cow and flew down the canyon and out across the llanos at dusk. The young girl was warned that all who witnessed a flyby of this winged bovine died soon after.

Orphan Mesa and the badlands at Ghost Ranch.

The most fearful spirit of the Yeso homestead was Vivaron. Seen only at sunset, this serpent *brujo* was a thirty-foot rattlesnake that lived under Mesa Huerfano, Orphan Mesa, a steep-sided butte that stood alone in the red sand lands southeast of the homestead.

With so much danger lurking just beyond the homestead's door stoop, the young Archuleta girl stayed close to home by day and never went outside after sundown.

It seems befitting that a brotherly misunderstanding, intensified by a well-deserved distrust of each other, ultimately ended the Archuletas' reign of terror at Yeso Canyon. One brother had delivered cattle to a buyer and, upon his return to the *ranchito*, told his hermano that for security purposes he had deposited the payment—gold coins—in an *olla* (ceramic jar) and buried it in a nearby hillside. The second Archuleta brother did not trust the first brother's intentions and demanded he produce the gold. A fight broke out, and before the location of the olla was revealed, the second brother had killed the first brother.

The surviving brother-murderer placed his hopes for retrieval of his gold on the mother and daughter: certain that his sister-in-law knew where her husband had hidden the payment, he told her she had twenty-four hours to produce it without consequences. If she did not, he would take the daughter and feed her to Vivaron.

It seems uncharacteristically trusting of the remaining Archuleta brother, but he left the mother and daughter alone and unattended in their dwelling that night. Perhaps he drank himself into an early evening stupor; or perhaps he believed the brujos were adequate guards of his hostages. But the mother and daughter overcame their fear of both the drunken brother and the spirits and stole out of the canyon on a burro. They rode all night down through the Chama Valley and, by morning, had reached the safety of a relative's home at San Juan Pueblo.

With only one brother and a few of his *hombres* remaining at the Yeso Canyon ranch, a posse of local men gathered their courage and raided the Archuleta hideout. They hanged the brother and what was left of his gang from the branches of the cottonwood tree that grew beside one of the casitas. They did not look for the hidden olla of gold coins, nor did they poke about the mesa sides or peer down into the well bottom for bones and bodies. Instead, the windows and doors of the brothers' casitas were boarded over and bolted closed, and Yeso

Canyon and this corner of the Piedra Lumbre under the cliffs were abandoned by the living.

In the first decades of the twentieth century, various sheep and cattle ranchers attempted to run their herds on the Piedra Lumbre's rangeland near the well-watered canyon. But the *maleficio* of the past held the beautiful badlands within its grip. Good grass and plenty of shade and water were to be found along el Rito del Yeso, but for the next twenty years no rancher in his right mind sent his herds to el Rancho de los Brujos. Shepherds followed flocks of sheep across the llanos to the southwest of the cliffs, but those who camped too close to the old ranchito of the Archuletas risked attracting the attention of the resident ghosts and witches whose whimpers and wails, whispers and erratic movements spooked people and livestock alike.

In 1918, a descendant of the notorious brothers, Juan Ignacio (Jose) Archuleta, filed for a homestead patent on the Rito del Yeso. In spite of the place's less-than-inviting reputation, Juan Ignacio and his wife must have realized the potential value of the property now legally recognized as Homestead Entry Survey (HES) No. 127. They did not move onto the homestead's 152.9 plated acres, but sold it to a local *rico*, Miguel Gonzales, in 1921. Gonzales lived in a grand hacienda on the Plaza Colorado grant near Abiquiú and was the owner of the village mercantile. Gonzales boasted the valley's largest sheep and cattle herds—his sheep numbered 150,000 animals in fifteen different sheep camps—and he already owned a large portion of the Piedra Lumbre grant adjacent to the Archuleta homestead.

Don Miguel gave the ghost stories little heed, and after acquiring the Ranch of the Witches, sent his *vaquero* to run cattle in the desert country under the cliffs. The hired cowboy told Don Miguel he was not afraid of the canyon's spirits and that he would live comfortably in the old homestead. But two weeks later, when Gonzales visited Yeso Canyon, he found his heretofore audacious employee living in a tent a good distance from the jacal dwelling.

"I could not stand the noises in the house," the young man told his boss. "All night I would hear a man and woman quarreling. . . . People tell me that a man and woman lived in the house all alone. They quarreled a great deal, and one day the woman disappeared. The man went away and has never been heard from since."[3]

Over the years there were numerous more encounters between the

Piedra Lumbre's cowboys and shepherds and the evil spirits of Yeso Canyon. By 1928, Gonzales had sold HES 127 to Alfredo Salazar, a sheep rancher who made his home in Cañones. Like Gonzales, Salazar had no intention of living at Yeso Canyon. In fact, Salazar cared so little for the brujo-burdened homestead that someone in his family was willing to risk losing the deed to the place in a poker game.

The precise details of this card game, like the olla of gold coins, are lost to modern memory in the sands of the Piedra Lumbre. Never recorded, the story of the fateful poker game between one Roy Pfaffle and a member of the Salazar family during which the deed for the Rito del Yeso changed hands, was passed along, told and retold over decades until fact, fable, myth, and history merged. Everyone seems to agree that it did, in fact, happen. Where it happened, who played, even the exact month and year of the game, were not deemed important enough to retell with the retelling. All anyone is certain of is that, in or around 1927 or early 1928, one Richard LeRoy Pfaffle of Alcalde, New Mexico, won a game of cards and walked away from the table with the deed to the homestead at Yeso Canyon.

Roy Pfaffle returned to his home at San Gabriel Ranch on the Rio Grande in the village of Alcalde, where he handed the deed to his wife, Carol Bishop Stanley. Stanley carried the deed to the courthouse in Tierra Amarilla and recorded HES 127 in her name on May 18, 1929. And at that time, the story of the place called the Ranch of the Witches took a turn into a narrative and a future that was to be the antithesis of its recent past.

Exactly what the middle-aged New Englander Carol Stanley knew in the late 1920s about the homestead's dark past can only be guessed. Stanley had traveled through the Piedra Lumbre dozens of times since her arrival in the Southwest before World War I, and she was surely privy to the legends of the canyon. But whatever Stanley had heard did not seem to lessen her appreciation of the place. And, except for good shade from the old cottonwood trees and the basic creature comforts afforded a desert abode that has a perennial source of water, the place at Yeso Canyon did not offer much in material amenities: only one of the two Archuleta casitas was standing, and it seemed to be well on its way back to the earth it was made from. The walls had begun to settle, every doorway was crooked, the cedar-stick ceilings were low, and the movements of mice sent dirt sifting down into the tiny rooms below.

But every window framed a spectacular view of the red and gold buttes and badlands, and to the south the line of the horizon was graced by the distinctive profile of Cerro Pedernal.

It seems an unlikely place for a newly divorced woman to go looking for a new start in life, but in 1931, following the breakup of her marriage to Pfaffle, and the collapse of their guest ranch in Alcalde, Carol Bishop Stanley packed up all that she owned, which included a Steinway grand piano and a Navajo rug collection, and with her English maid, Alice, moved into the ramshackle Archuleta homestead built nearly half a century before. With the arrival of this Boston expatriate, the Ranch of the Witches began its transformation from a feared haunt of disgruntled ghosts and nasty brujos to the beloved, faraway place called Ghost Ranch.

Stanley would own Ghost Ranch for only seven years and would be a full-time inhabitant of the place for just five. Yet without Stanley's bold move to the abandoned homestead in the high desert country beneath the shining cliffs, modern Ghost Ranch would most likely have never come to pass. Stanley's remarkable journey to the Piedra Lumbre is worth retracing because who she was, and who she knew and what they cared for, shaped the persona of Ghost Ranch for at least the next half-century. Her successors would build Ghost Ranch into the high-profile destination that it is today, but Stanley blazed the trail that enabled them to come here at all.

Stanley had been born and raised in upper-class Massachusetts and, by the 1930s, had traveled many times into the deep wild country of the Four Corners by horseback, buggy, and automobile. The primitive desert outback of New Mexico like what was found at Yeso Canyon had become the world Carol Stanley felt most at home in. Only the highs and the lows of Stanley's biography remain. Even what is known about Stanley suffers from the subjective coloration of individual memory and the exaggeration common to oral history. Stanley had no children and left no known diary. A handful of her letters offer pieces of her story in New Mexico, but the details of her professional and personal activities in Boston and Chicago before her journey to the Southwest in 1915 are poorly documented.

She was born Caroline Bishop Stanley on December 16, 1879, on Nahant Island, Massachusetts. Her extended family had lived in this colonial fishing community near Boston for generations, and the ex-

Carol Bishop Stanley (second row, right) and the staff of *The Neume* at the New England Conservatory of Music in 1905.

tended Bishop/Stanley familial connections included Cabots, Choates, and Perkinses—the wealthy and influential merchant families of Boston.

Stanley's father was a fisherman and an accountant, and although the family was not so wealthy as to be considered rich, they were prosperous enough to send their twenty-one-year-old daughter Carrie to the New England Conservatory of Music in 1900. Miss Carrie B. Stanley was a pleasant, sturdy-looking brunette, with a direct but unpretentious gaze. She worked on the staff of a literary quarterly, *The Neume*, and studied classical music and piano. When Stanley graduated from the Conservatory in 1905, she was a matronly twenty-five, yet she did what all women graduates did—went home to live with her family, where she sought a position as a music teacher.

Little is known about Stanley's comings and goings from 1905 until her arrival on the Arizona desert in 1915. She lived for some period of time in Boston, and then she took a bold step away from the Stanley household and went to Chicago, where she became involved with the social settlement movement. Stanley taught music at the Chicago Kindergarten Institute and began to move in a circle of educated and socially active women. Inspired and guided by Jane Addams of Chicago's Hull House, the settlement movement was championed by Anglo American women interested in bettering the lives of American immigrants. In her late twenties, Stanley joined this league of women who would later be called progressive idealists—educated, motivated women seeking meaningful work that led them out of a boring and useless existence in Victorian America. These women brought to the immigrant and poor of the settlement houses the belief that the arts were not the sole arena of the privileged. Music, Stanley's friends believed, was a birthright of all people, and music education a vital part of any person's development and growth. Widely held beliefs today, these ideas were hardly accepted and little voiced in the early 1900s.

Stanley's activities from 1905 until 1915 centered around her work as a teacher and a musician in Chicago and Boston, with no dates or exact locations for her sojourns until early 1915. At that time Stanley emerged solidly in the great American Southwest, where she was a guest for an extended period of time at the now-legendary trading post ranch of John and Louisa Wetherill in Kayenta. The explanation given for Stanley's move from what was presumably a comfortable and secure life in bustling industrial America to the undeveloped, exotic, but primitive Southwest had to do with a scuttled engagement. Apparently Carol (she gave up the name "Carrie" after college) Stanley fell in love with a musician, a violinist, in her homeport of Boston. The Stanley family might have been elated that their spinster daughter was finally to marry. Instead, the family viewed the musician an unsuitable suitor for their daughter and, the story goes, sent Stanley west to forget him.

Before World War I, a single Anglo woman who ventured into the Southwest was undertaking a journey on a par with a sojourn into an undeveloped foreign country. No woman would attempt such a trip without ample guidance by someone who knew the country. Stanley was most likely introduced to the Colorado Plateau and to the Wetherills by fellow musician and settlement house advocate Natalie Curtis. Curtis knew the Four Corners region intimately and may have traveled with Stanley by train from Chicago into the Southwest, or she may simply have provided Stanley with introductions.[4]

By 1915, Natalie Curtis had already distinguished herself among those pioneering Anglo Americans who had come into the Southwest to study and preserve the culture, language, and traditions of Native

America. Curtis studied classical music in New York and in Europe, but her professional life took a radical direction during her first visit to Arizona, in 1900. After hearing the songs and chants of the Native Americans, especially the Hopi, Curtis became passionate about music distinctive to the Native, non-white peoples of the world. Curtis made it her personal and professional mission to preserve Native American music. Beginning in 1903, she set up a recording workshop on the desert of the Hopi reservation in northern Arizona. Bedecked in decidedly un-Victorian khaki riding skirt, boots, and a wide-brimmed hat, Curtis carried her notebooks, wax cylinders, and camping gear on horseback and by wagon far into the rugged country of the Colorado Plateau. Curtis earned the trust of numerous Native American tribes (she adopted the Hopi name *Tawi-Mana*, Song Maid) and, in 1905, published her first major book, *Songs of Ancient America*. This was followed by what would become her most important published work, *The Indians' Book*, released in 1907, that included songs and stories from eighteen Native tribes in Arizona, New Mexico, and the Great Plains.[5]

From 1915 until 1917 Stanley went by horseback with Curtis into the Four Corners country at least four times. Theirs was no gentlewomen's sightseeing journey. Riding astride horses was a necessity, and Stanley and all women on the Southwest frontier learned to ride a western saddle in split skirts. Everyone slept on the ground, sometimes in a canvas tent, more often out under the stars. There were sleeping accommodations at trading posts and in government buildings near various Native communities. But these utilitarian, cramped shelters were rarely preferable to a soft stretch of sand in the pinion trees.

Stanley's inaugural trip into the Wetherills' desert outback most likely began at Holbrook or Williams, Arizona, in the fall of 1914, where one or more prearranged guides and cowboys met her train at the Santa Fe depot. The journey to Kayenta and the Wetherill trading post required a week or more on horseback through some of the most remote country in North America. There were a few primitive roads near the Anglo settlements along the railroad and connecting the small communities of miners and ranchers. But the modern, industrial world of Anglo America faded away from these chapped-lipped, dusty-haired, tanned, and trail-tested women as they rode deeper into the Native American world of the Colorado Plateau.

Carol Stanley at a desert campsite in the Four Corners Country in 1924.

Carol Stanley remained for an extended stay at the trading-post home of John and Louisa Wetherill in Kayenta in late 1914 and early 1915. Stanley did not return to Chicago or Boston for more than brief visits after 1915, and the Stanley family was surely more distraught about their daughter's new love—the desert Southwest—than they had ever been about her previous one.

Curtis may have stayed with Stanley at Kayenta also, but the account by Stanley's friend, Mary Cabot Wheelwright, of Stanley's initial visit and subsequent adventures with Louisa Wetherill does not mention Curtis.

> Mrs. Pfaffle [Stanley's later, married name] had come originally to the Southwest to stay with Mr. and Mrs. John Wetherell [*sic*] at Kayenta, Arizona, near the Four Corners, where four states meet, and at that time one of the wildest and most lawless parts of the West. . . . In those days pioneer anthropologists, archaeologists, and others used to stay at the Wetherell [*sic*] ranch, and they were among the first white people to realize the possibilities of studies of the Indians.[6]

At Kayenta, Stanley was amidst members of the royal family of Southwest archaeology. John Wetherill's family was credited with the "discovery" of the cliff dwellings of Mesa Verde in December of 1888. The discovery of the extensive cliff dwellings of Mesa Verde changed the Wetherill family's lives. Although they were amateurs learning the science of archaeology as they went, the Wetherills quickly became the foremost authorities on the locations and extent of the numerous Mesa Verde ruins, and they guided virtually every professional and amateur expedition into this great prehistoric community for the next decade.

During her stay with John and Louisa Wetherill, Stanley was given a glimpse of Native America few white people would ever know. Wheelwright described one of Stanley's adventures with Louisa Wetherill.

> Mrs. Pfaffle, coming straight from the East, had an extraordinary experience there. The federal government wanted to find a certain Ute Indian to try him for some crime. To Mrs. Wetherell [*sic*] an appeal was made to interview him and try to persuade him to give himself up. She took Carol Pfaffle with her and, traveling with horses for days they found the Indian at a Ute ceremony. Mrs. Wetherill persuaded him to come back to Kayenta with her. In telling me about it, Carol Pfaffle gave me an idea of the excitement she had felt in this adventure into the untouched wilderness, where she had met untamed Indians.[7]

The rustic but comfortable Wetherill home on the desert at Kayenta had an indigenous charm and aesthetic that, fifteen years later, Carol Stanley would replicate at the Yeso Canyon homestead on the high desert of the Piedra Lumbre. The simple design and frontier ambiance of the first adobe-and-wood buildings constructed by Stanley at Ghost Ranch owe much to the trading-post home of Louisa Wetherill. At once utilitarian and artistic, and celebrating the distinctive arts and crafts of indigenous America, this architectural and interior decoration style would soon be found replicated in homes across New Mexico and Arizona, and would gain national renown when it was formally recognized as a major design element of Santa Fe style.

In the summer of 1916, Stanley and Curtis were both living in rented rooms near the old plaza of Santa Fe, New Mexico. Stanley, now a seemingly confirmed spinster of thirty-six, was staying in the Hotel De

Vargas; Curtis, nearly forty, was renting rooms in a house on Buena Vista Street, a few blocks away. In the previous year, both Stanley and Curtis had left the Southwest to work and visit friends in Boston, New York, and Chicago. But both women were seeking a permanent home and work situation in New Mexico.

Santa Fe in 1916 was a small, friendly, personable town, and most of the newcomer Anglo Americans knew one another and lived in close proximity to the historic plaza district. Santa Fe was still an undiscovered paradise, a new colony for intellectual and artistic expatriates seeking a homeland untouched by the noise and industry of modern America. There were more horses and wagons than automobiles, and life in the capital city of New Mexico moved at a genteel pace. The Spanish language and traditional customs gave the capital of the new state of New Mexico an Old World European look and feel. Narrow dirt *caminos* led away from the plaza up into the foothills, where a new population of artists, writers, and intellectuals from all over the world were beginning to settle in what they liked to call the City Different. Burros laden with wood ambled along the alleys and streets, and horses were tied to hitching posts on the old plaza, where there were restaurants and eateries, boot and dress shops, and a new cinema.

Painters and writers who would become the nucleus of the Santa Fe artists colony arrived in Santa Fe in 1916, as did archaeologists and anthropologists involved with the excavation and study of the region's numerous prehistoric sites. Although Stanley and Curtis enjoyed the stimulating intellectual and creative environment of Santa Fe, the two women were seeking a home somewhere in the outer spaces of New Mexico. Earlier that year, in the spring of 1916, after a stay in a small, primitive house on the isolated Ramon Vigil Ranch in the Jemez Mountains, the two friends believed that they had found the place in New Mexico where they could set down permanent creative and personal roots.

The Ramon Vigil Ranch was on the remote and archaeologically rich Pajarito Plateau, twenty miles across the Rio Grande Valley from Santa Fe. Bordered on the southeast by the Rio Grande Canyon, this high plateau on the northeastern edge of the Jemez Mountains was a nearly inaccessible region of ponderosa forests, volcanic cliffs, high mesas, and deep canyons. The joint owners of the ranch, four Detroit automobile industrialists and one New Mexican, former Roosevelt Rough

Rider Ashley Pond, were looking for someone to develop and manage their Pajarito Club, a ranch resort they planned to visit several times a year for recreation.

The Ramon Vigil's southern boundary was the north rim of Frijoles Canyon—later Bandelier National Monument. The entire region was second to none in North America in the number and quality of Anasazi sites, many of which were already being excavated by Edgar Hewett, the founding director of the Museum of New Mexico. Stanley and Curtis were friends with the energetic, controversial, domineering, larger-than-life Hewett, who encouraged them to move onto the Ramon Vigil Ranch and develop a cultural center.

During long discussions in their rooms near the heart of old Santa Fe, Stanley and Curtis developed a plan to create a premier guest ranch. They envisioned their resort to include a respected archaeology museum that introduced newcomers to the prehistory of the region. Curtis and Stanley also wanted to display and sell Native arts and crafts. The promotion and sale of Native American art had been undertaken with some success by the Fred Harvey Indian Department at outlets along the Santa Fe Railway. But the Indian arts and crafts industry was new, and there was plenty of commercial room in New Mexico and Arizona for additional establishments that linked the traveling, buying public with the wares of Native artisans.

Neither Curtis, nor more recently Stanley, had "an income of any great amount," Roy Chapin, one of the Detroit owners (and the president of the Hudson Motor Company) wrote his partners, Henry B. Joy (president of the Packard Motor Car Company) and banker/brothers David L. and Paul R. Gray in July 1916. "Miss Stanley had hoped to finance the scheme . . . but she discovered recently that the Executor of her Mother's Estate had dissipated practically all of the funds and she is now in a position where her income is not enough to keep her going and as she puts it very plainly,—she must go to work."[8]

Although the Pajarito owners liked their proposal for a combination guest ranch and cultural center, Stanley and Curtis never moved onto the Ramon Vigil to implement their dream. Curtis struggled with fatigue and illness following a particularly arduous pack trip with Stanley in July that eventually placed Curtis in St. Vincent's Hospital in Santa Fe. Stanley monitored her friend's recovery at the hospital, but Curtis's recuperation was more closely watched by another acquaintance, painter Paul Burlin. Curtis and Burlin had begun to see one another in the summer of 1916, and he was a frequent visitor to Curtis's hospital room that fall. Curtis and Burlin were falling in love, and Carol Stanley would witness their marriage the following summer in Santa Fe.

Curtis's poor health forced her to withdraw from a late-summer expedition with Stanley and a New York friend, painter and musician Dorothy Kent. This journey into the Four Corners country was under the auspices of the newly formed Rocky Mountain Camp Company of Santa Fe. The three-week-long trip by horseback began in mid-September in Santa Fe and wove across northwestern New Mexico and into the Navajo country of the Colorado Plateau. This particular expedition made headlines because no one had ever attempted to ride horseback to the Indian Country of northern Arizona and southern Utah from Santa Fe. Upon their return in October, the *Santa Fe New Mexican* reported the success of this trailblazing adventure, adding that "heretofore it has been the custom of parties desiring to visit those points to outfit either at Gallup or Thoreau."[9]

Stanley understood that this trip could be history in the making, and before they departed Santa Fe, she wrote to Chapin from her room at the Hotel De Vargas. "I leave about the eleventh for a most wonderful trip, which lies about straight west all the 36th parallel from Española to the big Canon del Muerto in Arizona. I am intending there to ride northwest to Farmington New Mexico through those wild mountain trails—then about straight east to Taos, and back to Santa Fe, reaching here about October 3rd."[10]

Stanley urged Roy Chapin and his wife, who were planning a trip to New Mexico, to meet her and her traveling companions at the Fiesta of San Geronimo in Taos in late September. Stanley wrote Chapin, "We hope to get there, but are not sure we can as neither I nor anyone I know has ever covered the country through which we intend to return."[11]

If Chapin made it to Taos, Stanley never met up with him. On October 2 in Gallup, New Mexico, with Dorothy Kent as her witness, Stanley married one of the guides, Richard LeRoy Pfaffle. Kent and the horses, gear, and guides of the expedition headed back to Santa Fe, but the new Mr. and Mrs. Pfaffle headed out for a honeymoon camping trip.

The union certainly shocked Stanley's Boston family and probably surprised a few of her New Mexico friends when it was finally announced in the Santa Fe newspaper in late October. But the union was not actually as impulsive as it appeared. Stanley had met the cowboy-guide Roy Pfaffle on the passenger platform beside the narrow-gauge tracks of the Denver and Rio Grande Railroad in the town of Española, New Mexico, sometime in the spring of 1916.[12] Pfaffle was working at the Ramon Vigil Ranch, and he drove Stanley and Curtis up the cliff-hugging trail of a road to the Pajarito Plateau. Iowa-born Pfaffle had been living in northern New Mexico for several years by that time, and he knew the backcountry from his work as a forest ranger in the Jemez and Santa Fe National Forests. Pfaffle also had his own livery business in Española and hired out as an independent guide and outfitter.

Pfaffle joined forces with the new Rocky Mountain Camp Company in early summer, 1916, and continued to see Carol Stanley while she was living in Santa Fe. Pfaffle may have been with Stanley and Curtis on their illness-hampered camping trip in July, and he may have suggested that Stanley and Curtis join the Rocky Mountain Camp Co.'s record-setting cross-country expedition planned for early fall.

Both Stanley and Curtis were experienced riders and campers. Still, it is remarkable that these two nearly middle-aged women were invited to participate in such a demanding undertaking. The sense of remoteness and distance from civilization found in Canyon del Muerto, Canyon de Chelly, and on the vast stretch of desert to Rainbow Bridge in 1916 cannot be exaggerated. "No one who has not seen it can imagine the difficulties of the trail where it was necessary for the horses to climb up the slick rocks, or petrified sand dunes and where we went afoot and the horses follow Ben Wetherell's [*sic*] horse best as they could," Mary Wheelwright wrote of her journey across the same landscape with Stanley, in the 1920s. "At times I felt I could not possibly get through. At one point the trail was so steep that I could only get up by holding onto the tail of my horse. . . . Finally we came to the bridge and slept under the arch in full moonlight."[13]

Stanley had seen the Rainbow Bridge during her stay with the Wetherills in 1915. Stanley, Curtis, and now Dorothy Kent were members of a very small and remarkably hardy and self-reliant group of non-Native women who had visited and camped under the stars at the Rainbow Bridge prior to World War I. They carried everything they needed and not much more, although Miss Kent insisted on packing her violin across the difficult, slick rock trail to the canyon of the Rainbow Bridge where she serenaded her dusty, sunburned, chap-, hat-, and boot-bedecked audience with a concert—surely a first in the history of classical music, and in the story of this legendary monument.

Upon their return to New Mexico in late October, the new Mr. and Mrs. Pfaffle learned that the Ramon Vigil Ranch needed a new caretaker immediately. One of the ranch's owners, Pfaffle's former boss, Ashley Pond, had quit as on-site manager and, after severing his ties with the Detroit partners, had begun work on a new venture—the Los Alamos Boys' Ranch directly across the plateau from the Pajarito Club. Pfaffle quit his job with the Rocky Mountain Camp Company, and although he wanted to maintain his outfitting business from El Oñate Hotel in Española, the new Mr. and Mrs. Pfaffle decided to move up into the small house at the Ramon Vigil Ranch.

The winter and spring of 1916–17 were difficult times for the Pfaffles: they continued to operate their outfitting business in Española and organized and guided expeditions to Chaco Canyon, Mesa Verde, and the Natural Bridges of Utah. There was a severe drought that winter and spring, and although the Pfaffles had dozens of interested clients asking to stay at the ranch, they could accept only a few paying guests because they were hauling all of the water by hand from a well. All decisions about the ranch had to be cleared by the partners, and getting them to respond in a timely manner was a continual source of frustration for Carol. And then with the U.S. entry into World War I in April of 1917, the Detroit owners and their automotive manufacturing businesses were suddenly front and center in the American war industry. Carol Pfaffle wrote to Chapin before Christmas of 1917, "You and the other three owners are so busy in the great work that needs all your time and strength, that I know well you don't want to be bother[ed] with us. . . . The lack of bathroom facilities has lost us some people, and also quite a bit of money from some people who stayed, but who would have taken a private bath. . . . The canyon is terribly dry, and we are desperately worried lest the well go dry."[14]

Carol learned the highs and lows of guest-ranch management during a challenging two years at the Ramon Vigil. But in spite of the personal and financial insecurities generated by the war, the plateau's drought, and the absence of any real sense of long-term commitment from the

Detroit partners, Carol appreciated her time on the Pajarito's beautiful high country. "Spring is upon us," she wrote to Chapin in late February of 1918. "I wonder if you have any idea how lovely this canyon is in the spring when the cottonwoods begin to leaf out? The air is soft and balmy, and the whole world is full of sunlight, singing birds and hidden life."[15]

Even the Pfaffles' best efforts at the Ramon Vigil could not overcome the effects of the drought. By early March 1918, Carol wrote Chapin that "our sword of Damocles has fallen. The well has gone dry, and now, with a house full of people, we are hauling water from nearby canyons."[16]

The Detroit owners began to negotiate the sale of the Ramon Vigil Grant to Frank Bond of Española. Although Bond and Chapin suggested to the Pfaffles that they remain the guest ranch's managers, Carol and Roy left the Pajarito Plateau by early summer of 1918.

The Bishop's Ranch, soon called Bishop's Lodge, in the foothills of the Sangre de Cristo Mountains near Santa Fe, was looking for an experienced manager. The old chapel and grounds, once the retreat of the French Jesuit archbishop Jean Baptiste Lamy, had been bought by a Colorado man, James R. Thorpe. With nearly two years of ranch management behind them, the Pfaffles were considered experienced in the still-new dude ranch industry of the Southwest, and Thorpe hired them to supervise the renovation of the historic ranch. The Pfaffles' time at Bishop's Lodge was short-lived—within the year the owners fired Pfaffle because he was an "unpractical visionary"—but during that year they met and became business partners with a young cowboy named Jack Lambert, who would be an important addition to their lives for the next decade.[17]

Lambert was all of nineteen and a seasoned saddle bum and experienced drifter when he met Roy Pfaffle on the Santa Fe Plaza in 1918. Lambert had left Oklahoma at fourteen to become a professional cowboy, and his saddlebag résumé included work as a wild horse tamer, ranch hand, cattle puncher, and bridge builder in various parts of the West. Pfaffle and Lambert met in front of the Capital Pharmacy on the old plaza in Santa Fe in a conversation with Rocky Mountain Camp Company owner C. B. Ruggles. Ruggles introduced the affable Lambert to the older but equally affable Pfaffle, and Pfaffle told Lambert that he was managing a new guest ranch and had need of some hired help. Lambert went out to the village of Tesuque and, after looking the place over and meeting Carol Stanley Pfaffle, took the job with the new outfit.

Carol, Pfaffle, and Lambert enjoyed one another's company, and, when Roy Pfaffle was fired as manager of Bishop's Lodge, the three decided to open their own dude ranch. In late 1918, after selling the Onate Hotel, and gathering together what was left of Carol's inheritance, the Pfaffles bought a crumbling but historically rich and outstandingly beautiful rancho in Alcalde, New Mexico, on the Rio Grande River near San Juan Pueblo. Most of the adobe buildings were in ruins, but using what they had learned renovating the Ramon Vigil and Bishop's Lodge, Carol and the boys rebuilt and opened San Gabriel Ranch by 1920. The Pfaffles knew the best guides and wranglers in northern New Mexico, and with the good-natured, handsome, and dependable Jack Lambert as chief dude wrangler, San Gabriel was quickly considered among the best guest ranches in the Southwest.

San Gabriel Ranch enjoyed a decade at the forefront of the burgeoning New Mexico tourist industry. The ranch's location on the main road between Santa Fe and Taos made San Gabriel accessible to the legions of artists, writers, and sightseers moving up and down the Rio Grande Valley between New Mexico's bustling art colonies. Named for the first Spanish capital, established in 1598 a few miles downriver from the ranch, San Gabriel was the center of what the Santa Fe Railway's publicity department called "America's Most Famous Fifty Mile Square."

The opening of San Gabriel dovetailed perfectly with the railway's new national advertising campaign that promoted the natural and cultural wonders of the Southwest. The ranch was a featured destination on the Santa Fe's widely distributed map of the Four Corners region, and the San Gabriel dining room and patio garden became a regular lunch stop on the new auto tours sponsored by the Southwestern Indian Detours of the Fred Harvey Company, beginning in 1926.

At San Gabriel, Carol Stanley Pfaffle had the home she had longed for since her first visits to the Wetherills. And like Louisa Wetherill, Carol worked a seven-day week in summer heat and winter cold to maintain the ranch. She was hostess, accountant, publicity coordinator, meal supervisor, and personnel manager. Carol had no time to herself in the summer-autumn guest season. Life at San Gabriel, like all dude ranches, was a "continuous house-party," where a guest could do

Driver/guide Orville Cox took San Gabriel, and later Ghost Ranch, guests on auto excursions into the outback in the 1920s and 1930s. Here Cox and a San Gabriel touring car are being pulled out of the Rio Grande, c. 1921.

"just the things he or she wants to—and nothing else." Like all successful dude ranches, much of San Gabriel's appeal was its family-ranch atmosphere where real people—and real cowboys—lived.[18]

The casitas and rooms of San Gabriel were occupied from late June until October. Guests were almost always people Carol knew personally or professionally from Boston, New York, Chicago, and Cleveland, or they were recommended by friends and acquaintances. Most were wealthy and all were looking for a summer escape into a world distinctly different from modern America. The Pfaffles' ranch offered time out from high profile jobs and lives. "People dress simply," the San Gabriel Ranch brochure, "The Call of the Southwest," illustrated with original woodcuts by Gustave Baumann, explained, "and the general atmosphere is one of pleasant simplicity and charm."[19]

The Rockefeller family came during the summer to San Gabriel, and Archibald MacLeish and the directors of Carson Pirie Scott in Chicago returned each year. Princeton-based millionaire Arthur Pack and the writers and photographers of his popular periodical, *Nature* magazine, used San Gabriel as their base camp during research expeditions; and *New York Times* journalist Nicholas Roosevelt and Santa Fe Railway executive J. Sanford Otis of Chicago asked Carol and Lambert to arrange extensive pack trips into the desert for their families. "Sometimes I'd take whole families, or some of the Santa Fe Railway lawyers," Lambert remembered. "One summer I took four four-to-six week pack trips, one of them into three states. There was no pavement and not one fence between here and Gallup or the Grand Canyon."[20]

A young writer, Oliver La Farge, visted San Gabriel with his wife, Wanden. La Farge's work on and about the Navajos, culminating in his Pulitzer Prize–winning novel, *Laughing Boy*, in 1930, would have been of enormous personal interest to Carol, who, we can assume, shared with La Farge her own experiences among the Navajos with Natalie Curtis and with the Wetherills.

Willa Cather came to stay at San Gabriel with her traveling companion Edith Lewis in July of 1925. Cather and Lewis were on their way to Taos and planned to stay only a night. But the atmosphere of Carol's ranch appealed to Cather, and she remained a week and worked on the proofs of *The Professor's House* (which was, coincidentally, Cather's homage to Carol's friends, the Wetherill brothers) in the quiet seclusion of Carol's walled garden.[21]

Cather's visit to San Gabriel was during a time of great artistic revelation for the novelist. While in Santa Fe that summer, the idea for *Death Comes for the Archbishop* came to Cather in a single evening, and the remainder of the summer Cather was consumed by her ideas for the story. Cather's novel is based upon the life of the first archbishop of Santa Fe, the Frenchman Jean Baptiste Lamy, whose former retreat, Bishop's Lodge, had been renovated by Carol and Pfaffle some years before.

Even with guests as interesting as Willa Cather, by the end of the tourist season Carol was weary of her role as hotel keeper and tourist facilitator. Nearly every fall, Carol replenished her spirit by returning on horseback to the mountain and desert country. Roy Pfaffle remained at the ranch to oversee the animals and hired hands, and to pursue his passion for poker and horse racing. Carol, usually with Jack Lambert and a few of the other cowboys who lived at San Gabriel, packed up the horses and headed out for a few weeks in the big spaces known and unknown. They stayed at Hubbell's and Cozy McSparron's trading posts, camped beside familiar springs, and renewed friendships with Navajo friends as they crossed the reservation. "It was so inaccessible that you couldn't afford to forget anything," Lambert later recollected of those journeys into the Four Corners. "It was awesome and silent out there. . . . We rode by way of the Valle Grande, the Chaco Canyon ruins and west from Sheep Springs on the wagon road over Washington Pass to Lukachukai. We stayed with traders like Charlie Newcomb. . . . We rode past Chee Dodge's great big mansion down to Canyon de Chelly and camped on rims."[22]

Carol kept a detailed notebook of routes taken, landmarks, destinations, and the distances crossed each day that later became the mapped itinerary for guest expeditions. Carol's notes from a fifteen-day pack trip from Alcalde to Canyon de Chelly via Chaco Canyon included their arrival at Cañon del Muerto after two weeks on the trail. "Heavily timbered ridges. Beautiful scenery all the way to the top of Cañon del Muerto. A steep rocky trail too dangerous to ride down drops a thousand feet into the canyon, nearly an hour's walk to camp by the spring at the foot of the trail, within a short distance of the Mummy Cave, one of the most remarkable cave dwellings in the entire region."[23]

In the solitary winter months, Carol volunteered as a music teacher for the children of San Juan Pueblo and the village of Alcalde. In 1921, she wrote friends back east that her Christmas choir had some sixty voices. That next year, unnamed benefactors gave Carol two pianos—a Steinway concert grand and an upright—and she hoped to build a music room at the ranch. Carol wrote a friend, "I hope to do a great deal of work with the natives along the lines definitely taught me by Natalie."[24]

Absent from Carol's new home and life at the lovely ranch along the Rio Grande was her friend Natalie Curtis Burlin. If Curtis ever saw San Gabriel, it would have been during its years of reconstruction. Curtis and Burlin owned a home in Santa Fe, but they were away most of the year. Curtis's studies of folk music and Native songs had received international recognition, and she traveled all over the world giving lectures. In October of 1921, Curtis went to Paris with husband Paul Burlin, where she spoke to the International Congress on the History of Art in Paris. While crossing a Paris avenue, Curtis was struck and killed by an automobile. She was forty-six years old.

With friends Alice Corbin Henderson and Elizabeth (Elsie) Sergeant, Carol assembled a memorial service for Curtis in Santa Fe. Something rare and wonderful departed the Southwest when Natalie

Curtis died, and her passing was mourned as deeply among her Native American friends as it was among her Anglo ones.

Carol wrote to Natalie Curtis's mother, Mimsey, of an extraordinary encounter she had had at the Grand Canyon with one of Curtis's Hopi friends. "Just after news came of Natalie's death I met a Hopi whose uncle was Natalie's teacher for some time. I told him of her death. After a long silence he said 'But she cannot die. She is singing now—somewhere with her Hopi friends.' Then in spite of a small group of Americans (we were in the Harvey Curio room) he softly sang two songs she taught me and said 'She sang like Indian; have to have spirit of Indian for white woman to sing that way.'"[25]

In 1915, during her extended stay with the Wetherills, Carol had met a Navajo medicine man—a *cacique*, healer, and sand painter—named Hosteen Klah. Klah was a man of great authority and power among the Navajos, and he protected Carol and came to her rescue on at least one occasion during the tumultuous events surrounding tribal tensions with the U.S. government in the spring of 1915. Carol maintained a friendship with Klah after she moved to northern New Mexico and visited him on her numerous return sojourns to Navajoland.

Among Carol's first Boston friends to visit her new home at San Gabriel was Mary Cabot Wheelwright. Wheelwright was a wealthy forty-year-old spinster when she arrived in the Southwest. "I came initially to Alcalde," Wheelwright wrote in her autobiography, "to a 'dude ranch' kept by Mr. and Mrs. Pfaffle. Mr. Pfaffle was a descendant of Germans . . . and his wife was a Choate from Massachusetts—musical, imaginative and adventuresome. Their ranch was a wonderful introduction to the country."[26]

Wheelwright had founded the South End Music School in Boston before World War I, and she came to New Mexico on a personal pilgrimage to explore Native music and culture. With San Gabriel as her home base, and Carol Stanley Pfaffle as her guide, Wheelwright stepped into a new life on the last frontier of Native America. Like Carol seven years earlier, Wheelwright immediately fell in love with the place and the people.

Carol and Jack Lambert took Wheelwright on her first journey into the outback. They traveled by horseback to Canyon de Chelly, Chinle, and to the McSparron and Newcomb trading posts. Wheelwright especially wanted to attend a Navajo *Tleji*—Night Chant—and so Lambert led the women up a rugged trail over the Chuska Mountains to Nava. At the Newcomb Trading Post, Carol, Lambert, and Wheelwright learned that Klah was giving a *Yehbechei*, another Night Chant, at Kimpeto. It was seventy miles across the desert, but Lambert and the two women pushed their horses through blowing dust and stormy skies and reached Kimpeto just as it began to snow. "The dancers were to be seen through the whirling snow, while the fires blew out sideways," Wheelwright recalled. "Out of this turmoil appeared Klah, calm and benign. . . . He joined us for a while and I got a very strong impression of power from him."[27]

From this surreal encounter on the desert, Klah and Wheelwright began a friendship and collaboration that lasted the rest of their lives. With Klah's endorsement and cooperation, Wheelwright, in a manner reminiscent of Curtis two decades earlier, devoted her time and personal income to collecting and documenting sacred Navajo chants, myths, and songs. Klah also allowed Wheelwright to replicate his sand paintings, a taboo among his people.

After this journey into Navajoland, Wheelwright decided to make her home in New Mexico. She purchased the old Plaza de Los Luceros, adjacent to San Gabriel on the Rio Grande. After Carol's renovation of the property, Wheelwright made her residence at the hacienda and pursued what became an invaluable project on the traditions and religion of the Navajos. Klah and Wheelwright's collaborative work became the foundation of the Museum of Navajo Ceremonial Art, which opened in Santa Fe in 1937.

The Pfaffles acquired two additional properties by the late 1920s. The first was called Can Jilon Camp (the spelling was changed to "Canjilon" in the 1930s), and was a retreat in the Canjilon Mountains beside a trout stream in the high ponderosa country above the village of El Rito, forty-five miles from Alcalde. The camp had a large log house with a kitchen and common rooms, and rustic cabins and canvas tents for summer sleeping quarters. Staffed by a few wranglers and a cook, Can Jilon Camp offered a private paradise to those who wanted to be completely severed from the bustling world. The John D. Rockefeller family rented the camp for an entire summer in the late 1920s.

The second property acquired by the Pfaffles was a corral and a primitive, legend-laden dwelling tucked under the cliffs on the high red desert fifteen miles from the pueblo of Abiquiú.[28] This abandoned homestead at Yeso Canyon, won in the aforementioned card game, was contiguous with sixteen thousand acres of land on the Piedra Lumbre, also owned by San Gabriel Ranch. San Gabriel's horse expeditions bound for the Four Corners often followed the Chama River and crossed the Piedra Lumbre, and Carol had viewed the shining, variegated stone cliffs from a distance numerous times over the years. The decrepit homestead at Yeso Canyon—Carol called it Ghost Ranch in her account book in 1928—was in disrepair and nearly unusable, but the property offered a suitable stopover and a water and resupply post for the Pfaffles' pack trips headed into Indian Country.

The last few years of the 1920s were filled with duress for Carol Stanley Pfaffle. On the surface, San Gabriel appeared to be thriving. The ranch was at its prime and picture perfect, with plenty of guests and a skilled, dependable staff. Stanley kept abreast of San Gabriel's finances in an immense and intricately organized ledger tracing the ranch finances to the penny. But for all of her fastidious attention to the details of promotion, planning, and budgeting, Stanley could not stop the tide of national and personal events that would ultimately lead to the loss of her business, her marriage, and her beloved home on the Rio Grande.

The year 1927 had a foreboding beginning: Carol and Roy were driving the mountain road down from Can Jilon Camp when the car overturned and Carol's leg was injured, making it impossible for her to go east for her annual visit. Midsummer, Carol was not sleeping well and was complaining of migraine headaches. By the end of the year, Roy Pfaffle's gambling losses at both the card tables and racetracks of northern New Mexico had so depleted the ranch's profits that Carol mortgaged part of San Gabriel to her neighbor, Mary Wheelwright. This loan of twenty thousand dollars kept San Gabriel functioning another two years. But then the stock market crashed in 1929, and the once profitable world of New Mexico tourism evaporated literally overnight.

Jack Lambert was devoted to San Gabriel and might have stayed to help Carol through the financial crisis of 1929 but for the escalating alcohol addiction of Roy Pfaffle. Lambert could ignore Pfaffle's problems while he was out with guests on pack trips. But when he returned late summer from the Four Corners, Lambert could no longer tolerate the ill effects his friend's drinking had on San Gabriel. "When we got back I found Dick was drinking," Lambert said years later, "so I left to spend the winter in Phoenix."[29]

With her husband incapacitated by his addiction to alcohol, and with Jack Lambert departed, Carol was now left to manage San Gabriel on her own. In an attempt to protect her land holdings and her own emotional stability, Carol initiated divorce proceedings in 1930. She also made herself president of San Gabriel Ranch, Inc. By early summer of 1931, Roy Pfaffle's health was completely undermined by alcohol and tobacco—he was also a heavy smoker—and Carol placed him in a sanitarium in Pueblo, Colorado. A month later, Carol sent out a letter to her stockholders telling them that San Gabriel was through and that the mortgage holders would be forced to protect themselves by foreclosure.[30]

It was the end of an era in the life of Carol Bishop Stanley. She had to vacate San Gabriel and begin again somewhere else. She could have returned to Boston, where she held the official position as the black sheep in the Stanley clan. But the Southwest had become Carol's only home, and in 1931, at the age of fifty-one, Carol chose, again, to take the trail less traveled back into the unpeopled hinterland yet found in northern New Mexico.

With all that she owned and what was left of what she loved—her horses; a handful of loyal, and unemployed, cowboys, guides, and dude wranglers; one grand piano; and her English cook and confidante, Alice Pring—Carol gathered up the remnants of her life and resolutely set out to create a new home at the place called Ghost Ranch.

Two The Experience of Simplicity

We need to give some time to the arts of cherishing the things we adore, before they simply vanish. Maybe it will be like learning a skill: how to live in paradise.—WILLIAM KITTREDGE[1]

Although the population boom in New Mexico, especially Santa Fe and its immediate environs, continued in the 1930s, the Depression knocked the legs out from under the tourist industry. The ultrawealthy could still afford long summer retreats at guest ranches, but seasonal visitor traffic decreased dramatically in the Southwest. Everyone who made a living serving out-of-towners, from the small horse-pack trip guide to the Santa Fe Railway and its partner, the Fred Harvey Company, suffered profit losses from declining customer numbers and cut services or went out of business. The Santa Fe Railway introduced faster, more luxurious trains to accommodate the upscale clientele. And automobile manufacturers produced touring cars that were better equipped to carry people and their gear long distances. However, in New Mexico only those roads that connected major destinations underwent anything resembling improvement. Other roads remained the dirt, mud, and rock tracks they had always been, and wagon and automobile travelers embarked on journeys across a few miles or several states with ample food and water, spare mechanical parts, camping gear, and a sense of adventure, patience, and humor.

The road to Ghost Ranch was an easily overlooked trail defined by a pair of deep parallel ruts that departed the Colorado-bound road to Tierra Amarilla nearly midway across the sandy basin of the Piedra Lumbre. The first marker for the ranch road was a horse skull propped on top of the gatepost. Later, the horse skull was replaced by an ox skull and a primitive wooden sign with "Ghost Ranch" and an arrow pointing the way to the elusive ranch. But by all accounts (the most famous being Georgia O'Keeffe's), the road to el Rancho de los Brujos in the early 1930s was unmarked and hard to find, its exact location oft described as "somewhere out there" on the wide, hot expanse beneath the flat-topped, knife-thin mountain Pedernal, angling north and a bit east into the sandy red and gold hills to end directly at the foot of the Cliffs of Shining Stone. It was precisely Ghost Ranch's least desirable characteristics—its tainted past and subsequent shunning, and its physical distance from any community with even the meagerest of modern, civilized amenities—that preserved its pristine, untouched, unspoiled landscape until 1930.

While Stanley's circle of middle-aged friends in New Mexico were moving closer to town and setting up homes in Santa Fe and Taos, Stanley was moving farther from the beaten path. Abiquiú was not connected to the modern world by a railroad, as Española and Santa Fe were, and the road up the Chama River Valley to Abiquiú and north across the badland and mesa country of the Piedra Lumbre toward the county seat of Tierra Amarilla was sand and dirt in the dry season, clay and adobe mud in the wet season.

Young Betty Bartlett witnessed the metamorphosis of Ghost Ranch from a feared and avoided place to a beloved desert paradise. Betty was twenty when her father, Hartley W. Bartlett, came from New York to New Mexico to work as Stanley's business manager in 1931. Bartlett was an attorney and also an investor in Stanley's guest ranches. Newly widowed, Bartlett had closed up his Long Island home and come west with his only child hoping to save some of his investment by advising Stanley as the San Gabriel Ranch outfit transferred from Alcalde to her property near Abiquiú.

Betty spent one year in New Mexico, much of it shadowing Carol Stanley as she traveled back and forth between Alcalde, Santa Fe, and Ghost Ranch, which was briefly called San Gabriel. While Betty's father worked to balance the books and organize a financial plan to stabilize Stanley's business in the midst of both a killing drought that made the Midwest and Southwest into the Great Dust Bowl, and a national economic crisis that became the Great Depression, Betty explored the mesa and mountain country with Stanley's cowboys and guides.

With her Santa Fe friend, Mary Driscoll, Betty Bartlett motored up and down the dirt road between Stanley's two ranches. Professional driver Orville Cox taught the young women how to negotiate an automobile over the ever-challenging road conditions found throughout New Mexico in the early 1930s. "In those days any rain shower made roads slippery like axle grease," Betty Bartlett recalled of the summer of 1932, "and almost impossible to drive over until they dried. None of the roads were paved, so we never motored anywhere that we did not carry a tow rope, an axe, a shovel, a pail and other equipment, because sometimes we had to build a new road."[2]

Betty's father, Hartley Bartlett, had been a cavalry officer in World War I and carried a gun at all times in northern New Mexico. He reminded his daughter that this part of the United States was still a frontier. Although the Night Rider gang that had robbed Mary Wheelwright's estate in Alcalde had been caught and placed in prison, there were still cattle and horse rustlers. Even Stanley, who had lived for two decades in the wild places of the Southwest, would not stay at Ghost Ranch alone or unarmed. "This place can be dangerous," Stanley said, and instructed Betty to ride around Ghost Ranch always accompanied by one of the cowboys. "The Ghost Ranch I knew was primitive—no electricity, no running water, no heat except the corner fireplaces in each room. . . . The Ghost Ranch consisted of a tack house and two small buildings with a corral for horses or cattle, when they were not grazing the hillsides. The location beside colored cliffs was beautiful, snuggled next to a mesa plateau."[3]

The visits to the old homestead were worth the discomforts and risks involved. Betty Bartlett admired Stanley, who, in spite of migraine headaches and tiring and frequent trips to Santa Fe to handle legal and financial matters, found the time to revel in the gifts of space and silence found in the backcountry of New Mexico. Orville Cox took the women on automobile excursions, and Alice Pring, although herself suffering from various age-related ills, prepared Betty and Stanley wonderful meals in the tiny, makeshift kitchen in the casita under the cliffs.

The cowboys joined the women in the evenings and told stories by the hour, squatting on the ground. Later, Stanley would play her grand piano by the flickering candlelight in the old homestead. Betty and her father passed many a clear summer evening staring up at the dazzling sky of stars over the Piedra Lumbre while classical melodies spilled out

The restored interior of Ghost House, Stanley's home at Ghost Ranch in the early 1930s.

Ted Peabody, construction foreman of the Ghost Ranch headquarters, casitas, bunkhouse, Rancho de los Burros, and the Johnson House, c. 1937.

of the crooked Ghost House windows into the cool breeze that swept down the night canyon.

Even before construction of modern facilities began, the Ranch of the Witches began to undergo a profound transformation. Stanley began her new dream of a home at Ghost Ranch from the ground up. She was an experienced construction foreman by this time in her life, having participated in the renovations and additions at the Ramon Vigil Ranch, Bishop's Lodge, San Gabriel, and Wheelwright's home, Los Luceros. Stanley understood that a good guest ranch provided an environment that seamlessly combined the minimum but necessary creature comforts with the gifts indigenous to the wild and wonderful natural world the guests came to be part of for a few weeks.

Ted Peabody moved out to Ghost Ranch to oversee construction. Thousands of adobe bricks were made on site. Workers both male and female—men traditionally laid the walls and framed the roofs; women plastered both interior and exterior walls with mud plaster made from local clays and sands mixed with straw—were hired from Coyote and Youngsville. Because of the distance between Ghost Ranch and their homes, all workers remained on the ranch during the week and lived in a tent village along the Rito del Yeso during 1932 and 1933.

Stanley was up with the sun and at the construction site every day.

The newly completed Ghost Ranch headquarters, c. 1935.

The locals thought her a bit strange, but this divorced, middle-aged Anglo woman they came to call La Patrona, who spoke English and adequate Spanish with a Boston accent, soon became someone they very much respected. The first building constructed was the ranch's main headquarters. Stanley chose a slightly elevated site with a spectacular view of the cliffs to the north and east and of the wide, hot desert of the red badland country to the south to be the center of her new ranch. With Peabody, she designed a traditional flat-roofed adobe with viga ceilings and wood floors and double doors opening onto a south-facing portal. This five-room building housed a living room, pantry, kitchen, commissary, and office.

But headquarters was designed to introduce ranch guests to the magnificent world of the Piedra Lumbre: from the front portal newly arrived guests could survey the shimmering sand and stone landscape they were now part of. The narrow spire soon known as Chimney Rock was visible to the northwest. Ten miles southwest across the basin, the dark blue of the horizon followed the rugged topography of the Jemez

Mountains. And rising into the blue sky half a mile above the basin was the commanding profile of Pedernal, visible through every southern window and doorway of the simple, unassuming adobe building. Completed by the end of 1933, headquarters would become the heart and soul of modern Ghost Ranch.

The Ghost Ranch headquarters cost Carol Stanley more than three thousand dollars to construct. It was furnished with Spanish colonial furniture built by Ted Peabody and his son, Henry, and was decorated with baskets and Navajo rugs from Stanley's own collection. The understated, rustic elegance of Stanley's first building welcomed road-weary guests to Ghost Ranch for the next half century, at which time the original headquarters was lost in an electrical fire that burned it to the ground in the early spring of 1983.

As the headquarters building progressed, Peabody and the labor crew, which often included his son, Henry, simultaneously began work on new guest housing. By the end of 1934, Ghost Ranch had several more adobe guest cottages—Three Room House (later called Pine), Garden House, and a small adobe and log dwelling called the Log House, later renamed Cedar. An adobe bunkhouse, later named Corral Block, for wranglers, cowboys, guides, drivers, cooks, and other seasonal and permanent staff, was built down the hill below headquarters, near the horse corrals, poultry and turkey sheds, and saddle house. The generator (up and going by 1935) and the machine shop were placed at one end of the U-shaped Corral Block.

If Stanley was going to successfully undertake the ambitious task of starting over on a desert homestead as a more-than-middle-aged single woman, she was going to need a support staff of professionals. The cowboys, guides, and drivers who became part of Ghost Ranch were all men Stanley had known and worked with for many years. Stanley knew that the men who cared for the horses, and for the dudes who wanted to be around the horses, were often a guest ranch's primary ambassadors. A bad experience with a wrangler could end a guest's stay prematurely; conversely, a great experience with the staff could ensure a long relationship between a guest and a particular ranch. Dudes became partial to a particular dude ranch because of its facilities and location—and the facilities included the cowboys, whose primary responsibility was to lead often complete greenhorns safely and happily into and out of the wilderness. It was a job that required equal

The interior of a guest cottage at Ghost Ranch in 1936.

Ghost Ranch foreman Lloyd Miller, Stanley's second husband, at Ghost Ranch in 1932.

amounts of skill and charm. Having been a tenderfoot herself years before, Stanley knew what her guests needed and wanted in Ghost Ranch's wranglers.

Ghost Ranch's livestock, rangeland, and dudes were wrangled by an experienced group of men, most of whom had been with Stanley for years: the McKinley brothers, Jack, Marvin, and Lester, who were brothers to the infamous and now-imprisoned leader of the Night Riders, Bill McKinley; Alfred J. Jarmon, nicknamed Slim for his narrow physique and his habit of chewing upon but never smoking cigars; and people-shy but horse-smart Archie McKellor. Orville Cox, San Gabriel Ranch's ace mechanic, driver, and guide, agreed to oversee all of Ghost Ranch's vehicles and auto expeditions. And a cowboy named Lloyd Miller became the new ranch foreman.

Born in 1890 in Content, Texas, Lloyd Miller had worked in the Panhandle country as a cowboy and horse jockey and in the Rio Grande Valley as a professional hunter and guide before hooking up with San Gabriel Ranch as a wrangler in the mid-1920s. By the 1930s and his move with Stanley's outfit to Ghost Ranch, Miller's many years as the proverbial cow-punching drifter made for good storytelling around the guests' campfires. A favorite among the Ghost Ranch dudes was the story of Miller's youthful days as an unemployed jockey.

> On entering a new town, Lloyd would seek out the best-looking saloon and soon become engaged in the popular conversational topic—who owned the fastest horse. Feigning drunken bravado, he would presently offer to bet that the off horse in his shaggy-looking team could beat anything in town. Naturally, there were plenty of takers, and the next day a race would be arranged. The joker was that Lloyd's off horse had thoroughbred blood and was purposely kept looking seedy to lure the local suckers. The moment the race was over, Lloyd would collect on his bet and hurriedly leave town before the fleeced amateurs could organize their revenge.[4]

Miller was a small man with a quick and engaging smile. He earned Carol Stanley Pfaffle's trust as a wrangler during his several years at San Gabriel. And sometime between 1932 and 1934, Miller began to earn Miss Carol Stanley's affections too.

Jack McKinley was another Oklahoma-born cowboy who was trail boss for San Gabriel's horse and cattle stock, and who, with his brothers, came to Ghost Ranch to manage just about everything having to do with the Piedra Lumbre Cattle Company, established in the early 1930s. McKinley eventually distinguished himself among local cowboys by riding one of his best horses up the side of and onto the very top of Cerro Pedernal. According to his son, Henry, McKinley's only comment following this equestrian feat of nearly unimaginable difficulty was that he "wouldn't recommend it."[5]

Stanley had known Orville Cox since his days with the Rocky Mountain Camp Company, when he had a small office in La Fonda on the Santa Fe plaza. Now in his forties, Cox had initially come to New Mexico from North Carolina as a teenager in 1908 to await his death from tuberculosis. Cox survived and his family opened a sawmill in Cimarron, New Mexico. Orville Cox had a natural way with automobiles and mechanical devices and left the family business to take a job in Santa Fe with the new Rocky Mountain Camp Company in 1916. Cox was an avid reader and a self-taught historian and geologist, and

Head wrangler Jack McKinley at the Bennett House at Ghost Ranch in 1935.

by the time he joined the Pfaffles' San Gabriel Ranch in 1922, he was one of the most experienced tour guides in the Four Corners outback. Stanley knew that securing the now-married-with child Cox as the head driver and mechanic at Ghost Ranch in 1931 was essential to the new outfit's survival.

Slim Jarmon had worked with Stanley since his arrival to New Mexico in 1919. Jarmon's lungs were damaged by mustard gas in World War I, and he had left the Texas panhandle for the healing attributes of the high, dry climate of northern New Mexico. Although he had little formal education, at San Gabriel Slim found that his cattle, horse, mule, and campfire cooking skills, along with his soothing voice and amiable, low-key nature, gave him the necessary credentials to become a good dude wrangler. Jarmon led Nelson Rockefeller and his brothers several times into the southwestern outback and was famous for his ability, often on very short notice, to effortlessly organize and assemble a pack trip for a two-day fishing trip into the local mountains or a six-week excursion to the Grand Canyon.

Pete Dozier was a new employee but an old acquaintance of Stanley's when he moved into the bunkhouse at Ghost Ranch in 1931. Jose Pitman Guadalupe Dozier worked many years at San Gabriel's rival guest ranch, the Bishop's Lodge, where he was known as Frenchie or the Frenchman. (Dozier was actually only part French: his mother was a native of Santa Clara Pueblo who had married a half-English, half-French lawyer who had come west to teach at the small government Indian school on the Rio Grande in 1895.) During the 1920s, Pete and his younger brother, Tom, made a good living packing the rich and often famous into the outback on horseback. Pete worked for private outfits like the Bishop's Lodge; Tom worked with the Fred Harvey Company's Southwestern Indian Detours. Their brother, Edward, left the Española Valley to pursue a degree in anthropology and became the distinguished Dr. Edward P. Dozier, professor of anthropology at Stanford and at the University of Arizona. He also became a renowned author of books about his mother's people, the Tewa of the Rio Grande.

Archie McKellor never traded in his spurs for lodge life, but worked for Stanley as a cowboy's cowboy. McKellor, like Jack McKinley, was not by trade a dude wrangler. He was hired to follow and guide cattle, not people, about the open range. During McKinley's years with Stanley, McKinley became more flexible and worked with the dudes as well as the livestock. Although he was a no-nonsense, often gruff cowboy, handsome Jack McKinley had a natural frontier chivalry that made him extremely attractive to the guests, especially the ladies. But Archie McKellor wanted nothing to do with the tenderfoots paying good money to play cowboy, and he chose to live far from the dude ranching crowd, at the cow camps on the llanos of the Piedra Lumbre. Stanley needed someone like McKellor to follow the herd, and he happily took the job that gave him weeks at a time of complete solitude out under the sky with his bedroll, tarpaulin, camp kitchen, and a few good horses.

McKellor's reputation as the last of the real cowboys only served to heighten his mystique among the guests back at the ranch. Visiting dudettes found the shy man of the land irresistible. Throughout the summer months, McKellor's bachelor camp was frequently the destination of single, female guests who rode their horses out onto the Piedra Lumbre hoping for a glimpse of the mysterious loner.

Some of the Ghost Ranch staff—Jack McKinley, Orville Cox, and Slim Jarmon—had families, but because of the lack of housing and the distance over terrible roads to schools and medical facilities, wives and children did not move to the ranch. Living apart from one's family for employment reasons was an acceptable choice during the Depression. Jobs were scarce, and people took employment wherever they could find it. Many of the Ghost Ranch cowboys returned to visit their families several times a month, and they remained home for extended stays during the off season. This work arrangement especially suited former cowboys, who were accustomed to seasonal work as well as the freedoms that went with life in the out-of-doors. The only drawbacks were the problems common to all marriages that accommodated prolonged separation: spousal estrangement, loneliness, and infidelity. The stories of the Ghost Ranch cowboys, and their wives and families, would come to include all of these.

The small community of construction laborers and cowboys at Ghost Ranch in the early years of the 1930s was a tiny island of human activity and industriousness under the gleaming Cliffs of Shining Stone. The closest neighbor to Stanley's Yeso Canyon operation was Juan de Dios Gallegos, who lived at the Vadito de Chicos, the Crossing of the Willows, on the Chama River. De Dios's ranch was at the crossroads where the route west into Navajoland met the north-south road between Tierra Amarilla and Española. There was a wide, sandy crossing here where wagons and horses could ford the Chama River. In later years, a narrow bridge was built that was just wide enough for the first automobiles.

By 1931 de Dios was a living legend. Born in northern New Mexico in 1835 to Navajo and possibly Spanish parents, Juan de Dios Gallegos's life eventually spanned more than a century. An expert horseman and cowboy, de Dios had traveled extensively across North America and into Mexico before settling down with a family. He had been adopted when he was very young into the Gallegos family of Abiquiú, and the local lore claimed that he was the last of the *genízaro*—detribalized captives—in northern New Mexico. De Dios's Abiquiú-born wife was related to the influential Jose Maria Chavez, but de Dios raised his family at the ranch on the Piedra Lumbre.

The River Ranch, as it was called by Carol Stanley and the Anglos at Ghost Ranch, was a group of stone buildings nestled in the Chama *bosque*, with irrigated fields and a vegetable garden on the *bancos* above. The ranch was built by a Kentucky family who had come west and settled here in the 1800s. De Dios used the buildings for his family, and also for overnight visitors, as everyone passing through this part of northern New Mexico came to plan their journey with an overnight under the cottonwood trees at de Dios's Vadito de Chicos. In the 1920s, de Dios's informal hostelry even began to attract the Harvey cars and other guided tour groups.

It was a long drive to Santa Fe—several hours if the roads were dry and the vehicle trouble free—and trips to town were infrequent. Several times each month, Stanley, accompanied by Miller or Cox, and by her housekeeper and friend, Alice Pring, left the ranch and did errands in Santa Fe. Stanley's meticulously kept ledger book serves as a map of her purchases as well as her itinerary: lumber, nails, and miscellaneous building materials were purchased at Big Jo Lumber and at Santa Fe Builder's Supply; a diesel generator was bought from the Kramer mercantile at San Juan Pueblo; and general ranch supplies came from Wood Davis's Hardware Company in Santa Fe. For personal sundries Stanley went to the Capital Pharmacy on the Santa Fe plaza, and she perused the ladies' departments at J. C. Penney Company and Montgomery Ward, also on the old plaza. Laundry was taken to the Santa Fe Electric Laundry, and groceries were purchased from Kaune's Grocery. Once a month, Stanley treated herself to a shampoo, cut, and style at the De Vargas Beauty Shop. She still had friends living in Santa Fe—Dorothy Kent had a home now in Tesuque, and Alice Corbin Henderson and her husband, Will, still lived on Camino del Monte Sol—and after business meetings with her attorney, Francis Wilson, in his downtown office, Stanley met with her friends at La Fonda for lunch and conversation on the Harvey House patio.

Stanley was still marginally active in local art and cultural preservation groups and annually paid her ten-dollar fee to remain a member of the Archaeological Institute of America. But Stanley's unconventional choice for the extreme rural life found at Ghost Ranch had begun to distance her physically and emotionally from the Anglo society found in Santa Fe.

By late 1933, Ghost Ranch could comfortably accommodate eighteen to twenty guests, and Stanley needed the casitas fully occupied all of the summer and into the fall to break even. But the national economic depression was deepening, and tourist numbers were declining in New Mexico. With Lloyd Miller, Stanley was attempting to run the Piedra Lumbre Cattle Company, but with poor grass and a long-term drought, it was obvious that this venture was doomed.

Stanley had been in the dude business for more than twelve years and, at fifty-seven years of age, was losing the enthusiasm and patience needed to serve the needs and demands of even the best of guests. Stanley might have chosen to close the doors on her second ranch home had it not been for the timely arrival of three industrious, twentieth-century overachievers: Arthur Newton Pack, Edward H. Bennett, and Robert Wood Johnson. They were all three big names in American commerce and industry, with large, made-in-America fortunes. Pack and Bennett came knocking upon Stanley's crooked, low-slung front door within a few months of one another in the summer of 1933. Johnson would follow a year later.

All three would exert a lasting influence on Ghost Ranch, but Arthur Pack's would prove to be the most profound and providential. Stanley had first met Arthur Pack in 1929, when he had come to San Gabriel with members of his *Nature Magazine* staff. Pack was a professional writer and editor by trade, but he was as comfortable in the wild places yet found in the world as he was in his Ivy League hometown of Princeton. Born into a family that had already made their millions, Pack could have traveled the world as a man of leisure, a casual, uninvolved sightseer. Instead, Pack turned his love for and of the outdoors into an unwavering, lifelong crusade, and using his gift for the written word, helped to make environmental protection an American virtue via his magazine, books, and civic and political activities.

Pack's youngest daughter, Peggy, had suffered several serious bouts of pneumonia in previous winters, and by 1933, the family physician recommended the family leave Princeton for a home in a drier clime. Pack and his wife, Eleanor Brown—"Brownie"—had traveled into the Southwest several times by 1933, and had many friends with comfortable ranches in southern Arizona and New Mexico who offered the Pack family shelter. But it was to Stanley's new ranch on the high desert beyond Abiquiú that Pack was drawn. He had never seen Ghost Ranch, but Pack had been smitten by the landscape of the Piedra Lumbre several years before.

> A change of fortune, fate or destiny frequently creeps up on one unawares. I had no time to realize that the winter of 1932–33 was due to mark the end of a period in my life quite as definitive as had been the end of the first World War. Our younger daughter,

Arthur N. Pack in front of his Fairchild airplane with a relocated baby antelope at Ghost Ranch in 1934.

> Peggy, had a second serious bout with pneumonia, and so unfortunate were the after effects that our doctor recommended our taking her to a dry climate for at least two years. I thought of the gorgeous cliffs there in Navajo country. They had been like a magnet drawing me back to the Southwest, and now all at once here was a legitimate excuse which even our families and friends could recognize. We made our plans to go.[6]

The Pack family came by train to Lamy, New Mexico, in early June. Their entourage included Arthur and Brownie, their two daughters, Peggy and Norrie, their son, Vernon, and a nurse, Mary L. Duncan, whom the children called Nanny. The Pack family was met by a driver who drove them from Lamy to Abiquiú in a Lincoln touring car. It was a bumpy, hot, long, but beautiful journey to Abiquiú, where they stopped at Bode's General Store behind the old church on the village plaza. Martin Bode, the German proprietor, offered to accompany the family the final seventeen miles to Ghost Ranch. Pack was an experienced backcountry traveler, but he was grateful for Bode's company and conversation as the heavily loaded Lincoln drove up the narrow, dusty track into the Chama River Canyon. The dirt road inched and climbed along a high, narrow ledge above the river and wound around sharp, narrow curves as it passed through the deep gorge. The road through the Chama Canyon was hard on a vehicle, nerve-wracking on a driver, and downright terrifying for the passengers (young Norrie became carsick).

The road widened as it emerged from the red rock canyon onto the first spacious llanos of the Piedra Lumbre. The Pack family had their first view of Cerro Pedernal, which rose alone into the blue sky to the south. The winter of 1932–33 had brought good snows to northern New Mexico, and the grass on the Piedra Lumbre was tall and thick, giving a rare, lush quality to the high desert.

After a long, hot day of travel, the Pack family finally arrived at the place called Ghost Ranch.

> The main road of poorly graded clay had been rough enough, but after a dozen miles we turned off on a mere track marked only by a cow's skull propped against a rock, slid down an incredibly steep hill, crossed a creek on a narrow log bridge and wound up

A Ghost Ranch touring car in Monument Valley in October 1937.

> on the other side beneath a spectacular array of cliffs seen years before. . . .
>
> Close-in under the sheltering protection of magnificent buttes and sheer sandstone cliffs huddled a single low adobe building whose every door and window staggered crookedly. From it appeared a woman who spoke in cultured tones unmistakably Bostonian. "Welcome to Ghost Ranch," she said.[7]

Arthur Pack's fortune was not really remarkable among Stanley's guests; nor was his reputation particularly colorful or his accomplishments widely recognized. Although his appearance and demeanor were often compared to Edward, Prince of Wales, it is doubtful that, in the soft-spoken, gentle-mannered Arthur Pack, Stanley recognized Ghost Ranch's heir apparent. Stanley was simply glad to have a trusted friend and his family among her first guests at the fledgling Ghost Ranch, and she welcomed the tired and dusty travelers into the legendary Archuleta house under the cottonwoods.

After a supper prepared by Alice Pring, Stanley told the Pack family the stories of el Rancho de los Brujos, and entertained them later in the evening with a few classical favorites played on her Steinway. There was still no generator at Ghost Ranch, and the Pack's casita, like Stanley's house, was lit by candles and kerosene lamps. The night sky was clear and bright with the moon, and the family chose to sleep outside that first night. "That night . . . we spread our bedrolls outside under a pair of great cottonwood trees, which our hostess informed us had served only a few years before as gallows for the local cattle thieves. The cliffs surrounding us cast a shadow in the moonlight, and across the arroyo a pair of great horned owls hooted again and again. We agreed that this was indeed the place we were looking for to build a new home, and the next day bought a site from Carol."[8]

The next morning, Carol Stanley took Brownie and Arthur Pack out onto the Painted Desert below the great cliffs to look for a house site. They chose a flat, sandy plateau above the Arroyo Seco in the midst of the red hills several miles from ranch headquarters. To the north of the site a sheer wall of gold and pink cliffs rose two hundred feet into the sky. To the south was Pedernal.

With Stanley's guidance the Packs drew out the plans for a simple, U-shaped adobe house with rooms that opened onto a common portal that embraced the view of Pedernal. Every window framed some spectacular piece of the Painted Desert and red sand hills, the shimmering cliffs, or the far horizon line of mountains and mesas. The intimate immensity of the landscape of Ghost Ranch was nowhere more celebrated than at the house soon christened Rancho de los Burros, Ranch of the Burros.

Ted Peabody supervised the construction, which began immediately, of the house under the cliffs. The Pack family remained at Ghost Ranch that summer and fall and moved into the Ranch of the Burros by Christmas of 1933.

Pack's inherited fortune enabled him to effortlessly transplant his entire family to the faraway place of Ghost Ranch. But it was not just his father's money that made life at Ghost Ranch possible for Arthur Pack; his father's philosophies about people and land enabled Arthur Pack to appreciate the high desert paradise he had found at Ghost Ranch.

Arthur Pack's *Nature Magazine* and its sponsoring organization, the American Nature Association, based in Washington, D.C., were con-

Rancho de los Burros, the Pack family home at Ghost Ranch, under construction in 1933.

A view of Chimney Rock through a window in the Rancho de los Burros house while it was under construction.

sidered the voice of the young environmental movement by the early 1920s. But Pack was not the first in his family to find himself at the forefront of the American conservation movement. Pack was actually following the wide path into the field of environmental education blazed by his father, Charles Pack. "I lived and worked within the aura of my father's determination to become the greatest conservation leader of his time," Arthur explained in his unpublished autobiography. "My function was primarily to serve as an extension of the personality and unflagging zeal of Charles Lathrop Pack."[9]

Ironically, it was the Pack family's exploitation of American forests that had made them millionaires in the nineteenth century. Arthur's grandfather, George Willis Pack, began the lucrative family relationship with trees as a lumberman in the forests of Michigan and eventually owned the largest sawmill operation in the Northwest. Grandfather Pack had homes in Cleveland, Ohio; Port Huron, Michigan; Southampton, New York; and Asheville, North Carolina, where Pack Square still bears tribute to George's arrival there after the Civil War.

The family consciousness about trees and forests, and their possible demise at the hands of man, was awakened in the 1870s when Arthur Pack's father, Charles, went to Germany with his father, George. While George soaked in the healing waters at Carlsbad, young Charles Pack learned German from the daughter of the village forester. Charles also became acquainted with the Katz family, who had been part-owners of the Black Forest for more than two hundred years. The Katz brothers practiced selective cutting and reseeding: common practice today, in the 1870s, such premeditated and organized timber conservation was a novel and even questionable approach to lumbering.

Charles Pack returned to America and redirected the Pack family lumber business using the use/rest/reseed practices learned in Germany. By the first years of the twentieth century, Charles Pack had made his own millions several times over, and he used his money and influence to begin a one-man crusade to save the forests of North America. Pack explained in lectures and newspaper articles that if Americans did not decrease their rate of lumber consumption, and also begin extensive reseeding and replanting of the forests, America would be a treeless country by 1950.

Pack put his money behind his convictions and placed large amounts of the profits generated by the family sawmills back into the earth that had sprouted the Packs' magnificent fortune. He offered his expertise and services free of charge: Pack wrote a forestry primer, published it at his own expense, and distributed over five million copies to schools and forestry camps across the United States.

As the United States became a consumer society of seemingly unquenchable proportions, Pack reminded American society of its responsibility to the coming generations who could inherit an earth depleted of natural resources. He recognized, decades before it became a movement of global proportions, how the health of the environment directly impacted and determined the health of human society. Pack's forestry ideas impressed President Teddy Roosevelt, and, in 1908, he enlisted Pack into the National Conservation Congress, which appointed a commission to begin a national inventory of America's natural resources.

As world war threatened, Charles Pack urged Americans to become more self-sufficient. He sat down and wrote the *War Garden Victorious* primer that birthed the War Garden movement, and by 1917, Charles Pack was steering the National War Garden Commission that prompted three million Americans to create home gardens by 1918. After World War I, the global-conscious Pack founded the American Tree Association and personally financed the reseeding of Europe, shipping from Boston Harbor millions of packaged Douglas fir and Sitka spruce seeds to the battle-devastated lands of France, Italy, Great Britain, and Belgium.

Thus was the privileged yet activist environment that Arthur Newton Pack was born into in 1893. Arthur and his three siblings, Randolph, Lathrop, and Beulah, were raised in a household that valued personal, ecological, and social responsibility, where humans respected the earth and understood that they were in a relationship to the land and animals they shared the earth with. Arthur was the youngest son. He was by his own account small, shy, and awkward, more interested in books than sports or physical activity out of doors. Concerned about his third son's penchant for reading and sitting, Charles Pack sent the fifteen-year-old Arthur away from the comforts of Lakewood, New Jersey (where the Rockefellers and Goulds were neighbors), to a boarding school in the Adirondack Mountains. A former logging camp, the Ransom School for Boys immersed Arthur in college preparatory courses as well as boating, trailblazing, hiking, camping, and basic forestry practices. When the weather turned cold, Arthur and his classmates boarded a train for the Ransom School's winter campus on a Florida swamp, where the boys learned sailing and fishing skills in a little-known place called Coconut Grove. Although Arthur Pack would always have a quiet, thoughtful demeanor, the four years he spent in the mountains and on the sea gave him a self-confidence and affinity with the great outdoors that enabled him to pursue a professional life that often thrust him into the public eye.

In 1923, after attending Williams College and Harvard Business School, and with the financial backing of his father, Pack created *Nature Magazine* with his friend Percival Sheldon Risdale. *Nature* was devoted entirely to issues surrounding land and animals, and Pack's enthusiasm and knowledge about the natural world quickly attracted a subscribers list of more than 100,000 readers.

With *Nature* Pack simultaneously began his own nonprofit corporation, the American Nature Association, headquartered on 16th Street in Washington, D.C., a stone's throw from Pack's friends and allies at the National Geographic Society and in the White House. Pack and his organization received praise and encouragement from government officials, forestry management educators, and wildlife preservationists across the United States. But their cause faced a fundamental skepticism among average Americans, who were either disinterested in, or suspicious of, the whole philosophy surrounding the preservation of the earth's so-called gifts. "Trying to sell the idea of conservation of natural resources was rather like trying to promote religion," Arthur Pack wrote of his first years as a nature writer. "There existed a ready-made audience of those already converted to the cause, but the millions of ordinary citizens were simply not getting the message."[10]

By his early thirties, Pack had published his first book, *The Nature Almanac*, was at work on his second, *Our Vanishing Forests*, and was a much-in-demand speaker on the national lecture circuit. With *National Geographic, Nature Magazine* helped introduce the new genre of American nature writing and photography, and gave thousands of urban readers their first exposure to the yet-wild places and untamed species found in North America.

Pack was involved with all aspects of his magazine and wrote dozens of articles each year that involved research and photography expedi-

The newly completed Rancho de los Burros in 1933.

tions into the outback. His years at the Ransom School served him well, and there was no physical terrain that Pack was uncomfortable in.

Pack's partner in his adventures beginning in late 1919 was his wife, Eleanor Brown—called Brownie. By 1933, and the relocation of their family to Ghost Ranch, Arthur and Brownie had camped, hiked, boated, and motored across most of North America and Europe. But Brownie was not ready to settle down.

> One reads from time to time of women who have become explorers of the wild places of this earth, whether it be Africa, Alaska or the farthest jungles of the upper Amazon. The cause, perhaps, is a romanticism of the spirit which refuses to be confined within four walls or to be limited by the safety and security of family life,

Eleanor "Brownie" Pack photographing antelope at Ghost Ranch in 1934.

> preferring rather a rough sleeping bag under the stars to the finest mattress and linen upon a prosaic bed. . . . Such a person was Brownie.[11]

Arthur met Brownie at sister Beulah Pack's house party in the Adirondacks just after his return home at the end of World War I, during which he served as a captain with a U.S. aircraft armament division in England and France. Brownie was the daughter of a Connecticut doctor and a recent Wellesley graduate. Athletic and statuesque, Eleanor Brown had a self-absorbed confidence that made her both aloof and engaging.

Brownie's fascination with the natural world began when she was very young and explored the woods near her home, bird-watching, often alone on foot or in her canoe. Her parents took her for a stay on a Wyoming ranch before she began college, and from that day on Brownie's one and only ambition was to live in the West. Brownie's independence and unconventional pastimes in the wild intimidated women, but men found Brownie irresistible. Her eyes were intensely blue, and they locked onto people in a way that Arthur later called "mesmerizing." But then everything about Brownie was mesmerizing, and although Arthur suspected he was not the charming and adventurous white knight she was looking for, they fell in love and married only a few months after their meeting at Beulah's house party.

After a honeymoon on a boat off the coast of British Columbia, the Packs settled in Princeton. Brownie jumped into Arthur's professional life with energy and enthusiasm. She was involved in every aspect of Arthur's research and became a published nature photographer and author in her own right. When Pack and Risdale launched *Nature Magazine* in 1923, Brownie was as much a partner in the venture as the founders and wrote the garden section and coauthored articles for every issue.

The Packs had three children by 1927, but even her young family did not keep Brownie from her first love—outdoor adventure. The children were frequently left in the care of a governess while Arthur and Brownie led photographers, filmmakers, and writers on month-long expeditions into the hinterlands of North America. These expeditions brought to the American public the first motion pictures of mountain lions, antelope, mountain goats, bears, and all kinds of animals, and filled the pages of *Nature Magazine* with rare and wonderful photographs of birds and wildlife in their native habitat.

Every person who has ever called Ghost Ranch home for any length of time continues to call Ghost Ranch *home* for the rest of their lives. Although they would spend only a few years at the ranch, the Pack children would not be an exception. In the summer of 1933, Eleanor, known as Norrie, ten; Margaret, called Peggy, six; and Vernon, seven, sunk their hands and their hearts into the sand of the place called Ghost Ranch as if they had been born upon it.[12]

Theirs was a privileged but not a pampered existence, and much of the Pack children's experiences at Ghost Ranch paralleled their father's time at the Ransom School. Towheaded, petite Peggy quickly regained her health in the high, dry air of the Piedra Lumbre and, with Norrie and Vernon, spent the long summer days out of doors exploring the badlands and canyons of the Piedra Lumbre. With daily instruction from the ranch cowboys, the sisters became adept horsewomen and soon took their horses out for long rides into steep and difficult terrain.

The burros for which the Pack house was named were brought to Ghost Ranch from a canyon near Abiquiú where there was a wild herd in the 1930s. Pack learned that the local ranchers considered the wild burros—descendants of burros brought in with the copper miners of the late 1800s—a nuisance and were shooting them for sport. With Jack McKinley, Slim Jarmon, and a young Princeton grad named Frank Hibben, who had come to New Mexico with the Pack family, Pack organized a burro roundup. The men spent three days in Copper Canyon and, after much effort and frustration, managed to capture three of the wild burros and bring them back to Ghost Ranch. The Ghost Ranch herd continued to grow over the next few years, with both wild and domesticated burros given to the Packs, who kept them in a corral near their house under the cliffs.

The burros were tamed using a method favored in California at the time: a log was tied to each burro and after days of dragging the dead weight about behind them, the animals were docile and approachable. The burros became the responsibility of the Pack children, who learned the individual quirks of Connie, Bonnie, Blanca, Pinky, and Old Egypt, and handled them accordingly. "Connie you had to climb on bareback," Peggy Pack remembered a half-century later. "Bonnie was okay with the saddle, but she didn't like anyone on her bareback—she'd buck them right off. They were all wild."

Pinky was considered the least stubborn, and was favored by the children because he had a lively step—rare among burros—and would actually reach a destination with little or no balking or bucking. "They were such little things," Norrie Pack recalled, "if they bucked you off, you wouldn't get hurt. I got bucked off numerous times by a burro . . . but it wasn't like a horse. . . . You didn't have far to fall!"

With fall came a regular school routine for the Pack children. Frank Hibben served as their tutor, and classes based on the Calvert School curriculum were held in one of Stanley's casitas, soon renamed the School House by the children. The Pack children's daily routine included feeding, saddling, and then riding the burros the two and a half miles over the desert to Ghost Ranch headquarters. Snow, rain, sleet, heat, or sandstorm, the Pack children rose at dawn to tend their burros and then head out across the badlands for school. "Once I remember the burros simply would not go," Norrie Pack recalled of 1934. "It was snowing; it was miserable out, and my mother got in her car and came

Norrie, Peggy, and Vernon Pack on the burros at the house that was named for them, 1934.

Frank Hibben tutoring Norrie and Vernon Pack on the portal of Rancho de los Burros in 1934.

up behind them and nudged them to go from the rear . . . with the car! Far be it that she would take us to school!"

Their tutor, Frank Hibben, was studying for his master's degree in zoology, and lived at Ghost Ranch in 1933 and 1934. He needed specimens and, with Brownie's blessing, paid the Pack girls fifty cents apiece for dead rattlesnakes he then skinned and sent back to the Cleveland Museum. Norrie Pack remembers their snake hunting expeditions. "We'd go out and kill them with a rock, and then when they stopped moving—and in the middle of the day sometimes they still wriggled around—we'd hook them on the end of a stick and then try to get on our horses, or burros, and ride them back to the ranch. And the horses did not like this one single bit. It was a little difficult. But fifty cents was an awful lot of money."

Although everyone at Ghost Ranch went to great lengths to avoid the shy, poisonous prairie rattlers that were often found underfoot. The Burros House was unknowingly built upon an established rattlesnake community, and members of the Pack family developed the habit of using an extra-long stride through the doorways to the portal in order to avoid startling a snake sunning on the threshold.

A twenty-by-sixty-foot, concrete-lined swimming pool was built in the ground alongside the Rito del Yeso half a mile from the mouth of Yeso Canyon. Summer afternoons could be blistering hot at Ghost Ranch, but a quick dip in the chilly, spring-fed pool was enough to temporarily reverse heat-induced lethargy. There was an adobe bathhouse but no other amenities. However, the setting was spectacular, and sunbathers on the narrow pinion-and-juniper-edged deck gazed up at a deep blue sky edged by a sheer red wall of cliffs to the north and east, Chimney Rock to the west, and Pedernal to the south.

By 1934, Stanley had mortgaged most of her land—one-third of the Piedra Lumbre Land Grant, or about sixteen thousand acres—to Pack. Pack had also become a partner in the Piedra Lumbre Cattle Company, although it was already evident that the drought-ravaged and overgrazed land could not support even a small herd of cattle; the company was defunct by 1935.

Pack did not need to pursue a profitable business on the Piedra Lumbre, but he did enjoy the challenges and physical labor involved with livestock and, within his first year at Ghost Ranch, began to purchase palomino horses. Pack bought two fillies and a stallion, Brujo, from a quarter horse breeder named Warren Shoemaker and began to breed what would become a highly respected line of registered palominos. Over the next decade, Pack registered more than ten of the Ghost Ranch horses with the American Quarter Horse Association, and Pack's palominos became highly prized among western breeders. Descendants of the Ghost Ranch palominos became pivotal to the successful linebreeding program of Hank Weiscamp of Alamosa, Colorado, whose horses are regarded by breeders and ranchers as among the finest quarter horses in the West.

Although Pack's horses were used for pleasure riding around the dusty, rugged terrain of the Piedra Lumbre, they were always groomed to perfection. "Mr. Pack used to baby his horses," rancher Hank Weiscamp recalled, "and they always looked like they had just stepped out of a show ring."[13]

Pack was not as disconnected from mainstream America as he might have appeared. He had begun to take flying lessons in Princeton and, by the end of 1933, had his pilot's license. After moving to Ghost Ranch, a runway was scraped out of the hard desert near the Burros House, and Pack kept his new Fairchild airplane in a small hangar under the cliffs. Pack used the plane for short trips to Santa Fe and Albuquerque and also became a competent cross-country traveler, often flying solo from New Mexico to New Jersey for business.

From his desk at the Burros House Pack remained an active general in the battles waged by the American conservation movement. Pack continued to work as editor of *Nature Magazine* and also remained president of the American Nature Association. Polite, deferential, soft-spoken Arthur Pack showed his defiant side in his monthly column "Conservation," where he bluntly articulated his opinions "on the vital issues affecting our use, and abuse of natural resources, including wildlife," and declared that the American Nature Association's purpose was to assist "Americans to play a militant part in the attainment of constructive conservation aims."[14]

In 1934, as the Taylor bill and its controversial proposals for public land usage—which regulated, among many other things, grazing rights—became the law of the land, Pack joined the new Southwestern Conservation League (SCL). Pack was in favor of the Taylor laws, but he also understood that there needed to be grassroots community support if public lands were to be truly protected. The New Mexico-based SCL was among the first organizations in the United States to bring cattle and sheep ranchers, game and fish agencies, and conservation groups to the same table to discuss the regulations and protection policies for public lands. Pack explained the importance of the league's initial meetings in an article published in *New Mexico Magazine* in 1934.

> It was almost the first time in history that all these groups had ever been gotten together in the Southwest on a basis of mutual understanding, mutual trust, and mutual cooperation. . . . There is much that needs to be done to attain real conservation, protection against erosion, protection against the multitude of factors of man's occupancy, which have disturbed the balance of nature.[15]

Pack had witnessed firsthand the irreversible changes brought to the wild by people and advocated federal action that would legally and formally distinguish land that was wilderness from land that was national park. Franklin Roosevelt's New Deal gave enormous amounts of money to the development of state and municipal parks. Parks were well and good to Pack and his conservation colleagues, but they saw how increased levels of outdoor recreation, aided by improved and even encouraged automobile accessibility into national parks, was threatening the wilderness yet found in those national parks. Pack's American Nature Association joined forces with the National Parks Association, the Wilderness Society, and the Emergency Conservation Council and publicly criticized the U.S. Park Service's management of national parklands. Pack and his colleagues called for real protection of the last great places—meaning little or no recreational and extractive use. "These proto-environmentalists were advocating a new landscape ideal—wilderness—that embodied the notion that preservation should be for its own sake, not for the sake of efficient multiple use (forests) or for the sake of public enjoyment of nature (parks)."[16]

Pack's initial optimism about successful cooperative local and federal conservation efforts was probably challenged over the next few decades as the goals of environmentalists and the needs of the cattle and sheep growers in the United States took opposing sides on a regular and often hostile level. But Pack's and his allies' efforts to inform the public about the fragility of the environment did lay the foundation for land-use policies responsive to the goals of conservationists, ranchers, farmers, recreationists, and civic groups, and anticipated the eventual need for global land-use management and environmental laws.

At Ghost Ranch, Arthur Pack had found a home that most people would have called a paradise, aloof from the despair and desperation experienced by the vast majority of Americans during the Great Depression. He and his family were privileged expatriates waiting out the thirties deep in the indigenous Southwest, where people and communities functioned in a self-sufficient manner much as they always had. But Pack was different from others in his aristocratic circle because he was not simply biding his time until the American economic crisis passed. Pack believed the real treasures in life were not material goods and acquisitions, but were the simple joys found in the simple life. Pack was downsizing permanently and was happy enough to settle down into a routine at Ghost Ranch that moved between his writing desk, the small vegetable garden, the docile burros, and the blue-blooded palominos.

Pack's thoughts on the subject of modern life became his third book, *The Challenge of Leisure*, in which he shared his views on Americans and their addiction to what he called the Big Four: "the automobile, the moving picture, the radio, and competitive sports organized on a grand, go-getter scale."[17] Pack understood that his life of leisure was a luxury afforded only the wealthy. Even so, he believed that most people, wealthy and not, avoided real leisure time and were bored by it. The challenge of leisure was to learn to use it well; and to Arthur Pack, leisure time was nowhere better spent than in wild places. "Literally and figuratively, those who live beyond the reach of cement pavement have their feet on the ground," Pack wrote.[18]

Pack's approach to living brought him admiration from a small circle of friends who admired his devotion to a life close to nature. But his lack of desire to circulate and compete in the outer world sparked a growing discontent in his wife. Brownie had married a white knight who loved, as she did, the woods and outer places; but she also wanted that knight to seek the jousting and attentions of center court.

While Arthur was becoming drawn into the daily routine of running Ghost Ranch, Brownie was becoming more certain that she did not want to be tied to the responsibilities of a guest ranch. Throughout their first year at the Burros House, while Pack was spending more and more time at ranch headquarters, Brownie was spending more and more time with young Frank Hibben. And by the summer of 1935, Brownie would make this arrangement formal when she up and left Arthur and Ghost Ranch for a life with the aspiring archaeologist.

Within a few weeks of the Pack family's 1933 arrival at Ghost Ranch, a second family of wealth and influence wound their way to Stanley's Piedra Lumbre doorstep. Early one July morning, Edward H. Bennett, a semiretired Chicago architect, drove out of Santa Fe toward Abiquiú with his son, Ted Junior. Father and son had grown bored with the polo-playing crowd that gathered each day at Arthur Cable's summer home in Tesuque, where the Bennetts were staying, and so left the rest of the Bennett family—Joe, Betty, and stepmother, Olive—in Tesuque and drove north up the Chama River looking for a place they had heard about called Ghost Ranch. Ted Junior remembered that inaugural journey to the Piedra Lumbre: "From Espanola to the ranch was forty miles of washboard road, and the Chevy acted as though it had no wheels and we were being dragged along. Finally the trip was over and we were there. We were greeted by Carol Stanley, a person of great charm, and given some iced tea. Father and I both loved the place at sight. The colors were unbelievable, many small hills reaching to a row of cliffs that seemed to rise from nowhere with great chimneys among them, of colored sandstone. It was breathtaking."[19]

It is likely that Stanley knew Edward Bennett at least by name and certainly by reputation. San Gabriel guests had included numerous people from Bennett's Chicago circle: the Harvey family of Harvey House fame, Archibald MacLeish of Carson Pirie Scott, and members of the J. Sanford and Stuart Otis families that worked with the Santa Fe Railway.

Bennett Senior had achieved international recognition as one of the primary architects associated with the Chicago Plan. In 1909, with Daniel Burnham, Edward H. Bennett developed the urban plan that fundamentally suggested how the city of Chicago should grow in the twentieth century. Their now-famous plan included the reclamation and greening of the lake shore, the straightening of the Chicago River, the double-decking of Wacker Drive, and the promotion and preservation of a greenbelt of forest preserves. Bennett also designed Buckingham Fountain, the centerpiece of Chicago's Grant Park.

The Plan of Chicago was not just about architecture and structural designs, but included socioenvironmental proposals to initiate better living conditions for Chicago residents—housing and zoning codes and designated public parks. What Bennett and his colleagues created for Chicago became a model for growth in other American cities, and Bennett's expertise was sought by planners in Washington, D.C., Detroit, Portland, Brooklyn, and Ottawa, Canada.

Although retired, Bennett was a frequent visitor to Washington, D.C., where he dined with congressmen and presidential aides who sought his advice on changes and additions to the Federal Triangle region of the capital. He was also working on the Century of Progress World's Fair that would open in Chicago in 1934. Bennett was in New Mexico to get away from the professional pressures that pursued him, but it was not until he came to be sipping tea and swapping stories in Stanley's primitive house under the shining cliffs that he felt he was truly *away*. Father and son Bennett asked to see the new guest ranch under construction, and after a quick tour of a just-completed adobe

Edward H. Bennett Sr. at Ghost Ranch in 1937.

guest house, Ted Senior told Stanley that he and young Ted would return the next day with the rest of the family for an extended summer stay.

The Bennett family returned and remained the rest of the summer at Ghost Ranch. The children rode horses with the ranch cowboys and hiked and roamed the Piedra Lumbre just as the Pack children did. Edward Bennett and his second wife, Olive, became friends with Carol Stanley, and before they left in August, Stanley agreed to sell them 212 acres under the cliffs to the west of ranch headquarters, where they could build a summer home.

The Bennetts chose a house site half a mile across the sand land from the Packs', directly below the massive chimney formation called Puerto del Cielo, Gate to Heaven. The Bennett and Pack houses would be walking distance from each other, but were situated among the red and yellow sand hills so as to be completely private and hidden from each other.

Bennett's Lake Forest office diary the fall of 1933 documents his daily progress on two very different projects: the Apex Building in the Federal Triangle that necessitated many journeys to Washington and often to the White House; and the "EHB House in New Mexico."[20] The Washington project would tie up Bennett's energies for years, but the house in New Mexico went quickly. Plans were finalized by late September, and the construction of the Bennett adobe, called Casa Monte Rojo, the Red Hill House, began by early October. Stanley and Peabody were still working on the Pack house, but they simultaneously began the Bennett house.

Casa Monte Rojo was completed by July of 1934, and the Bennett family began semiannual visits to Ghost Ranch. Each year until World War II, they arrived in mid- to late-July and returned to Chicago after Labor Day. Bennett and his wife, Olive, also came for several weeks each March to open the house, and to watch winter depart and spring arrive on the Piedra Lumbre.

Bennett drew up the actual building plans for his desert house, but the design was based upon the traditional pueblo-style plan Stanley had used for the Pack house: U-shaped and flat roofed, the major architectural consideration of the Bennett adobe, like the Packs', was the placement of windows and doors so as to frame the house's spectacular views of the cliffs to the north, the red and gold sand land to the

The Edward H. Bennett House, Casa Monte Rojo (later called Casa del Sol), in 1937.

east and west, and to the south some twenty miles across the valley, Pedernal rising into the blue sky.

A garage housed the large generator and batteries; keeping the electrical system working was nearly a full-time job at the Bennett house, just as it was at Ghost Ranch headquarters and over at the Packs' home. The Bennett house, again like its neighbor, had a large rattlesnake population—some eighteen were killed during construction—and occupants learned to step carefully and cautiously across the door stoops.

The daily summer duties of Harvard undergrad Ted Junior included the maintenance of the generator and the extermination of the rattlesnake-attracting mice that were determined to make the garage their new home.

> Among other things I had partial share in care of the batteries and a primary duty in care of the mice. We had a Fairbanks Morse electric generator, with its accompanying 55 2-volt batteries. They worked in a sort of cumshaw arrangement: the batteries started the generator, and the latter charged the batteries. The batteries made the juice for the house and the water pump in the well. The mice took more care. It sounds cruel, but they attracted rattlesnakes and had to be got rid of. I used to make sandwiches of white bread with a sort of chemical jam—I forget what it was—but it looked delicious. . . . Father, incidentally was a menace to the rattlers; he accounted for many with rocks thrown.[21]

The Bennett teenagers rode horses and took the "Clay Car"—a remarkably indestructible Lincoln owned by Stanley that had survived a dunking in the Chama River—on adventures across the Piedra Lumbre. There were overnight trips to Santa Fe, but most of the summer was passed on Ghost Ranch, where the family swam in the pool, hiked into the canyons, watched the Friday-night rodeo, and dressed up for the Saturday evening *baille*—dance—held each week for the visiting dudes, dudettes, and resident staff and cowboys.

As a young man, Edward Bennett Sr. had studied in Paris at the École des Beaux-Arts, where he had become an accomplished watercolorist. His paints had been put aside for decades, but at Ghost Ranch the sixty-plus-year-old Bennett found time to pursue his own art again and taught himself to paint with oils. Bennett spent many an afternoon painting out of doors under a tent rigged to the side of the family Ford parked out in the desert. Bennett may have been the first to render the Ghost Ranch cliffs in oils on canvas, but his efforts would soon be eclipsed and diminished with the arrival to the Piedra Lumbre in the next year of Georgia O'Keeffe.

In the early 1930s, Arthur and Brownie Pack's circle of friends in New Jersey briefly included aviator Charles Lindbergh and his wife, Anne. In 1931, Charles and Anne and their new baby boy lived in the Packs' neighborhood in Princeton. Lindbergh had completed his solo flight across the Atlantic in 1927, and the now-world-famous aviator and his wife and young son, Charles Junior, were looking for a home to purchase in the nearby countryside.

The Packs and the Lindberghs became friends and spent casual afternoons and evenings together. Brownie's brother, Alfred, a pilot and a psychiatrist, often joined the two couples for dinner, and the men stayed up late into the night talking about aviation and medicine. Brownie Pack and Anne Lindbergh both enjoyed classical music and on several occasions went into New York to attend lectures and concerts together. "Anne and I used to have wonderful times together," Brownie recalled of those days. "Lindbergh wasn't interested in music. And if we were without him, no one ever recognized her.

"I think that we were their only friends in Princeton, besides the real estate woman. . . . They didn't want to get involved."

The Lindberghs moved out of Princeton and onto a quiet farm in the country near Hopewell, New Jersey. Brownie continued to visit Anne at her country house. "Unfortunately our acquaintance with the Lindberghs was destined to be short lived," Arthur Pack wrote years later. "They moved to their new home in the nearby countryside and there the cruel kidnapping and murder of the baby took place, with all the blaze of subsequent publicity which drove Charles and Anne out of this country to spend several years quietly in England."[22]

The March 1, 1932, kidnapping of the Lindbergh baby sent a shock wave through the Packs' community of friends and associates that included many wealthy and high-profile families. The Princeton community was further traumatized when two and a half weeks after the Lindbergh baby kidnapping, in the wee hours of the morning of March 19,

1932, an intruder cut through the screen of the second-floor nursery window at the home of Johnson & Johnson heir J. Seward Johnson. The Johnson home, an enormous stone mansion on the Raritan River called Merriewold, had recently been the target of an attempted burglary, and with the Lindbergh kidnapping, the staff was on high alert.

The intruder was seen by the children's nurse, who sounded the alarm that brought Seward Johnson, gun in hand, racing down the hall into his infant daughter Diana's bedroom. The intruder fled back through the window, but Johnson managed to shoot him in the leg as he descended the vines that grew on the house. The wounded burglar escaped that night but was caught several days later in a local diner. In a police lineup, Seward Johnson identified the man as the same one who had broken into his home several weeks before.

The Merriewold burglar was sent to the state penitentiary, but to the Johnson children, it felt as if they had been sent to prison: the estate grounds were wrapped in barbed wire, searchlights swept the lawns, and bars were placed over all windows.

The police never ascertained whether the convicted felon was planning a burglary or a kidnapping. But with the Lindbergh family's nightmare, only a few miles away, still unsolved, even a professional security system and on-site bodyguards for his four young children did not assuage Seward Johnson's fears of additional kidnapping attempts. By the early summer of 1932, Seward Johnson packed up his children and their entourage of nannies, nurses, cooks, and bodyguards and fled to his wife's family home in Bermuda.

Seward Johnson was the younger brother of Robert Wood Johnson II, who in 1932 had taken the helm of their family's enormous pharmaceutical company, Johnson & Johnson. Seward was not the businessman that his brother Bob was, but he carried the title of Johnson & Johnson vice president and treasurer.

Bob Johnson and his second wife, actress and model Maggie Shea, had moved into one of Princeton's most historic homes, Morven, in 1930. The Johnsons were soon part of the Princeton civic and social circle that included the Packs—their yards shared a back wall—and the two couples began to meet for dinners. They began what was to become a satisfying and stimulating friendship for all of them: Bob and Arthur both became pilots, and Maggie and Brownie were both serious wildlife photographers. The Johnsons and Packs soon vacationed together, especially to places that offered time in the wilderness. One such Pack-Johnson expedition included a small, handpicked group that Pack led into the northern Canadian Rockies. Bob Johnson was the designated volunteer first-aid specialist for the entourage of professional and amateur photographers. One of the latter was a young Princeton undergrad named Laurence S. "Larry" Rockefeller, whose father, John D. Rockefeller, was a family friend of Arthur Pack's from childhood days spent in Lakewood, New Jersey.

This particular summer sojourn into the outback of British Columbia lasted a month, and camping gear and photographic equipment were carried on horseback. It was not designed to be a sightseeing holiday; the expedition's camps were days from civilization, and everyone was expected to pull their own weight. Before the group departed Larry's dad told Pack that he wanted Laurence "to do some real work and not just go along for the ride."[23] Pack assigned Larry the seemingly endless but vital chore of providing fuel wood for the group's various campsites. "In the process [Larry] made the mistake of splitting his foot with the axe when we were several days out from any doctor or hospital."[24]

Bob Johnson leapt to young Larry's aid and proved that he was far more than just the CEO of the largest pharmaceutical company in the world: Robert Wood Johnson could actually put to good and expert use the products his company made. From his state-of-the-art first aid kit "Bob did a remarkable job" and cleaned, sterilized, and sutured Larry's wounded foot back together.[25]

Although they moved in different circles professionally, Pack admired Bob Johnson, a "dynamic, restless, unconventional businessman with a sense of humor as well as a sense of duty."[26] In 1933, the Johnson & Johnson Company's sole manufacturing plant was in New Brunswick, with annual sales of about $11 million. In the next decade, under Robert Wood II's leadership, J & J would expand worldwide to include some ninety manufacturing plants with annual sales of $700 million in 120 countries![27]

Numerous personal reasons prompted Bob and Maggie Johnson to follow the Packs to Ghost Ranch in the summer of 1934. The Johnsons could afford to holiday in the finest resorts in the world—their residence on Hog Island in Nassau hosted winter parties for royalty—but after hearing Arthur's stories about the beauty and peace of Ghost

Ranch, they came in midsummer to stay in one of Stanley's rustic, no-frills casitas, where they partook of the simple life.

Bob Johnson was not given to taking a lot of time off from his professional duties, but during his brief visit to the desert of the Piedra Lumbre in the summer of 1934, he found something that he wanted more of in his life: simple pleasures shared with friends and family. The Packs' and Bennetts' summer life at Ghost Ranch seemed to give both the adults and the children exactly what they wanted and needed—freedom and togetherness. The Johnsons had tried unsuccessfully to have a child since their marriage, in 1930, and had adopted a baby, Sheila, earlier that year; their lives were now centered on their new daughter. With the Packs' encouragement, Bob and Maggie Johnson made a lease agreement with Stanley for land upon which "to build a house, have a garden, etc. on what is known as Ghost Ranch."[28]

Bob Johnson hired Edward Bennett to draw up the building plans for his Ghost Ranch retreat. Although the other members of the ranch community suggested that the Johnsons consider a design similar to the single-story, rambling adobe *ranchos* of the Pack and Bennett families, Bob Johnson insisted on a simple two-story rectangle. Bennett thought Johnson's design choice a poor one, but he did what he was asked and began drawing the plans for the RWJ house when he returned to Lake Forest in early September of 1934. The first draft of the plans for what would become the one-and-only two-story structure at Ghost Ranch was sent out on September 20, with final revisions exchanged between Johnson's and Bennett's offices by late October.

Carol Stanley again oversaw the payroll and kept the account book for the RWJ residence, and Ted Peabody was foreman of the crew. By this time, the construction crew of men and women from local villages had worked on Stanley's ranch for more than two years. The construction crew formed a close-knit community, and there was at least one marriage—Herman and Georgia Salazar—the result of the socializing between the young men and women living at what Stanley called the Mexican Camp.

Employment opportunities were few to nonexistent in Rio Arriba County, especially during the Depression. From 1932 until 1936 there was the rare situation at Ghost Ranch where construction projects financed by the ultrawealthy provided local men and women with almost full-time work for several years.

Seward and Robert Wood Johnson's house at Ghost Ranch in 1936.

The Johnson brothers and their families joined the seasonal resident community at Ghost Ranch in the summer of 1935. Bob, Maggie, and Sheila Johnson moved into their two-story adobe with Sheila's nursemaid and with their bodyguard, Clay Wolf. The house was small and spartan: the first floor had a living room, kitchen, dining area, and a bedroom for the baby and the nanny. A steep flight of stairs up the center of the house went to the second-floor bedrooms: to the west was Maggie Johnson's private suite with a large bathroom whose footed bathtub had an unobstructed view of Pedernal; to the east, Robert Wood's smaller bedroom and bath.

Among the other ranch residents the Johnson house was commonly referred to as "the box." Ted Bennett Jr. remembers that even Bob Johnson later regretted his insistence on the aesthetically unremarkable rectangular design, and "afterwards said to Father (Edward Bennett Sr.) that he wished he had taken his advice because it did just look like a box."[29]

Bob Johnson sang Ghost Ranch's praises to his brother, Seward, who was living with his family in Bermuda, and in late summer of 1935, Seward decided to come and see the place for himself. Seward brought his wife and four children, accompanied by their nurse and personal

Maggie (Mrs. Robert Wood Johnson) and her daughter Sheila at Ghost Ranch in the summer of 1936.

bodyguard, on a private train to Lamy, where they were met by a private car that brought them to Ghost Ranch. The Johnson house was not large enough to accommodate both Bob's and Seward's families, so Seward's family stayed in one of Stanley's larger guest cottages.

Although Seward's children were accompanied at all times by John Holsworth, a former policeman and professional bodyguard, they were not particularly aware of the security that surrounded their young lives. They did notice, however, that at Ghost Ranch they stepped into a daily routine that included a freedom of movement, and an absence of parental scrutiny, unknown anywhere else in their world.

The Seward Johnson children, like the Pack clan, spent most of their daylight hours on horseback. Three-year-old Diana stayed close to her nurse, but the elder three, Mary Lea (whose baby face graced the cans of J & J baby powder in 1928), Elaine, and Seward, took great pleasure in riding hard and fast into the mesa land. Their Brooklynite bodyguard John Holsworth had few riding skills and no sense of direction on the Piedra Lumbre's sprawling sand lands, and the Johnson children made a sport of losing Holsworth in the desert. Like Clay Wolf, Holsworth carried a pistol at all times—the children had no idea why—but both bodyguards had cause to use their weapons only when the ranch rattlesnakes came too close to their young wards—or to themselves.

Slim Jarmon and the ranch cowboys took the Johnson children on overnight camping trips into the mountains and on long rides up the Rito del Yeso for picnics on the high, grassy meadows above Box Canyon. At least once a week, the adults joined the children for rides up the long trail to Mesa Montosa for a campfire supper on the high cliffs overlooking the ranch. Slim, Pete Dozier, and Clarence, another resident wrangler, rode ahead and prepared a camp-style gourmet meal for the riders and then taught the children camp songs as the fire died down to embers. When Pedernal was a dark form in the indigo summer sky everyone remounted their horses and slowly descended the starlit trail back to the ranch.

"There was a good feeling at Ghost Ranch," Elaine Johnson Wolde remembers of her childhood summer days on the Piedra Lumbre. "It was very safe, very separate. The family never left the ranch at all. Ever. We children felt very independent, and had our own grand time away from the parents, doing our own thing."

Neither Bob nor Seward invited many visitors to their desert home.

Those friends who did receive an invitation to Ghost Ranch were given a stern warning by the Johnson brothers the day they arrived: the first guy who talks about business goes home.

The Johnson brothers' sister, Evangeline, was among those invited to Ghost Ranch, and she came several times a summer from Taos, where she vacationed with her husband, composer Leopold Stokowski. The Stokowskis had begun to come to New Mexico several years before the Johnson & Johnson brothers' discovery of Ghost Ranch. Stokowski, the progressive, experimental, and controversial director of the Philadelphia Orchestra, was among those creative artists brought to Taos by Mabel Dodge Luhan for inclusion in her elite circle of brilliant friends. In 1931, the Stokowskis made the first of many visits to Luhan's celebrated home at the foot of Taos Mountain. Stokowski was pursuing new musical forms in his own work and, through Mabel's Taos Indian husband, Tony Lujan (Mabel changed the spelling to "Luhan" because she was afraid her eastern friends wouldn't know how to pronounce "Lujan"), was introduced to Pueblo ceremonial chants and rhythms. After his first visit to the Southwest, Stokowski wanted to learn everything he could about Indian culture and music and returned in 1932, and for the next several summers, with his recording equipment.

The Stokowskis were a startlingly handsome couple: Evangeline was raven haired and willowy. Although she was married to an internationally recognized personality, Evangeline was spirited and independent in her own right, athletic and outspoken, and piloted her own plane by the time she was twenty-five. Her exotic sense of fashion influenced her friends, including Mabel Dodge, who allowed Evangeline to restyle her hair on one of her visits to Taos in the mid-1930s. Leopold Stokowski was every bit as beautiful as Evangelinee—tall and slender, with a finely chiseled face and light-blonde hair.

By 1935 and the Stokowskis' first visit to Ghost Ranch, Leopold had resigned his position with the Philadelphia Orchestra and was shifting his musical energies to new opportunities in Hollywood. Stokowski's work with Walt Disney on the film *Fantasia* would soon dominate his life (and his interest in actress Greta Garbo would soon after bring an end to his marriage to Evangeline), but in 1935 and 1936, the Stokowskis and their two daughters were frequently the Johnson brothers' guests at Ghost Ranch.

Evangeline and Leopold Stokowski brought Tony Lujan and Mabel

Dodge with them to Ghost Ranch, and their colorful, dramatic arrival always sent a ripple of excitement through the summer community of guests and residents. Stokowski was widely recognized, as was Mabel Dodge. Tony Lujan, although less well known, was stunning with his long braids, blanketed torso, and dark skin. Stokowski and Lujan spent the mornings playing music in the Johnson living room, where there was a piano for Stokowski to play while Lujan drummed and chanted.

Young Ted Bennett had become friends with Bob and Seward Johnson and their families, but Ted did not know that their sister, Evangeline, was married to the world-famous composer. Ted recognized Tony Lujan and other members of the famous Taos crowd, but even after seeing someone who resembled Stokowski sitting with them in the Ghost Ranch dining room, Ted didn't believe it was the famous composer.

> One day we were visited, to my amazement, by Tony Lujan and his entourage. I had found that getting Tony Lujan to go somewhere he didn't want to was like moving a stone house. The group consisted among others of Mabel Dodge, Dorothy Brett, and a man who looked somewhat like the pictures of Leopold Stokowski. They all had luncheon, and looked about for something to do. Meanwhile I had Goodyear, my old friend from St. Mark's, with me and we decided to climb a mountain. I said to Goodyear, "I'll bet that guy thinks he looks like Stokowski." . . . When we finally returned to the ranch, we were approached by Bob Johnson, who had been with the Lujans and said they had been looking for us since they knew how much I liked music and that they had had a clambake, with Tony playing his drums and Stokowski (for it was indeed he) tuning the piano. I wished I had stayed.[30]

Ted missed out on Tony Lujan and Leopold Stokowski's impromptu concert, but there were other opportunities to hear Native music, as Ghost Ranch hosted weekly performances by dancers and singers from San Juan Pueblo. "Many of these men and women were most graceful experts in their tribal ceremonies, and performed around huge bonfires," Arthur Pack wrote. "Leopold Stokowski, several times one of our guests, appeared fascinated by the strange mixture of their musi-

The dining room at the Ghost Ranch headquarters in 1936.

cal time, which is unfettered by standard rules of music and yet produces a throbbing rhythm that seems to re-echo all night in one's dreams."[31]

At the end of the summer of 1935, Seward Johnson's private railroad car departed Lamy with Dorthy Burnham, the young daughter of a Piedra Lumbre homesteader. Dorthy's father, Dave Burnham, worked for Stanley as a fence builder and blacksmith and was a popular "squares caller" for the Saturday evening square dances held throughout the summer. The Burnham family owned land on the eastern side of the Piedra Lumbre, several miles over the high mesas from Ghost Ranch. Their house was a sizable and well-crafted stone-and-timber dugout that, in spite of its partially underground location, had a fine view of Pedernal and the Chama River as it crossed the desert basin far below.

Dorthy Burnham had struggled with polio since childhood and, unable to walk, had become an expert horsewoman. Dorthy was a teenager in the summer of 1935 when the Johnsons became interested in her plight and offered to take her back to see medical experts in New York. Dorthy's parents gave their consent, and Dorthy lived with the Johnsons through the winter. After consultations and corrective surgery paid for by the Johnsons, Dorthy returned home to New Mexico able to walk in "ordinary" shoes. Even so, for the rest of her life, horses continued to be Dorthy's favorite means of transportation.

By 1935, although Ghost Ranch was owned by Carol Stanley, it was underwritten by Arthur Pack. Stanley's financial situation had not improved since her divorce from Pfaffle and, even with the Pack, Bennett, and Johnson families' continued interest in the ranch, she was hardly breaking even. However, Stanley's personal life had improved: since her move to Ghost Ranch, Stanley had formed a romantic liaison with foreman Lloyd Miller. As Stanley and Miller began to discuss their future together, it became evident that Ghost Ranch was too expensive an operation for Stanley's beleaguered inheritance to support. Perhaps Pack suggested to Stanley that he should buy her out, or maybe Stanley and Miller approached Pack with the idea. History has not recorded this conversation, but for reasons undoubtedly both financial and personal, on March 1, 1935, Stanley sold all of Ghost Ranch to Arthur Pack. "It became evident that Carol couldn't keep the place," Ted Bennett Jr.

remembered. "For all her charm, there wasn't enough money coming in. Arthur Pack wanted to buy it from her, and this turned out to be a blessing in disguise. For a naturalist, he was very wealthy, and the considerable cost of the Piedra Lumbre grant was no burden to him."[32]

Stanley sold Ghost Ranch and all of her land holdings on the Piedra Lumbre Land Grant—some sixteen thousand acres—plus all of her interests in the Piedra Lumbre Cattle Company to Arthur Newton Pack for the sum of seventy-five thousand dollars. Pack was now sole proprietor of the place called Ghost Ranch: buildings, sheds and barns, wells, generators, furniture, dishes, automobiles, wagons, farm and ranch equipment, burros, horses, several Jersey cows and calves, one bull, one hundred and fifty chickens, twenty-five ducks, eighty-six turkeys, and one sow. The deal even included much of Stanley's Indian art collection that decorated the guest cottages.

Pack asked Stanley to remain in residency at Ghost Ranch until the end of 1935. Brownie Pack had made it absolutely clear to her husband that she had no interest in becoming Ghost Ranch's new hostess. Pack needed Stanley's onsite expertise to keep the ranch running smoothly through the coming summer guest season. Pack also needed Lloyd Miller to remain at the ranch for at least the duration of the guest season, and if Stanley left, Miller would follow.

According to Brownie Pack, "Stanley and Miller enjoyed each other's company and fell in love over several years." Miller was a weathered but not worn middle-aged cowboy with a movie star smile and a quick wit. "Lloyd was a rather lightly built fellow," Frank Hibben remembered, "but very much of a cowboy. Very much of a man."

On November 14, 1935, at the United Brethren Church in Chamita, New Mexico, Lloyd Miller became Carol Stanley's second husband. They shared the same birth date—December 16—eleven years apart: Stanley was fifty-six the day they married, although on the marriage license she laid claim to only forty-nine of her years. Miller claimed all forty-five of his.

In early 1936, the Millers bought and moved onto a small ranch, Cottonwood, on the Rio Grande River near Alcalde. They did not want to open a guest ranch but planned to breed and raise quarter horses. The Millers struggled over the next few years to establish Cottonwood as a viable racehorse ranch. Lloyd was not a drinker, but he loved the racetrack and he liked to bet on the horses. "After Carol sold the ranch

. . . it was a disaster," Brownie Pack recalled half a century later, "because [Lloyd] really did like to gamble, and lost a lot of her money."

Cottonwood Ranch did acquire several good stallions, but they were expensive to buy and expensive to keep. By 1940, the Millers' quarter horse operation had more debts than income, and the Millers were forced into bankruptcy. "We all saw it coming," Dorthy Burnham Fredericks recalled. "Carol turned her money over to Lloyd just like she had to Pfaffle before him. Carol began to avoid her old friends—never went to lunches at La Fonda or any social event where she might meet people who knew what had happened. Carol couldn't take the humiliation of being broke twice by men."

Stanley's twenty-year maid and confidante, Alice Pring, returned to the East. The Millers sold what they could and gave what they could not carry to Ted Peabody to store in his house in Española. Dorthy Burnham Fredericks recalls that Carol Stanley and Lloyd Miller departed New Mexico "with one good quarter horse stallion and a borrowed saddle"—the Steinway grand piano was sold—and set up house in a humble dwelling in Arboles, Colorado, where Carol worked as the postmistress. "Carol's health wasn't good," Dorthy Burnham Fredericks remembers, "but she was doing all the cooking and wearing patched jeans after a whole life with a cook and a maid and fine dresses and pressed shirts."

The Millers lived in quiet oblivion until Stanley's death in December of 1948 to thrombosis of a coronary artery. Stanley was buried near Pagosa Springs. Although it was a long drive over the high mountains in winter snow, Dorthy Burnham Fredericks remembers that "all the cowboys showed up for her funeral. All of them."

Brownie Pack was not enthusiastic about her husband's acquisition of Ghost Ranch in early 1935. She had already made her dislike of the guest ranch business clear to Pack, and when Pack bought the ranch he knew full well that the management of Ghost Ranch would be his alone. Norrie Pack recognized how different her parents' needs were by the summer of 1935. "What got to her [Brownie] was that my father really wanted to settle down. He didn't want to go traveling around the world anymore. He wanted to settle down here, which he said was the most beautiful place in the world anyway. . . . He had to run this guest ranch . . . and she absolutely did not want any part of that."

Brownie kept occupied with her own activities and friends—photographing the children and their animals, visiting and driving to beautiful places with Maggie Johnson, and accompanying Frank Hibben on long jaunts in search of archaeological ruins. The daylong excursions with Hibben should have troubled Pack, but he believed that the young man was too young for Brownie—she was twelve years Hibben's elder—and that this infatuation, like several before back in New Jersey, would run its course and be forgotten. But Pack was wrong.

Pack learned of Brownie's decision to leave their marriage and their life at Ghost Ranch in the midsummer of 1935 while visiting his neighbors, Edward and Olive Bennett. Young Ted had been sent to retrieve the Bennett and Pack families' mail from headquarters and, when he returned to the Bennett house, he handed Pack the letter that brought his world crashing down around him. "Arthur Pack was the man who was having tea with my parents when I brought home the mail. A letter from his wife, Brownie, said she had run off with Frank Hibben from Princeton. . . . I was sorry I had got the mail."[33]

Hibben had become a permanent fixture at the Pack home in Princeton when still an undergrad. Hibben was studying biology and anthropology and wanted to learn wild-animal photography, and so had begun to accompany Arthur and Brownie on treks into the wild. By 1933, Frank Hibben had traveled with the Packs to Alaska, Florida, and the Bahamas. Pack may have been blind to Brownie's and Hibben's interest in one another, but Frank Hibben's parents were not. Pack later recalled how, during Princeton's graduation festivities in 1933, Hibben's father had taken him aside "to express appreciation of what we had been doing for their son. He asked if I had considered the danger of keeping the young man so much with us. I laughed. I had seen this sort of thing happen before and I was sure Brownie would soon get over this attachment as she had the others."[34]

After his graduation from Princeton, Hibben followed the Pack family to New Mexico and lived at Ghost Ranch in 1934 and 1935. His primary duty was to tutor the children, but he also liked to work with the ranch cowboys. Hibben rode with Pack and McKinley to round up the first wild burros and then was a trail hand on a cattle drive from Santa Fe to the Piedra Lumbre. "Jack McKinley and Shorty Skelton and I got five hundred cattle at Lamy and we drove them up to the Ghost Ranch," Hibben later recalled of that first summer. "We had to go through a few fences and get some keys to locked gates and things like that. But it was, as far as I was concerned, the old trail days, you know. Of course, I got a big bang out of it!"

There was a large herd of wild horses that roamed the Piedra Lumbre basin and the Jemez Mountains in the 1930s. Hibben went with the ranch cowboys on their semiannual wild-horse roundups, which were dangerous affairs for even the most experienced riders. "They were all nice to me. . . . I didn't know anything about anything. Jack McKinley taught me how to take care of horses. He said, 'Remember that a horse is a beautiful animal but has a brain about as big as your fist, and he can kill you.' And so, on that premise, we showed a great respect for horses!"

Lloyd Miller taught Hibben hunting and tracking, and introduced Hibben to numerous unexcavated archaeology sites in remote canyons and mesa tops throughout northern New Mexico. "Lloyd knew the country real well . . . and he showed me a lot of the ruins. He showed me the first Gallina ruins, which I didn't realize at the time were different."

Everyone in the Pack family was involved with Hibben's archaeological projects, and the Rancho de los Burros house under the cliffs became Hibben's desert laboratory. Arthur Pack returned home each day to find potsherds, reconstructed ceramic vessels, flint chips, and arrowheads from Hibben's, Brownie's, and the children's wanderings spread out across the tabletops and windowsills of the house.

In the spring of 1935, Pack asked Hibben to help him reintroduce pronghorn antelope to the Piedra Lumbre. Pack and rancher Charlie Belden, of the Pitch Fork Ranch in Wyoming, had devised a plan to transport young antelope back to Ghost Ranch in Pack's Fairchild airplane. Other attempts to relocate antelope overland by train or truck—which subjected the animals to inoculations at state lines—had failed because the long trip proved too stressful for the high-strung pronghorn. Pack and Belden figured their method using air transport might be successful because the journey could be done in one day, and the antelope would not suffer from prolonged handling and containment.

The young antelope were rounded up at Belden's ranch and prepared for the flight to New Mexico. Hibben recalls, "We had them tranquilized and also tied up. It was a very hard thing to do. I spent my time with the antelope to try to soothe them, reassure them. Their legs are so slender, if they got just one leg loose, they'd break it and kill themselves. We'd use nicotine sulfate, which is very deadly, because if you give them just a little too much, it kills them. A little too little, it doesn't faze them at all."

Pack and Hibben repeated this journey several times and successfully brought several dozen antelope to Ghost Ranch. Pack's antelope relocation effort received much regional publicity, and he was asked to transport additional planeloads of antelope fawns to conservation and wildlife groups in Arizona and California.

The young antelope were kept in a corral at the Packs' house under the cliffs until they were old enough to release into the wild. The Pack children bottle-fed the babies. "It was our job, as kids, to feed them," Norrie Pack remembered. "They were in a pen in the backyard. Dad didn't just let them loose on the mesa, they were little, they were babies. We fed them with ginger ale bottles with nipples on them. . . . We became attached to them and didn't want them to be let loose, but dad said let them loose on the range. . . . They stayed around for a while, until the next season, when the does began to have babies."

Pack was not ignorant; he understood that Hibben's interests were always professionally and personally self-serving. But Pack considered young Hibben to be as brilliant as he was brash and bold, and even underwrote Hibben's study of mountain lions that became his master's thesis at the University of New Mexico (UNM). Pack did not underestimate Hibben so much as he underestimated Brownie's attraction to Hibben. "[Hibben] had an awful lot of charm," fellow archaeologist Alden Hayes recalled of the young Hibben. "You could see why Brownie left old Arthur Pack."[35]

Looking back at the years leading up to Brownie's elopement with Frank Hibben, her departure from Ghost Ranch that summer day should have come as no surprise. But to those who lived that day, it was shocking. With the note of Brownie's elopement in his hand, Arthur Pack, dazed and speechless, departed the Bennetts' house. He returned to Rancho de los Burros, the beautiful and, until that moment, tranquil home under the cliffs. Pack paced from room to room seeking clues as to what he should do. Ghost Ranch was busy with people—the Johnson families, various Princeton friends, a few guests who were newcomers to the Piedra Lumbre. Pack's children were with their governess swimming or riding. But there was no one to give Pack solace and advice.

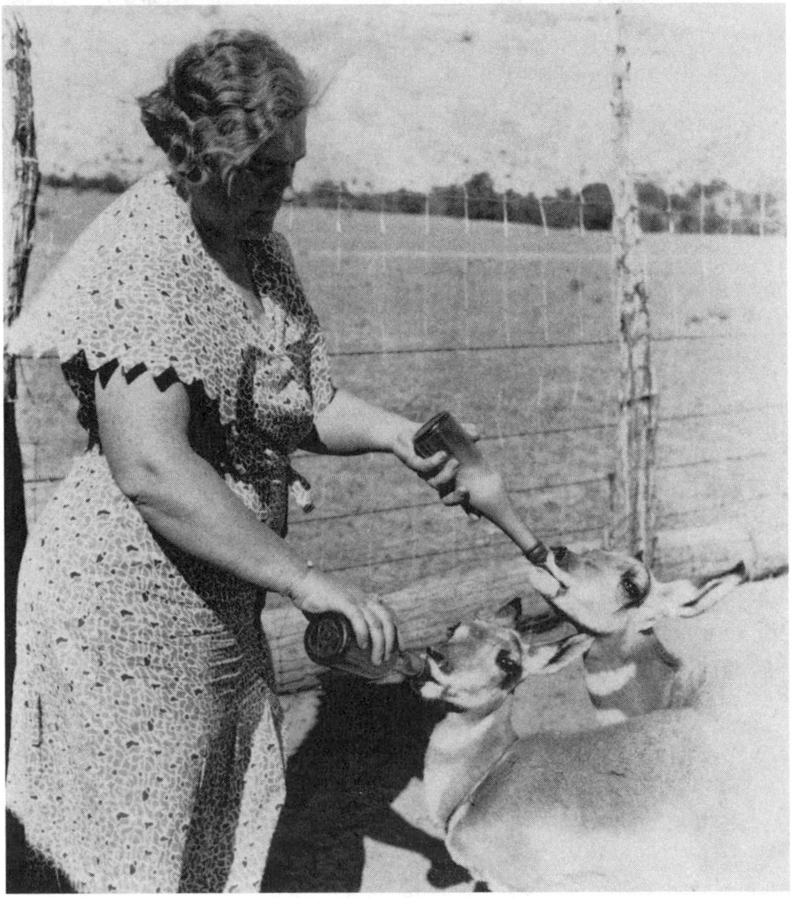

Mary Duncan, the Pack children's nanny, feeding the baby antelope in 1934. Duncan died at Ghost Ranch in 1936 after she was gored by an adult buck antelope.

Pack decided he needed to talk with his good friend and lawyer, Judge Botts, in Albuquerque. Breaking the aviator's rule to never fly when compromised by mental confusion or emotional distress, Pack "pushed out my little green airplane, automatically went through the remembered checks of oil, fuel and trim, and a few minutes later was speeding down the Chama valley."[36]

Pack flew into a layer of low clouds almost immediately and realized too late that he was trapped. "The deck of cloud beneath me now seemed to extend in every direction to the horizon, and the hole through which I had flown had closed and was no longer visible. I had no radio, no way of asking for human help, and my supply of gas could not last indefinitely."[37]

Pack sought divine guidance. It was apparently granted, as Pack's airplane miraculously avoided collision with the major mountains that surrounded the plane on three sides while it descended blindly through the opaque white. "I caught a glimpse of a wet black road over which the cloud bottom seemed to hold about a hundred feet above the ground . . . and as I hugged the black ribbon of highway under the clouds as closely as the telegraph poles would permit, a strip of dirt runway miraculously appeared. A moment more and I was safely down, taxiing towards a small shack where a man stood beside a car in drizzling rain. He was there, he said, to meet an expected mail plane but he now felt sure it wouldn't be coming in this weather."[38]

Pack took a room at La Fonda on the plaza. After a fitful night with little sleep, Pack flew on to Albuquerque where, with the counsel of his friend and attorney C. M. Botts, he began to legally and emotionally reconstruct his life.

The divorce settlement signed that fall granted Brownie Pack custody of the girls, Peggy and Norrie; Vernon would remain with his father at Ghost Ranch. Following Brownie's marriage to Frank Hibben in 1936, the girls were placed in private boarding schools. Hibben completed his master's at UNM, and the new Mr. and Mrs. Hibben moved to Cambridge, Massachusetts, where he completed his Ph.D. at Harvard.[39]

Following Pack's own remarriage, Brownie insisted on a new out-of-court custody agreement that stipulated that the girls would not visit Ghost Ranch until they were twenty-one. Brownie was not worried about losing her daughters to Arthur's new wife; she was worried about losing them to Ghost Ranch. "Ghost Ranch meant more to me than anything in my whole life," Peggy Pack said years later. "I really loved the country. The country and the horses. . . . That's what broke me up more than the divorce was having to leave the ranch and the horses."

The summer of 1935 saw the demise of a second marriage at Ghost Ranch—that of Jack and Margaret McKinley. Handsome, debonair wrangler Jack McKinley caught the eye of a wealthy, and married, ranch guest named Ardith Johnston. Ironically, it was as the nurse to Ardith Johnston's children that Margaret McKinley had first come from Boston to New Mexico—to San Gabriel Ranch—and met Jack McKinley, in the late 1920s. But friendship and loyalty seemed to be out of favor that summer, and although Ardith was vacationing at Ghost Ranch with her husband and four children, she found enough time alone with Jack McKinley to fall in love with him. Within a few weeks of their arrival, Mr. Johnston announced that he was leaving the ranch with the children and divorcing Mrs. Johnston. And soon after this disclosure, Jack McKinley announced to his wife, Maggie, that he was leaving the ranch to tour Europe with the estranged Mrs. Johnston.

The McKinleys were divorced by the end of the year. Pack, also newly divorced, needed a resident governess for Vernon, and for the girls when they visited, and offered Margaret McKinley a job and a house at Ghost Ranch. And although Jack McKinley and Ardith Johnston returned from Europe and set up their home at the Diamond K Ranch near Glorietta, New Mexico, Pack became legal guardian for the McKinley children, Wayne, Henry, and Barbara, who, with Vernon Pack, lived year-round at Ghost Ranch until they left for college.

Pack spent the next year rebuilding a life for himself at Ghost Ranch. The girls were allowed to join their father and brother at Ghost Ranch for Christmas of 1935, but after their departure, Pack moved everything he owned out of Rancho de los Burros. He set up a new home in Stanley's old residence, the Yeso homestead that was now called Ghost House, and began a very long, lonely winter on the Piedra Lumbre.

The spirits of the canyon that haunted Pack were all personal, and although he was grateful for the beauty of the Piedra Lumbre, and the landscape that each day "seemed to weave a gentler spell," his nights were "bad beyond belief." Pack left Ghost Ranch in midwinter and flew himself east for a long visit among friends in Princeton.[40]

Pack continued to promote Ghost Ranch with his nature films and stories, and, when he returned to New Mexico in 1936, he was determined to make his new life as a single father and dude ranch owner work. This was to be Pack's first summer without Carol Stanley steering the ranch through the hectic guest season. While he was in Princeton, Pack sought out friends to fill summer positions at Ghost Ranch. The sons of professors were invited to come and work for room, board, and a small stipend. And Janet Jepson, the wife of Pack's friend, geology professor Glenn Jepson, offered to come and spend ten weeks working as the ranch hostess.

Spring came and Pack worked alongside the ranch gardener, Archie Galbraith, a fearless fellow who came to Ghost Ranch from a job as a prison guard in Canyon City, Colorado. Pack and Galbraith landscaped headquarters, enlarged the vegetable and flower gardens, and pruned the old orchard. Pack had always found pleasure in physical chores, and that spring in particular he welcomed the chance to sink his hands into the good soil that reconnected him to the place of Ghost Ranch.

In late spring, Pack awoke one morning to the pleasing but abnormal sound of rushing water. He climbed from his narrow bed in the tiny, low-ceiling bedroom of Ghost House and walked outside to find that the water from Yeso Canyon that flowed down the acequia he and Galbraith had recently cleaned and enlarged was gushing out of sight into an apparently bottomless hole in the ground. After a morning of investigation, Pack and Galbraith decided that the irrigation water had found the old well dug by the Archuletas forty years before. Pack knew the stories of the murderous brothers and with Galbraith pumped out the water and probed about the bottom of the reopened well for bones and/or treasure. They found neither. The well was filled in again, and the legends of buried bodies and buried gold remained legends, the truth of the long-ago times known only by the spirits.

Pack's daughters arrived for the summer in late May to spend what would be their last summer with their father and brother at Ghost Ranch. Pack's construction crew was just completing work on an adobe house up the hill behind headquarters to accommodate Pack and his extended family—Vernon, Maggie McKinley and her three children, and his two daughters when they were allowed to visit.

Pack and Ghost Ranch were ready for the summer when Phoebe

Ghost House (formerly the Archuleta homestead) and the ranch garden in 1937.

Finley, the daughter of Pack's old friend and colleague, Bill Finley, came to visit the ranch with her mother, Irene. Pack hardly recognized Phoebe, whom he had not seen since she was a child. Phoebe, a University of Oregon graduate, was now an attractive and confident young woman, and Pack invited her to go along with several friends and wranglers on a preseason camping trip to Lost Lake.

During those few days among the ponderosa pine–covered mountains above Ghost Ranch, Pack and Finley fell in love. On their last night out, Arthur and Phoebe sat alone over the dying embers of the cook fire, sipping warmed rum and grapefruit juice following a cold rain that had sent everyone else to their tents. Pack asked Finley, who was fourteen years his junior, to marry him.

Although he hardly knew her when he proposed, Phoebe Finley was like family to Arthur Pack. Bill and Irene Finley had been part of Pack's inner circle of friends and colleagues since the early 1920s, when Bill Finley wrote a monthly column as *Nature Magazine*'s western field representative. By 1936 and the wedding of his daughter to one of his closest friends, Finley was one of the world's most widely published nature photographers. Finley, in partnership with his wife, spent summers in the backcountry of North America photographing birds and wildlife, eventually amassing fifty thousand still photographs and 200,000 feet of movie film. Finley's nature films—produced in an informative and narrative style soon emulated by Walt Disney—were shown in theaters nationwide, and his photos and stories were regularly featured in *National Geographic, Life, Atlantic Monthly, Colliers, Field and Stream*, and *Ladies Home Journal*.

Bill Finley, like Charles Pack and Natalie Curtis, used his personal friendship with President Theodore Roosevelt to sway federal policy in favor of his personal cause: wildlife protection. Finley's influence with Roosevelt resulted in the establishment of the first federal wildlife sanctuary in the West, Three Arch Rocks, on the Oregon coast. In 1911 Finley became Oregon's first fish and game commissioner, and for the next few decades he actively participated in every major decision concerning the welfare of wildlife in the state of Oregon and the Northwest. Dr. Finley (Oregon State College gave him an honorary doctorate of science) also served as field naturalist for the Audubon Society for more than twenty years, and he was an influential and outspoken leader of the National Wildlife Federation. To this day, Finley's photographs of a family of California condors, taken in 1906 with friend Herman Bohlman, are considered the most complete photographic record made of this vanishing species.

Bill Finley was a famous colleague, but he was also Arthur Pack's best friend. Over several decades, Finley and Pack took many trips into the backcountry together to do research and photography for *Nature Magazine*. Their intimate research of a species often involved complicated camouflage and costuming: At Glacier Park, the men designed a white-flannel mountain goat disguise complete with horns and whiskers; and to photograph moose they hid "behind a flimsy blind of baby evergreens" while an angry bull moose stalked them, "sticking his horns in from the other side, while [Pack's] hands clattered in the film changing bag."[41]

Finley was seventeen years older than Pack but, even after he became Pack's father-in-law, was like a brother to him. Deeply committed to preserving the land and animals they loved, Pack and Finley also shared a sense of humor about themselves and their work that was the foundation of their lifelong friendship. "I have thought often of the days when you and I traveled the mountains together," Pack wrote to Finley years later, "and sat tired and thirsty upon some crag to share the last refreshing orange from the tail pocket of your cruiser's shirt. And I recall once when the tempting morsel slipped from your fingers and bounded a thousand feet into space before either of us had a single bite. . . . 'That,' you said, 'is why oranges won't grow in the Rockies. They won't stay put.'"[42]

Phoebe Katherine Finley's upbringing mirrored Arthur Pack's in several important ways: the daughter of a famous and dedicated conservationist team, Phoebe Finley was as comfortable camping in the Sonoran Desert as she was in the high Rockies or on the Oregon coastline. Home was found in the great good places of the earth, and Phoebe Finley was a perfectly suited partner for Pack and the life he offered her at the bright, high desert place called Ghost Ranch.

The marriage of Phoebe Finley and Arthur Pack took place on the portal of the Ghost Ranch headquarters on June 11, 1936. (Six days earlier, Brownie had become Mrs. Frank Hibben.) The Pack children, Norrie, Peggy, and Vernon, joined Phoebe's parents and grandparents as witnesses to the ceremony conducted by the Reverend Schlotterbeck of the United Brethren Church in Española. Schlotterbeck, the

Phoebe Pack on the porch of the Ghost Ranch headquarters in 1937.

same minister who had married Carol Stanley and Lloyd Miller, had apparently heard every legend, myth, rumor, and horror story about Rancho de los Brujos and was extremely uncomfortable to be standing upon the infamous land. The ceremony itself was short and to the point, and, following the champagne toast for the new bride and groom, the good Reverend Schlotterbeck walked briskly to his car and drove quickly away from Ghost Ranch in a cloud of dust.

Summer guests were due to arrive in the next few days, so there was no time for the Packs to take a honeymoon. The newlyweds were driven in a brightly painted wagon to the newest guest cottage up the hill from headquarters. The Pack children and their nanny, Mary, moved into their own casita. The Finleys returned to Oregon, the last of the summer staff of college students arrived and moved into Corral Block, and the new Mr. and Mrs. Pack opened Ghost Ranch for the summer season.

Ghost Ranch seemed to have acquired a tamer persona. However, within twenty-four hours of the Pack wedding, the unpredictable spirits of the Piedra Lumbre reminded the people of the ranch that this was, still and all, a wild place: the Pack children's nanny, Mary L. Duncan, died after she was gored by one of the buck antelope.

Duncan had gone alone that evening out into the red hills to visit the baby antelope. Like everyone at Ghost Ranch, she had developed an affection for the herd of young antelope when they arrived in Pack's Fairchild in the spring of 1935. While the Pack family lived at Rancho de los Burros, the animals were kept in the corral beside the house. The pronghorn had become accustomed to people feeding them and handling them and were tame and playful. When they were old enough to be turned loose on the llanos in the late fall, the antelope did not immediately move out onto the open range of the ranch, but remained in contact with the Pack family and the ranch staff.

By spring of 1936, the relocated herd had its first crop of fawns. Although the older antelope were still relatively calm around people, and often grazed close to the Rancho de los Burros house, and even the main ranch, they had begun to acclimate to the Piedra Lumbre, and to adopt the necessary instinct for survival on the high desert. After the baby antelope were born, although they were not being raised by people, Duncan and the Pack children drove out to visit them on the desert.

Pack and the ranch cowboys had noticed that, following the birth of the babies, one of the young bucks, called Bucky, had become protective and was sometimes confrontational with humans. The children had been warned to stay away from Bucky, who was, after all, simply doing what nature told him to do: protect the young.

On that fateful evening of the goring, Pack became worried as night descended and Duncan was nowhere to be found. The men organized a search party at headquarters, but just as they began to depart, Duncan's pickup truck appeared on the road at the lower end of the field. The truck idled along slowly, wavering side to side, before coming to a stop. When Pack reached the truck, Duncan was slumped over the steering wheel, unconscious.

The men carried Duncan's bloodied and bruised body up to headquarters, and Slim Jarmon was sent to find the doctor at the nearby Civilian Conservation Corps (CCC) camp. Duncan lived through the night but, even with medical attention from the CCC physician, died by morning. The doctor's report stated that although she had been brutally gored by the buck, her wounds were not mortal: Mary Duncan died of shock.

Duncan's death shocked the ranch community and left the Pack children devastated. Even before Brownie and Arthur Pack's separation and divorce, Duncan had become the three children's primary caretaker and confidante. (Vernon had his own tutor, Thomas "Tuck" Ross, in the summer of 1936 and then attended Millbrook School in Amenia, New York.) Since the divorce, Mary Duncan had become the person the children trusted the most.

The Pack children were unaware of their nanny's accident and were not told until the next morning of her death. Duncan's body was placed in Ghost House, where it lay covered by a sheet on a table until it was placed into a coffin and flown back to Pennsylvania for burial by her family.

Janet Jepson and her husband Glenn arrived at Ghost Ranch within twenty-four hours of Mary Duncan's death. Glenn Jepson was on his way to lead a Princeton field camp in Wyoming, and Janet, unaware that there was a new Mrs. Pack, assumed she had a job as ranch hostess for the summer. In the whirlwind surrounding their romance and marriage, Pack had forgotten that he had asked Janet Jepson to come and work as ranch hostess. Pack's initial reaction to the Jepsons' arrival at his doorstep on June 14 was embarrassment. This was quickly replaced by relief: the Pack children were without a nanny, and in the lovely Janet Jepson, Pack saw the answer to very urgent prayers. He asked Jepson if she would stay and be the children's governess. Jepson was an energetic twenty-two-year-old and, although she had never taken care of children, understood the extent of their loss and their need. "The children were at loose ends," Jepson recalled. "Their Nanny was as close to them as anyone they knew. I took the job and spent the summer of 1936 as their governess. I called myself the Kid Wrangler."

Jepson stepped into the life of Ghost Ranch with effortless ease. She rode horses with the children, taught them lessons on the headquarters portal, took them swimming each day in the Yeso pool beneath the cliff they came to call Ice Cream Rock, and took them for picnics in the lumbering Pierce Arrow. Jepson's only time off was after the children were tucked into bed, at which time she joined the other summer staffers playing poker, swapping stories, and singing songs with the cowboys in the bunkhouse.

Ghost Ranch was soon lively with its regular crowd of seasonal returnees, including the Johnson & Johnson families and their nannies and bodyguards and the extended family of Edward Bennett at the house of Monte Rojo. Under Pack's guidance Ghost Ranch became everything that Carol Stanley had dreamed it might become. What Pack did not know about dude ranching he made up for with energy and enthusiasm, and his family fortune gave him freedom from the profit/loss burden that weighed down other guest ranch owners. The 1930s, an era that brought more failures than successes to ventures connected to the New Mexican tourist industry, would be the golden years of Ghost Ranch.

Peabody's crew built more casitas near ranch headquarters at the foot of the mesa, and after cleaning and reopening the acequias dug by the Archuleta brothers nearly half a century before, a large vegetable garden was laid out. The orchard of old fruit trees was pruned, and young apple, cherry, and apricot trees were planted. The ranch had its own dairy herd (although Maggie Johnson sent Clay Wolf to Abiquiú each day for pasteurized milk), and all of the beef, lamb, turkey, chicken, and duck served in the ranch dining room was ranch raised.

Phoebe Pack introduced new recipes to the ranch menu. Although Phoebe relied on common, all-American, time-tested recipes handed down to her from her mother, she had so many requests from guests for those recipes that she finally published them in a small booklet. She warned her audience, however, that the secret to her food was not to be found in the individual ingredients, but was rather the combination of people and place that resulted in a dining experience that reflected the special, magical ambience found only at Ghost Ranch. "The secret of many a menu lies rather in its suitability to time, place and mood. . . . Food without the personal ministrations of host and hostess, without the background of friendly talk and Nature's best backdrop may never please the palate half so well. . . . We know that it is the combination of all these elements which has pleased you here."[43]

Pack invested in the publication of brochures that described both the ranch's natural beauty and its owners close-to-the-earth philosophy. "The Ghost Ranch is a real ranch all the year round—not the usual artificial 'dude' ranch or cottage hotel. It offers no golf course, tennis courts, nor other amusement of the country-club variety, for its charm lies in an atmosphere and philosophy contrasting with the everlasting hurry and rush of society, business, and politics—a practical experience in simplicity."[44]

That Ghost Ranch was a real, working ranch—it still had a small herd of cattle and Pack's prize palominos grazing the pastures—and not just another false-fronted dude resort was a source of pride to the ranch cowboys. Pulitzer Prize–winning author Oliver La Farge became a fan of the ranch wranglers and frequently came up from Santa Fe to participate in Ghost Ranch cattle drives and roundups with Slim, Pete, Clarence, Archie, and the rest of the cowboys, all of whom he genuinely respected and admired. La Farge wrote about the skills peculiar to their dual role as horse and dude wranglers in an article published in *Vogue Magazine* in May of 1936.

> Any good dude ranch has to keep one or more attractive fellows with a natural gift for carrying ladies' pocketbooks. It has to have competent men with even tempers, who won't tell the richest guest they ever corralled to go plumb to hell and stay there, or saddle up and ride off, offended, at the height of the busy season, or try to drink a gallon of redeye every time they pass through a town with a bar in it.
>
> It also has to have men who will ride twenty-four hours straight

> and think nothing of it, who can tough it out for a week hunting horses, with no bedding and little grub, who can handle animals, and, if need be, people, through every accident of rain and storm and sand. A world of hard work lies behind the smooth running that brings your saddled horse to you every morning.[45]

Pack asked La Farge to write a few paragraphs about Ghost Ranch for publicity purposes. Afraid that he would be asked for similar testimonials for other guest ranches, La Farge declined Pack's request, although he did so apologetically. "I put off answering you in the first place, because I didn't want to turn down your request if I could help it. . . . I have refused to do much this type of thing for Captain Oakley, as well as for other outfits not in any way to be classed with yours. . . . I don't see, then, how I can do it for you without getting into hot water. . . . I have a warm feeling for your outfit, and dislike turning you down."[46]

La Farge did, however, defend the authenticity of the Ghost Ranch cowboys in a letter to a mutual friend and ranch guest, Henry Goddard Leach, following Leach's editorial in *Forum and Century* magazine that referred to the Ghost Ranch cowboys as "Yankees." Leach was an old friend of Pack's, and came to Ghost Ranch with his family for long visits in the 1930s. (Leach was also very close friends with Willa Cather, and in 1927 his *Forum* magazine was the first to publish, in serial form, what was to become the book *Death Comes for the Archbishop*.) Leach described his journey from the Santa Fe depot at Lamy across the ninety-three miles to Ghost Ranch. "A Yankee cowboy drove me this distance in his car . . . and Yankee cowboys met me with gentle horses at the ranch."[47] La Farge wrote Pack, "I've written [Leach] that I didn't think they'd be pleased."[48]

The ranch hands were *not* pleased with Leach's statement, although Leach did tell his readers that "these vigorous young men were saturated with politeness" and were "grand seigniors of courtesy." For all his jibes at the wranglers, Leach loved the Piedra Lumbre and, in his two-page editorial, spoke for everyone who ever came to Ghost Ranch and fell under its spell. "The first morning may seem to you too grand and expansive, with no familiar thing. The gorgeous wild flowers may seem too strange to you. But every succeeding day will surely seduce you."[49]

Three Georgia O'Keeffe and Ghost Ranch

Living out here has just meant happiness. Sometimes I think I'm half-mad with love for this place. —GEORGIA O'KEEFFE[1]

Arthur Pack would eventually own more than thirty thousand acres of the Piedra Lumbre, and Ghost Ranch would reach from the painted sands beneath the Cliffs of Shining Stone across the Chama River to the pinion and juniper foothills of Pedernal. Yet to the greater world Ghost Ranch would not be remembered as the place where the Packs lived, or where the Johnson & Johnson brothers summered and the Bennett family vacationed. Even the Archuleta brothers would fade into historical anonymity. The place called Ghost Ranch would achieve international recognition and celebrity status because of one woman, painter Georgia O'Keeffe. O'Keeffe's legal claim to the place she called the Faraway Nearby would encompass only ten acres, but her personal, creative, and emotional investment in the landscape of Ghost Ranch would eventually transcend borders and boundaries. Like all great love stories, the story of the place called Ghost Ranch and the story of the painter called Georgia O'Keeffe cannot be separated. To tell the story of one you must tell the story of the other.

Georgia O'Keeffe had begun to form a relationship with New Mexico prior to the summer of 1934 and her first visit to Ghost Ranch. O'Keeffe had already fallen in love with the landscape of the Four Corners, having spent the summers of 1929 and 1930 in Taos at the Los Gallos home of Mabel Dodge Luhan and the summer of 1931 at the H & M Ranch near San Gabriel Ranch in Alcalde. Summers in the heat and light and space endemic to northern New Mexico transformed O'Keeffe: she learned how to drive in New Mexico, and alone and with friends spent the long summer days hiking and exploring, sunbathing, and sketching. Each fall, O'Keeffe returned to her husband, Alfred Stieglitz, and their Manhattan life a new woman. "I realize I must be different than when I came out," O'Keeffe wrote her friend Rebecca Strand, "but it seems so long ago that I can't remember what I was like—so I can't lapse back to it—I can only be as I am—and I feel terribly alive—."[2]

O'Keeffe's life with Stieglitz was firmly rooted in the modern art scene of New York City, and she remained committed to him and their marriage in spite of her intensifying attraction to the country and the life she found in the Southwest. However, after three summers in New Mexico, O'Keeffe was deeply enamored with the region and admitted to a friend that she loved the place "almost as passionately as I can love a person."[3] O'Keeffe's attraction to New Mexico and her incontrovertible need to be there for longer and longer periods of time would pose the only real threat to her marriage to Stieglitz. "I am divided between my man and a life with him—and some thing of the outdoors—of your world—that is in my blood—and that I know I will never get rid of—" she wrote a friend in New Mexico, "I have to get along with my divided self the best way I can—"[4]

Northern New Mexico exerted a hypnotic power on O'Keeffe, and by her fifth summer visit to the region, the high desert mesa and mountain region had become synonymous with an emotional and artistic freedom the painter could not live without. Following physical illness that kept O'Keeffe away from the Southwest for three summers, she returned to the H & M Ranch in Alcalde in June of 1934 determined to anchor her emotional and creative life in the northern New Mexico country she had begun to call the Faraway.

In 1934, O'Keeffe wanted New Mexico, but she did not want to be involved with the social life that thrived in Taos and Santa Fe. She returned to the H & M Ranch, but even a small guest ranch in the tiny village of Alcalde offered too much exposure to people and their dramas. For the first time in her forty-six-year-old life, O'Keeffe began to think about keeping house in New Mexico, about finding "someplace where the people do not run me crazy—"[5] O'Keeffe's time had come to be alone in the landscape she loved. "As one chooses between the country and the human being," O'Keeffe wrote a friend, "the country becomes much more wonderful."[6]

To paint and work away from unwanted interruptions and social calls, O'Keeffe left Alcalde each morning and drove alone up the Chama River Valley toward Abiquiú. With her canvas and paints set up in the rear of the car, O'Keeffe could stop and park by the road and spend entire days painting. But she could also hike up into the sand hills and mesas, or walk along the Chama River in the shade of the cottonwood bosque. There were hamlets and ranchitos, and men working in the irrigated fields of corn and alfalfa, but O'Keeffe was left to herself in the rural valley south of Abiquiú.

In the previous winter in New York, O'Keeffe had heard about a spectacular, high desert plateau called the Piedra Lumbre, which was found a few miles north of Abiquiú. David McAlpin, the grandnephew of John D. Rockefeller, had told O'Keeffe about his Princeton neighbors, Arthur and Brownie Pack, and their recent move to a new home in northern New Mexico. McAlpin had worked with Pack on various civic and religious projects in Princeton, and he had heard that the Packs' new adobe home on the Piedra Lumbre plateau was situated in nothing less than "the best place in the world"—a place called Ghost Ranch.[7]

O'Keeffe was intrigued, but it wasn't until late July of 1934, after O'Keeffe had been back in New Mexico for more than a month, that she went to see the place touted as the best for herself. O'Keeffe did not go alone on this sojourn, but was accompanied by her Alcalde neighbor, Charles Collier. Collier, the son of John Collier, commissioner of Indian affairs, had never been to Ghost Ranch. But he had seen the Piedra Lumbre, and he agreed that the high desert below Pedernal was country O'Keeffe needed to see. O'Keeffe had heard enough about the incomparable magnificence of this place and, in midsummer, set out with young Collier to see Ghost Ranch for herself.

It was to be both a glorious and a frustrating day for O'Keeffe and her companion. After winding up the dirt track past Abiquiú, and braving the ever-narrowing and precarious dirt road into and up through the Chama Canyon, O'Keeffe's Model A emerged onto the bright expanse of the Piedra Lumbre below the *cuchilla* (knife) of Pedernal. In the July heat, the Cliffs of Shining Stone were a distant narrow band of shimmering gold and red miles away across the sandy llanos. The rough and dusty road followed the Chama River to the crossing at the Vadito de Chicos Ranch of old Juan de Dios, and then headed northwest across the basin up onto the hot sand land toward Navajo Canyon. As the road

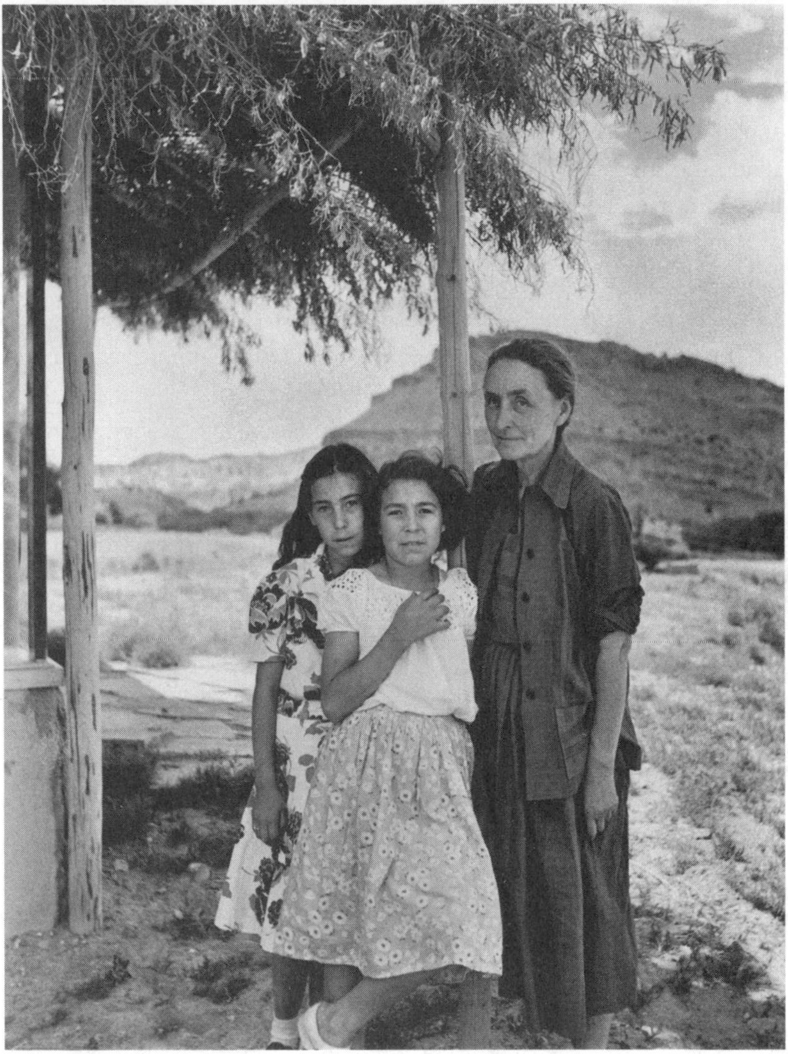

Georgia O'Keeffe with her young Abiquiú friends Rosie and Louisa Trujillo in 1951. Rosie Trujillo McCall later lived at Ghost Ranch with her family, where she was the supervisor of housekeeping. Her husband, Ray, was head of maintenance, and her sister Lou also worked at Ghost Ranch for many years.

neared the northwest edge of the basin, the famous, luminous cliffs finally assumed their true size and stature, and the sheer sandstone walls rose hundreds of feet above the desert floor into the blue sky.

O'Keeffe and Collier could see the place called Ghost Ranch, but they could find no sign and no road that led to Ghost Ranch. They turned around and retraced their tracks but still found no road that cut across the rugged arroyos and red sandy badlands toward the cliffs. They finally gave up. Sundown began to turn the walls to fire, and O'Keeffe and Collier departed the Piedra Lumbre without finding the fabled ranch.

O'Keeffe was frustrated that day. Even so, it was love at first sight: before she had placed a foot onto the land of Ghost Ranch, O'Keeffe was completely smitten by its rugged, spare beauty and its raw wildness. O'Keeffe knew she had found what she was looking for. "Perfectly mad looking country—hills and cliffs and washes too crazy to imagine all thrown up into the air by god and let tumble where they would. It was certainly as spectacular as anything I've ever seen—and that was pretty good."[8]

A few days later, while driving her Model A past the Kramer mercantile at San Juan Pueblo, O'Keeffe noticed a parked vehicle with *GR* painted on its door. She stopped and waited for the driver to return. When he did, O'Keeffe asked for *precise* directions to the elusive ranch on the Piedra Lumbre. The driver—possibly Orville Cox or Slim Jarmon, or perhaps Ted Peabody picking up building supplies—explained *exactly* where the ranch road departed the main road on the desert basin. He also told O'Keeffe that there was no sign on the gate, but that Ghost Ranch's private road was marked by a skull (either a horse or a cow—it was frequently stolen and replaced by whatever animal skull was readily available) hung on a post.

O'Keeffe immediately set out in her Model A to find Ghost Ranch and, with poetic perfection that August day, easily found the horse skull marking the gate. She drove her Ford several miles on the private road that wound up and down across the sandy, sage- and pinion-speckled hills to the last stony rise and her first view of Ghost Ranch. "I knew the minute I got up here that this was where I would live."[9]

Ghost Ranch claimed O'Keeffe that summer day, and O'Keeffe claimed Ghost Ranch. There were other people already living in the painted badlands, and O'Keeffe would never own more than a tiny piece of the good country, but these details would forever be insignificant to their relationship: the place below the cliffs on the desert basin of Pedernal was O'Keeffe's world. She knew it immediately, and from that day forward into the next five decades, the unspoiled, spacious, hot, wild, and wonderful faraway place called Ghost Ranch was the physical, creative, and spiritual center of Georgia O'Keeffe's life. "It was a new world," O'Keeffe said years later. "And I thought this was my world."[10]

O'Keeffe's arrival to Ghost Ranch in midsummer of 1934 began with a conversation with Carol Stanley in the crooked doorway of the old Yeso Canyon homestead. Stanley explained to O'Keeffe, whom she had met in 1929 when O'Keeffe stopped for lunch at San Gabriel Ranch with Mabel Dodge Luhan, that all of the Ghost Ranch casitas were taken for the month of August. There was, however, a room in one of the cottages that was unoccupied for one night. To O'Keeffe, one night in this magic place was better than nothing, and she re-drove the forty bumpy miles back down the valley to Alcalde, retrieved her clothes, and returned to Ghost Ranch by evening.

During O'Keeffe's inaugural night at Ghost Ranch the son of one of Stanley's summer guests developed appendicitis, and the family left before dawn to seek emergency medical attention in Santa Fe. Stanley knew they would not return, and she told O'Keeffe in the morning that one of the casitas was now unoccupied for the remainder of the month. "I went immediately to Ghost Ranch to stay," O'Keeffe said years later, "And I never left."[11]

O'Keeffe moved into and remained in the vacated casita at Ghost Ranch until her departure for New York in the fall. Although O'Keeffe was already a nationally recognized painter and personality, her arrival at Ghost Ranch in the summer of 1934 was only of passing interest to the other ranch residents: The Pack family was fully ensconced in their new Rancho de los Burros home out under the cliffs; Casa Monte Rojo was completed, and the Bennett family were enjoying their first summer vacation on the Piedra Lumbre. And by late summer, Bob and Maggie Johnson would make their inaugural visit to Ghost Ranch and begin plans for their own adobe home.

The Ghost Ranch summer community had virtually doubled in size since 1932, but ranch visitors did not come to spend their time socializing with other guests. Still, Ghost Ranch was called a dude ranch, and for all its isolation and pristine open space, O'Keeffe worried that the place could be ruined by the kind of people who came to stay at a dude ranch. "Ghost Ranch was a dude ranch, I was told—and I thought dude ranchers were a lower form of life. . . . I wasn't sure I could live with dude ranchers."[12]

But O'Keeffe learned that first summer that she *could* live with dude ranchers if it meant she could live at Ghost Ranch. She also learned over the next few summers that among those "dudes" were people who would become close, lifelong friends.

Beginning in 1934 and for the next few summers, O'Keeffe lived in close proximity to the other ranch guests. O'Keeffe fiercely guarded her solitude and virtually ignored the other people coming and going at the ranch. But O'Keeffe also understood that to maintain such a distance from civilization in the extreme high desert, New Mexican outback, she needed the services and expertise of the Ghost Ranch community.

Until she moved out to the Burros House under the cliffs in the summer of 1937, O'Keeffe did not have her own kitchen facilities, and she took her meals with the other guests in the ranch dining room in headquarters. The other diners learned to leave Miss O'Keeffe to herself unless she initiated conversation.

"When you got to know Georgia, she was a very, very nice person," friend Dorothy Brett said of O'Keeffe. "But she had a rather cold front that made things a little difficult for her and for everybody else. It's a horrid thing to say, but I think she was bored with people."[13]

At Ghost Ranch in the summer season there were two shifts for each meal: the children, their nannies, tutors, bodyguards, and other caretakers ate first, followed by a more formal gathering of the adults. O'Keeffe did join the adults and even enjoyed the company of several—O'Keeffe and Brownie Pack formed an immediate friendship, and David McAlpin and his Rockefeller cousins were soon ranch regulars whom O'Keeffe enjoyed socializing with. And although O'Keeffe formed a famous dislike for Bob Johnson, she was drawn to his energetic, vivacious wife, Maggie, and later became close friends with Seward Johnson's second wife, Esther. "All the people are very nice," O'Keeffe wrote Stieglitz. "They are all people with their children of all ages and they come for the outdoor things they can do."[14]

As O'Keeffe came to know the cowboys and wranglers around the ranch, she was drawn to the jovial mealtime shared by the resident staff. O'Keeffe became friends with Pete Dozier, Jack McKinley, and Slim Jarmon, and always accepted an invitation to their no-frills mess hall in Corral Block, where the conversation was apt to be colorful, irreverent, informative, and good humored. Laverna Galbraith, Archie's wife, often cooked the staff supper, and O'Keeffe wrote Stieglitz that she liked "La Verna's food best and eating with all of them at night is enough for me."[15]

O'Keeffe stayed at Ghost Ranch just over a month that first summer. But O'Keeffe knew when she left that she had found her place, and when she returned to Ghost Ranch in June of 1935, O'Keeffe settled into Garden House for a six-month stay. In doing so, O'Keeffe was declaring to her husband, her friends, and to herself, that her relationship with New Mexico, with Ghost Ranch, was no longer casual. O'Keeffe began to define the borders of her home country, of her world. Ghost Ranch was now O'Keeffe's Place and everyone knew it.

O'Keeffe sunk her heart and her creative spirit into the ageless and mysterious landscape of the Piedra Lumbre, whose forms and colors were exotic and familiar to her at once. "Bad lands roll away outside the door—hill after hill—red hills of apparently the same sort of earth that you mix with oil to make paint. All the earth colors of the painter's palette are out there in the many miles of bad lands. The light naples yellow through the ochers—orange and red and purple earth—even the soft earth greens."[16]

Garden House was located at the east end of the ranch's large and luscious vegetable garden. O'Keeffe made a point of becoming friendly with the gardeners, who always obliged her need for a fresh carrot or a handful of vine-ripened strawberries. But during the daylight hours, and often into the night, O'Keeffe was rarely found in or around ranch headquarters. After breakfast O'Keeffe headed out in her Ford or on foot into the wide country that began at her doorstep. The bright, open spaces of the high desert summer were O'Keeffe's destination, and she drove into the sand hills, hiked out under the buttes and cliffs, and rode horseback into the canyons that wound onto the mesa tops and into the mountains.

O'Keeffe lavishly and lovingly painted the topography of her new home. She set up her canvas and her paints in the rear of the Ford, where she was shaded from the blistering sun, and painted every piece of her world. O'Keeffe's plein air studio encompassed all of the Piedra

Garden House at Ghost Ranch in 1936. O'Keeffe spent several summers here. This casita, built by Stanley's crew, was later the ranch's health center.

Lumbre; her subjects were the stones and cliffs, sky, bones, clouds, shadows, dried desert trees, and tiny desert flowers. The only interruptions to the primal silence were the buzzing of the cicadas and the calls of the resident ravens that echoed off the cliffs. The badlands under the cliffs were gritty and dusty, and the summer sun turned O'Keeffe's skin deep brown. The heat of the high desert reached a blistering pitch by noon, at which time O'Keeffe often joined the rest of the ranch community for the ritual siesta.

Like an ancient, silent companion, Cerro Pedernal was always on the horizon to the southwest. The slender, angular mountain became a central subject in O'Keeffe's paintings. Pedernal had a powerful, mythological reputation in the New Mexican landscape thousands of years before O'Keeffe came to portray the mountain. But the intensity and scope of O'Keeffe's affection for Pedernal, rendered in form and color in numerous paintings over half a century, irrevocably merged the persona of the mountain with the painter.

To the greater world of people unfamiliar with the raw materials that inhabit the high desert of northern New Mexico, the subjects of O'Keeffe's canvasses were impersonal objets d'art, embellished and abstracted artifacts, untethered to the real world. But O'Keeffe was actually painting the timeless story of animals and plants and people in and of a place. Her canvases rendered the complex, multilayered primordial world that existed around and beside her at Ghost Ranch.

O'Keeffe never painted portraits of the people coexisting in her world at Ghost Ranch. Even so, for those who walked this land, lived this time at this place, O'Keeffe's paintings were often portraits of their world that contained familiar images and recalled experiences that were part of the collective memory of the Ghost Ranch community.

O'Keeffe's six-month stay at Ghost Ranch in 1935 coincided with the tumultuous midsummer departures of Brownie Pack with Frank Hibben, and Jack McKinley with Ardith Johnston. O'Keeffe had come to know and like Brownie Pack before her dramatic exit from the Piedra Lumbre. Brownie, like O'Keeffe, disliked the traditional roles most women embraced, and was happiest in her Levi's and broad-brimmed hat exploring new territory on horseback or in an automobile out under the open sky. Both women loved classical music, and when Arthur was away on business, O'Keeffe and Brownie spent evening hours at the Packs' Burros House listening to favorite recordings of Bach or Beethoven. "We were friends immediately," Brownie Pack recalled years later, "and loved the same things."

Brownie had a fearless sense of adventure that was attractive to O'Keeffe. The two women packed picnic lunches and, with Brownie behind the wheel of the Model A, took off for long days under the wide, hot sky. "We began to take picnics and explore weird canyons and get stuck in the mud . . . in an old Ford thing. We got stuck in the Chama River once. . . . Oh, we had all sorts of times. . . . We'd go out and find beautiful places, and then O'Keeffe would go back and paint them if they appealed to her."

Frank Hibben was working on his master's thesis about New Mexico mountain lions—locally called cougars—and gave O'Keeffe photographs he had taken of the native lions in the wild. When Hibben learned of O'Keeffe's interest in collecting and painting bones, he brought her various animal skulls. "I had one deer skull and she admired that, and then I got her a cow skull . . . and then I got her a couple more deer skulls, and a bear skull. I don't think she ever painted that one! I thought she was going to paint a lion, but I don't think she ever did!"

The drought of the 1930s devastated the wild and domestic animals of New Mexico. The carcasses of horses and cattle, coyote and deer, were found everywhere on the Piedra Lumbre. By 1935, and the enforcement of the Taylor Grazing Laws, which called for the removal of all domestic animals from federal range lands, the llanos and sierras of the Piedra Lumbre became the graveyard for hundreds of wild horses exterminated by government sharpshooters. Although these mustangs—reputed to be descendants of horses brought from California in the 1820s over the Old Spanish Trail that crossed the Piedra Lumbre—had never been handled by humans, and were virtually impossible to catch, the wild horses were deemed domestic by the government. When the mustangs could not be rounded up and held for adoption, the horses became legal shooting targets. "The bones were everywhere," Dorthy Burnham Fredericks remembers. "Of course O'Keeffe painted them. They were *everywhere*."

O'Keeffe's bone collecting had actually begun during her first summer visits to Taos and Alcalde. The bones were O'Keeffe's tangible, touchable reminders of the wordless wonders she found and felt in New Mexico, and she had begun to ship barrels of the smooth, sun-

O'Keeffe and bones found on the Piedra Lumbre desert at Ghost Ranch. Photograph by Ansel Adams, 1937.

bleached bones back to New York in 1929. "I have wanted to paint the desert and I haven't known how. I always think that I can not stay with it long enough. So I brought home the bleached bones as my symbols of the desert. To me they are as beautiful as anything I know. To me they are strangely more living than the animals walking around—hair, eyes and all with their tails switching. The bones seem to cut sharply to the center of something that is keenly alive on the desert even tho' it is vast and empty and untouchable—and knows no kindness with all its beauty."[17]

Most of the ranch cowboys had never seen O'Keeffe's paintings, but they were appreciative of her bone collection and began to collect bones to give her. Jack McKinley became friends with O'Keeffe after he began to bring her skulls he found while riding the range. "O'Keeffe and my father got along real well," son Henry McKinley recalled. "Dad used to go out and bring her skulls. She told me this herself—that he used to go and bring her skulls all the time. And O'Keeffe told me that Jack McKinley made a very dashing figure, you know, with his silk handkerchief around his neck, and his hat and chaps. O'Keeffe thought the world of him."

Although O'Keeffe would not discuss art and painting with Edward Bennett Sr., who was, like her, driving out onto the desert and painting plein air from the back of his car, they did become friends over tea and conversation at the Casa Monte Rojo house under the cliffs. O'Keeffe loved her Model A and enjoyed mastering the difficult roads of northern New Mexico. Her conversations with Bennett were frequently about their experiences with various automobiles. The Bennetts had driven two vehicles cross-country from Chicago to Ghost Ranch and had also bought one of Ghost Ranch's retired but indestructible Lincolns—a 1923 model known among the staff as the "Clay Car." O'Keeffe compared notes with Bennett about better automobiles coming onto the market, the difficulty of keeping tires from puncturing, and the conditions of the local roads. And sometimes the conversation on the Bennett portal beneath the Puerto del Cielo turned to the location of skeletons and bleached bones, and particularly to one outstandingly fine skull that graced a beam of the Bennetts' covered porch. "[O'Keeffe] used to kid my father about the ram's head that adorned our portal," Ted Bennett remembered, "saying she would come and take it some night."[18]

O'Keeffe made paintings of a ram's skull that may or may not have been based on the coveted specimen owned by the Bennetts. However, several of O'Keeffe's paintings titled "Ram's Skull" were actually renditions based on a locally renowned Angora goat's skull. The billy goat whose skull became O'Keeffe's ram's skull model belonged to Dorthy Burnham, the young girl who went east with the Johnsons for foot surgery. After Dorthy's billy goat died, the carcass was hung in a tree near the Burnham homestead east of Ghost Ranch. The family dogs made a game of trying to de-tree the animal corpse and managed to chew the tips of the old goat's horns. The goat's skull eventually made its way to O'Keeffe's well-known bone collection, where it became the subject of several canvasses that referred to it as a ram's head. The goat's skull may have been misidentified, but its dog-chewed horns were accurately depicted in the paintings "Ram's Head, White Hollyhock-Hills, 1935" and "Ram's Skull with Brown Leaves, 1936."

The young antelope enchanted O'Keeffe as they did everyone at Ghost Ranch, and she was impressed by Pack's devotion to the pronghorn's survival in the first summer after their arrival in 1934. "The road from the Pack house to the main house was so bad that when it rained [Pack] had to ride over on a burro to get the fourteen gallons of milk to feed them."[19]

When O'Keeffe drove her Ford out on the three-mile road to the Bennetts' or Packs' houses under the cliffs to the red badlands to paint and hike, the antelope often ran alongside the car. After she bought an open roadster, O'Keeffe worried that the young pronghorn might try to jump into the back of the automobile. Following the goring and death of Mary Duncan, the children's nanny, the guilty buck antelope was kept briefly in a pen near Rancho de los Burros, where O'Keeffe set up a studio in 1936. "I think he knew I was afraid of him. He would stand and look at me—come and eat from my hand—then hook my hand with his horn as if it were his natural gesture. Sometimes the coyote that was the pet of the house would be lying beside the pen like a dog."[20]

The buck was later shot and his skull given to O'Keeffe, who years later placed it in several of her paintings of the Piedra Lumbre. The antelope skull hovering in the sky above Pedernal was a playful, magical painting to the outside world, but to those who lived at Ghost Ranch and knew the story of the nanny and the antelope, the death of Mary Duncan was quietly and elegantly memorialized in "Antelope Head with Pedernal, 1953."

O'Keeffe became acquainted with old Juan de Dios, whose Vadito de Chicos crossing of the Chama River she had used several times since her first excursions about northern New Mexico in 1929. O'Keeffe admired the independent, elderly half-Navajo, half-Spanish de Dios, who was one hundred years old in 1935. O'Keeffe also admired de Dios's two giant oxen, and frequently reminded him that when one of the animals should die, she very much wanted the skull.

In 1935 one of the oxen did, indeed, die. Jack McKinley and Slim Jarmon and the rest of the ranch cowboys were invited to share a meal of the ox's meat, which everyone agreed was as edible as stiff boot leather. And when she arrived for the summer, de Dios gave O'Keeffe the giant skull. O'Keeffe did a simple drawing of the ox skull and, although she rarely gave away her work, gave the drawing to Arthur Pack, who was recovering from the painful and humiliating departure of Brownie with Frank Hibben. Pack was the first to admit his ignorance about art, especially O'Keeffe's, but he greatly appreciated the gesture and the gift, although he mistook the drawing to be that of a cow's skull. "She tried to be a friend," Pack wrote in his memoir, "even bringing me one day as a gift a perfect drawing of a cow's skull which I then and there adopted as the insignia and trade mark of the Ghost Ranch."[21]

Pack and O'Keeffe often disagreed as to what was best for Ghost Ranch, and their forty-year friendship weathered stormy silences, mild to moderate misunderstandings, and several irreconcilable differences of opinion. But over the years, Pack, in partnership with his second wife, Phoebe, became O'Keeffe's time-and-trail-tested compadres—neighbors on the frontier, where shared hardships and triumphs forged trusted friendships. O'Keeffe could be thoughtless and even rude to her neighbors, but she could also be generous and forthcoming. The Packs learned to maintain an even-tempered, even aloof, attitude toward O'Keeffe. As the years progressed and their understanding of one another deepened, Pack and O'Keeffe came to be friends who tolerated one another's differences and shortcomings. Pack forgave O'Keeffe her numerous and often tactless demands, and O'Keeffe forgave Pack his ignorance of all things artistic. "He didn't understand art at all," Pack's daughter, Peggy, remembered. "And O'Keeffe knew this and accepted it. Still, one day she asked him to come over and visit

The Ghost Ranch ox skull and sign marking road to the ranch. Photograph by Ansel Adams, 1937.

her. She said, 'Arthur, I now have something to show you. And you're going to get this one.' She had painted this great big painting of the blue with the clouds in it. She said to Arthur, 'Okay, what's that?' And my father said, 'Oh, Georgia, that's easy! That's clouds seen from an airplane.' He was so proud of himself."

After he purchased Ghost Ranch, Pack had to spend a good deal of his daily energy throughout the summer seeing that O'Keeffe was comfortable and happy. Most of her wishes Pack was able to grant: O'Keeffe was always given the casita she preferred, and by 1936, the Packs were able to give her a studio at the Burros House in which to work. The Packs instructed all Ghost Ranch guests to leave O'Keeffe alone and were told that unless O'Keeffe initiated it, conversation with the artist was discouraged, even if she was seated at the same supper table. The guides and wranglers also accommodated O'Keeffe: Orville Cox and Pete Dozier especially rearranged their schedules whenever O'Keeffe or her guests needed a personal driver or a guide.

In spite of Pack's best efforts to please O'Keeffe, he was still the target of her temper on many occasions. She wrote a friend about one such confrontation. "I gave him one of my best trimmings—I had been mad at him long enough to have it all very clear in my mind and in fine order and I spared him nothing—I drew all the blood I wanted to and wiped my knife clean on what was left of him. He didn't have a leg to stand on—In a way it was pretty awful but it was what I thought and felt and I hammered it in one nail after another."[22]

Before she met O'Keeffe, Phoebe Finley was forewarned of O'Keeffe's blunt dismissal of people she perceived as superfluous to her life and work. But Phoebe Finley was a confident young woman and, although she greatly respected O'Keeffe, was not in awe of the famous artist. Phoebe Pack first met O'Keeffe out under the noon sun on the desert airstrip at Ghost Ranch in early summer of 1936.

> When I first met Georgia, who I always called Georgia, I was with Arthur, also the Johnsons and the Bennetts. They were all standing around and Arthur introduced me. He said, "Georgia, I'd like you to meet my new wife." Georgia stood looking at me for a minute. I reached out my hand and I said, "Hi Georgia!" She came back with her hand and said, "How are *you*, Phoebe!" She

Orville Cox and Georgia O'Keeffe at Canyon de Chelly.
Photograph by Ansel Adams, 1937.

was absolutely floored that anybody would approach her on a man to man basis. . . . Georgia was a very unique person. There's no question about that. Her aim in life was art and her painting . . . not people.

A month-long quarrel with O'Keeffe could be instigated by some singular, almost insignificant event. One such summer spat at Ghost Ranch began when Phoebe refused to give O'Keeffe a freshly baked cake. "I had just baked a cake for dinner and Georgia saw it in the kitchen. Georgia told me it was her housekeeper's birthday and she wanted the cake. I said, 'No! What would my guests eat tonight?' Georgia said, 'Bake another one!' I said, again, 'No.' Georgia was very miffed. But she got over it in a couple of months! We remained friends!"

The ranch vegetable garden was also the source of much Pack-O'Keeffe negotiation. Phoebe Pack used to say that the carrots dug up especially for O'Keeffe cost the Packs a dollar apiece in the 1930s. "O'Keeffe would come and ask for two carrots. Or a ripe melon. The only ripe melon. And then Arthur had to take somebody off the garden who was working and say, 'Go down and dig two carrots for Miss O'Keeffe.' We felt this was kind of a drain. The people in the garden were all busy. She did that almost every day. And she'd take what she wanted, anyway, like no one else existed."

Phoebe Pack and O'Keeffe had many such domestic encounters in the next several decades, and, although Phoebe was well known to stand her ground to O'Keeffe's sometimes difficult requests, Phoebe eventually came to the conclusion that "with people like Georgia, it's a heck of a lot easier to do what they want."[23]

For reasons unclear to the ranch community, O'Keeffe openly and vocally disliked Robert Wood Johnson. "There were certain people that Georgia just couldn't tolerate," Phoebe Pack remembered. "She couldn't see Bob Johnson without making a crude or cruel remark. She'd say something like, 'Why don't you keep off this property and then I wouldn't be bothered or annoyed by you.'"

O'Keeffe may have assumed this adversarial position toward Bob Johnson following his decision to not purchase one of her paintings. In 1935, the Johnsons were interested in buying one of O'Keeffe's paintings of a morning glory and met with Alfred Stieglitz in New York.

Robert Wood Johnson did not know Stieglitz, but Ghost Ranch's seemingly isolated world had a way of trickling beyond the ranch's borders into the greater world they all circulated in back east, and Stieglitz knew a great deal about Bob and Maggie Johnson prior to their meeting. He knew they were fabulously wealthy, and Stieglitz also knew, presumably through his wife, that the Johnsons had been unable to conceive a much-wanted baby. (Maggie Johnson had miscarried after mountain climbing in New Mexico.) Stieglitz decided to use this personal information in their negotiations about the painting. Arthur Pack later paraphrased Stieglitz's proposal to the Johnsons.

"You want a baby! You cannot have one—I know these things. But you can have an O'Keeffe painting. For this, you will give her two years of creative life, which will need fifteen thousand dollars."[24]

Stieglitz essentially suggested that Bob Johnson pay more than twice the going price in the 1930s for an O'Keeffe painting. The actual amount of the O'Keeffe was not prohibitive to the chairman of Johnson & Johnson, but Stieglitz's cavalier attitude toward the couple's ongoing struggles to become parents, and his flagrant inflation of the painting's market value, apparently perturbed and possibly insulted Bob Johnson. Several weeks later Stieglitz learned the Johnsons would not be buying the painting after all. "Dear Mr. Stieglitz," Maggie Johnson wrote, "You will be glad to know that we have adopted a baby. Sorry about the O'Keeffe."[25]

Bob and Maggie Johnson returned to Ghost Ranch in 1936 with their newly adopted daughter, Sheila. O'Keeffe was cool to Bob Johnson, but if she was miffed with Maggie, it did not have a lasting effect on their friendship. Maggie continued to be one of only a very select few Ghost Ranch summer people who dined and socialized with O'Keeffe.

Following a pack trip into the mountains during which one of the hired hands cut his foot and was taken to the hospital, O'Keeffe went with Maggie and her bodyguard/chauffeur, Clay Wolf, to inform the hired hand's family of their son's accident. It was a fifteen-mile drive across the basin to the family's modest home in a village beneath Pedernal. The hired man's family spoke only Spanish, so Pete Dozier went with them to translate. Reaching the family's home proved to be an ordeal, and the glimpse into the world of a traditional Nuevo Mexicano family left a lasting impression on Maggie Johnson and O'Keeffe, who wrote Stieglitz.

> We got stuck in a little broken bridge—crossed a hay field—a stream—stones to step on very far apart—a field that had just been irrigated and was very wet—then the house up a little hill—a dog barking at us all the while out of the dark—Clay got a shovel and went back to dig the car out while Maggie with Pete to interpret told the family—they were so distressed—a very old man—quite blind and thin but very alive in his way of moving about and gesticulating—Pete was so quiet and gentle with him—The house was very poor but neat and orderly—I was interested in it all.[26]

O'Keeffe had met ranch hand Pete Dozier several years before in Taos, when he was employed by Mabel Dodge Luhan. By all accounts, Pete Dozier had an exceptional and remarkable *presence*, and everyone who met him remembered him. Slightly built and soft spoken, with high, chiseled cheekbones and an easy smile, Dozier was an exotic and refined cowboy. Fluent in English, Spanish, and Tewa, Pete Dozier gracefully straddled Indian and non-Indian worlds. O'Keeffe often sought out Dozier at Ghost Ranch social functions. She wrote to Stieglitz, "Last night the children gave a play that the governess wrote and helped them with—It was given out on the porch after supper,—was very amusing. . . . After that they danced. I only looked on with Pete, one of the ranch hands—half Indian and half a very good French line—He was working for Mabel when I was in Taos and has been here a couple of years. He is very handsome and a beautiful dancer when he dances but he sat by me most of the evening."[27]

In the summer of 1937, O'Keeffe did a painting of a sunflower that Maggie Johnson brought to her one morning. Maggie's young nephew, Seward Johnson Jr., was visiting the ranch while O'Keeffe was working on the new canvas, titled "A Sun Flower from Maggie." Maggie introduced Seward to O'Keeffe and, throughout the summer, Seward shared with O'Keeffe the treasures he found on his walks in the badlands. The Johnson children, like O'Keeffe, filled their casita windowsills with smooth stones and pieces of dried wood picked up on the desert. O'Keeffe particularly admired a piece of mica Seward carried in his pocket, and one morning she proposed a trade to the five-year-old. "I thought maybe O'Keeffe was going to give me a small painting for my piece of mica," Seward Johnson Jr. remembered of their transaction that summer day. "She said she had just finished a painting of a sunflower. But instead of a painting, she came back to me with the sunflower itself, the 'model.' O'Keeffe tied a handkerchief around it and gave the sunflower to me. To a small boy, it was very special. I took it to bed with me that night, held tightly in my hand. Of course, it didn't last very long."

The sunflower did not last long in little Seward's hand, but the mica became a permanent treasure in O'Keeffe's windowsill collection. Forty years later, Seward Johnson Jr. and O'Keeffe met again. He reminded her of their trade—the sunflower for the chunk of mica. "I told her, in jest of course, that she still owed me for that beautiful piece of mica. A sunflower! I had been just a small boy! I asked if she remembered? O'Keeffe got a twinkle in her eye, and nodded and laughed!"

Several summers later, Seward Jr.'s new stepmother, Esther Underwood (Seward Sr.'s second wife), joined the Johnson gatherings at Ghost Ranch. Essie was small, elegant, and self-confident, and became one of O'Keeffe's most trusted friends. During the long Manhattan winters, when the sun and the space and sky of the New Mexican summer seemed to be light-years away, O'Keeffe often left the city for quiet weekends at the Johnson farm in Oldwick, New Jersey.

In spite of parental instruction to the contrary, the Pack sisters, Norrie and Peggy, frequently made O'Keeffe's plein air studio their morning destination. Their summer days were spent on horse- or burroback, and although their first encounters with the reclusive painter were accidental, finding O'Keeffe soon became the purpose of the Pack sisters' excursions into the sand land.

"Peggy and I were very conscious of O'Keeffe being around here in the summer because we were always searching for her," Eleanor Pack Liddell remembered. "We'd get our horses and just ride around and look for her car. We were bound to run into her. She wasn't very friendly—why should she be to us? We were really bothering her. She was trying to paint and we'd hang over her shoulder and look at what she was painting! She really didn't like that. One day, in order to get rid of us, she gave us a Hershey bar. That was a bad mistake: we searched all the harder the next day!"

Arthur Pack never heard about his daughters' antics—neither O'Keeffe nor the sisters spoke of their sand-land encounters. Years later, when they began to see reproductions of the canvases they had seen on O'Keeffe's easel in the open desert, Norrie and Peggy Pack realized what they had been privy to. "I can remember one day coming upon her," Eleanor Pack Liddell recalled, "and she was doing one of her paintings with a skull in the sky . . . a skull in the sky!"

Jack McKinley's children also learned that O'Keeffe could be warm and welcoming one day, and cool and dismissive to them the next. One morning O'Keeffe would see the children and invite them in to the Burros House, where she was working, and serve them lemonade and cookies, whereas the next day she would shoo them away or ignore them completely.

Arthur Pack understood how the ranch children offered a bridge between the temperamental artist and Ghost Ranch, and even used them when he needed to smooth ruffled feathers. Following one confrontation with O'Keeffe, Pack filled a basket with fresh produce from his garden and sent the McKinley children on their burros to visit O'Keeffe. O'Keeffe wrote a friend about the children's visit with the peace offering that included the following:

> Carrots
> 16 beets
> 2 cauliflower
> 2 cabbages
> 3 large head of lettuce—
> I had to laugh—[28]

Ghost Ranch had more than twenty thousand acres of private desert that abutted national forest to the north. Still, O'Keeffe's plein air studio was frequently—and literally—overrun by ranch people and livestock. After her successful winter of foot surgery in New York, Dorthy Burnham returned to Ghost Ranch and worked with the ranch's string of horses. During one morning roundup on the badlands west of the ranch, Burnham's corral-bound herd nearly trampled O'Keeffe. Burnham remembered, "I was running horses across the desert—you don't walk horses, like cattle, you get them running and then you don't stop them until they're where you want them to be. I came up and over a ridge at a hard run. And there was O'Keeffe, sitting in front of her canvas. I couldn't stop them: the horses just thundered right past her, around her, the whole herd, and left her sitting in a huge cloud of red dust!"

In spite of O'Keeffe's instructions to the contrary, Pack and the Ghost Ranch staff kept a distant eye upon O'Keeffe. Although she was usually alone, people knew where O'Keeffe was and how long she had been gone. The Piedra Lumbre was a vast and unpredictable landscape where humans could still find themselves in dangerous situations. Heat prostration, dehydration, snake bite, flash flood, broken bones from a missed step on a steep trail—it was easy to get into trouble on the desert. O'Keeffe knew Pack and his cowboys kept an eye on her comings and goings, but it was a small price to pay for the personal and creative freedoms inherent in a Ghost Ranch summer.

The Garden House casita that was O'Keeffe's summer home from 1934 through 1936 was part of the cluster of guest cottages nestled close to Ghost House. It was small and tidy, with a fine view of the garden and with Pedernal peeking through the orchard. But the casita had no space for canvases and paints, and, as she had during her summers at Alcalde, O'Keeffe painted under the sky or used her Ford with the back seats folded down for her studio.

O'Keeffe had driven past Pack's Rancho de los Burros home dozens of times during the summers of 1934 and 1935. Like the Bennett house, the Pack home was located in the center of what O'Keeffe now considered the best country on earth, with windows and doors framing unfettered views of the painted sand lands, stone cliffs, and the faraway horizon that included Pedernal. The house was also three miles from ranch headquarters.

When O'Keeffe returned to Ghost Ranch in 1936, Pack had moved out of the Rancho de los Burros house and was building a modest new adobe home behind the ranch headquarters for himself and his new bride. Most of the Pack family furniture was left at the abandoned family home out under the cliffs, and the Burros House now served as a guesthouse for Arthur and Phoebe's visiting friends and family.

Carl Edward Glock and his father, a former classmate of Pack's at Williams College, were housed in Rancho de los Burros in 1936. Carl had just graduated from high school and, with his dad, had "car camped" cross-country from Pittsburgh to Ghost Ranch. After a week vacationing as Pack's guests at the ranch, Carl accepted Pack's suggestion that he remain and work as a "ranch hand" for room and board.

Glock lived at the Burros House that summer and remembers that O'Keeffe began to use one of the rooms for a studio. Although Glock's primary duties were in the ranch kitchen or down at the corrals, he and another summer staffer, Tim Pfeiffer, a Princeton undergrad, were asked to drive Miss O'Keeffe about the valley on painting excursions and into town on errands and social calls. Maggie Johnson often went along on these sojourns, which could also include camping in the outback for two or three days. Both Glock and Pfeiffer enjoyed their time with the famous painter and her friends, although it meant long days on the hot desert with little to do but stretch out under a tree and nap.

Glock and Pfeiffer became experienced chauffeurs and, like their mentor, Orville Cox, began to drive guests in the ranch Lincoln on overnight journeys to Santa Fe, Taos, and even across the Four Corners country to Mesa Verde, Acoma, and to the late-summer Indian ceremonial festivities at Gallup. Pack also asked the two young men to keep his desert airstrip free of prairie dogs. Glock and Pfeiffer spent countless hours under the July sun inventing ways to clear the packed sand runway of the animals' deadly, plane-toppling holes—a thankless and ultimately fruitless task. "I even tried gassing them with exhaust from vehicles," Glock remembered, "but discovered they always had extra entrances."

Once a week, Glock and Pfeiffer carried a satchel with the ranch checks and receipts into the bank in Española. Pack gave Glock a loaded pistol to carry in the Lincoln because the return trip included the same bag filled with cash for the Ghost Ranch payroll. There were no more banditos using Yeso Canyon for their stolen cattle, but Ghost Ranch was still very much on the frontier, and highway robbery was still very much a concern among New Mexican travelers.

O'Keeffe's official living quarters were in Garden House that summer, but Glock remembers that she began to spend more and more of her time at her studio in Rancho de los Burros. By midsummer O'Keeffe had begun to sleep at the Burros House and, in some unspoken yet recognizable way, had begun to claim the adobe in the badlands as her own.

Glock and Pfeiffer became pals that summer with Janet Jepson, the Pack children's summer governess, and the threesome often spent their days off hiking into the canyon country or riding into the mountains. Jepson had studied astronomy at Vassar, and the night skies over the Piedra Lumbre were a stargazer's dreams come true. Jepson slept out under the open sky whenever her duties allowed it, often throwing

Princeton undergrad Tim Pfeiffer and Georgia O'Keeffe at Ghost Ranch in 1936.

down her sleeping bag on the roof of the cottage she shared with the Pack children near ranch headquarters. But Glock told Jepson that the best stargazing was found on the roof at Rancho de los Burros. Jepson recalled that night:

> I heard that O'Keeffe was away for a few days, and so I asked Arthur Pack if I could take my sleeping bag out and sleep on the roof of Rancho de los Burros. He thought that would be just fine, so I drove over in the old Pierce Arrow, climbed up the ladder and threw down my bag for a night on the roof. Sometime during the night, very late, I heard a car drive in. It was O'Keeffe. She saw my car and knew someone was there, and began to call out, "Who's there?!" I answered from the roof, "It's me, Janet Jepson, up on the roof!"
>
> O'Keeffe climbed up the ladder in the dark but she did not climb onto the roof. I sat up in my bag, and she stood on the ladder, silhouetted against the stars and the night sky, and we had a very pleasant conversation. O'Keeffe was interested in my husband, Glenn's, work at Princeton where he was a professor of geology and paleontology.
>
> We spoke like that for a while. And then she told me to enjoy the stars. She said good night and climbed back down the ladder and went to her room and went to bed. I remained on the glorious roof all night.

O'Keeffe's propriety of Ghost Ranch was so complete by the summer of 1937 that she did not feel it was necessary to inform the Packs if and when she was coming to the ranch to stay. In mid-July, O'Keeffe arrived unannounced to find that Arthur and Phoebe Pack had a full ranch, with every room in every casita occupied. O'Keeffe suggested that the Packs rearrange the other guests so that there was a vacant cottage for her to move into. Pack ignored this suggestion and instead offered O'Keeffe a room at Rancho de los Burros. O'Keeffe gleefully agreed to the arrangement, and from that summer forward the house under the cliffs belonged to O'Keeffe: "As soon as I saw it, I knew I must have it," O'Keeffe said years later of the Burros House. "I can't understand people who want something badly but don't grab for it. I grabbed."[29]

Moving into the Burros House in July of 1937 was as much a milestone in O'Keeffe's creative and emotional life as the finding of the road to Ghost Ranch had been three years earlier. At Ghost Ranch O'Keeffe found her place, her world; and in the House of the Burros she found the center of her world.

Vernon Pack's summer tutor, Nathaniel Abbot, and his wife, Clara, were already staying in the Burros House, as was Carl Glock, there for his second summer at the ranch. But O'Keeffe's housemates had work that kept them at the main ranch throughout the day, and they returned to Rancho de los Burros after supper. The adobe was essentially O'Keeffe's private space, and she set up a studio and a bedroom and used the kitchen for private meals. With three miles between herself and the ranch community, O'Keeffe could walk and paint, stare at the cliffs, and sit on the top of a sand hill, virtually alone in the wide good country. "All my association with [the house]," O'Keeffe said years later, "is a kind of freedom."[30]

O'Keeffe was smitten by the house and its surreal location front and center in the desert kingdom of Pedernal. The cliffs of multihued sandstone rose to the north (O'Keeffe called the seven-hundred-foot-high stone walls that filled the north windows "her curtains"[31] and arranged her bed so that she could watch the sky over the desert at night), Pedernal and the deep blue mountains of the Jemez defined the south, and the red and gold sand hills, buttes, spires, and stone-strewn arroyos spilled up and down to the east, west, and everywhere in between. The size of the sky and land appeared limitless, and the sensation of a place inhabiting infinite space dwarfed the adobe house, but also gave everyone living within it a sense of a cosmic timelessness. O'Keeffe repeatedly attempted to explain the extraordinary setting of Rancho de los Burros.

> It's the most wonderful place you can imagine. It's so beautiful there. It's ridiculous. In front of my house there are low scrub bushes and cottonwood trees and, further out, a line of hills. And then I have this mountain. . . .
>
> At the back door are the red hills and the cliffs and the sands—the bad lands. I go out of my back door and walk for 15 minutes and I am some place that I've never been before, where it seems that no one has ever been before me."[32]

The moon, like the cliffs, the roof, and Pedernal, was a primary character in O'Keeffe's daily life at Ghost Ranch. The flat-topped roof of the Burros House became O'Keeffe's evening perch from which she observed the comings and goings of her celestial companion on the landscape. "I've been up on the roof watching the moon come up—the sky very dark—the moon large and lopsided—and very soft—a strange white light creeping across the far away to the dark sky—the cliffs all black—it was weird and strangely beautiful."[33]

Over the next few summers O'Keeffe lived and worked at Rancho de los Burros. She began to "undecorate" the house to suit her minimalist liking: unneeded furniture and excess clutter was cleared out of her rooms. The rose bushes were uprooted and O'Keeffe began to water the sage that grew between the flagstones of the patio. The bones, stones, and dried cedar and pinion wood that O'Keeffe found on her daily walks across the red hills soon covered the portal's walls and window ledges. The rattlesnake population, however, was not impressed by O'Keeffe's arrival, and they continued to claim the portal. O'Keeffe learned that, if a door was left ajar, the interior rooms were also the territory of her reptilian desert cohabitants. O'Keeffe was duly respectful of the prairie rattlers, but she did not let them dampen her enthusiasm for the paradise she found at Rancho de los Burros.

It was a seamless existence; the colors, forms, sounds, and smells of the outer world of the Piedra Lumbre swept through the house's doorways and windows day and night. The world of people faded into the hot air. There were no distractions. O'Keeffe's only companion at Rancho de los Burros was the landscape itself. The mundane universe ceased to exist as O'Keeffe was immersed in an environment that reminded her daily, hourly, that the natural world was complex and multifaceted far beyond her understanding.

O'Keeffe's paintings were portraits of the macro and micro worlds that she was immersed in at Rancho de los Burros:

My Backyard
Red Hills
Red Hills Blue Sky
Red Hills with White Cloud
Horn and Feathers

The House I Live In
Cedar Tree with Lavender Hills
Hollyhock Pink with Pedernal
Red Hills with Pedernal
From the Faraway Nearby

Looking south from the house and patio, Pedernal's angular form dominates the horizon from dawn until dusk. Beneath the night sky of sparkling stars, or partnered with the luminous moon, the flint-topped Cerro is the single most powerful element in a landscape of mythic, primordial forms. Pedernal became O'Keeffe's favorite subject, and after dozens of paintings and renderings, the mountain became as much an icon to the natural world as O'Keeffe was to the art world. After decades on the Piedra Lumbre, O'Keeffe simply and bluntly established her claim to Pedernal. "It's my private mountain. It belongs to me. God told me if I painted it enough, I could have it."[34]

The flat roof of the Burros House became as much a part of O'Keeffe's living quarters as the rooms enclosed by adobe walls below. "You live out here and you become very aware of change. . . . I climb up that ladder onto my roof there, and I can just stare out at the hills. I've been known to spend weeks up there, looking at how they've washed into new shapes. You can go up there and feel how good the world is."[35]

The handmade pine ladder left at the house by Arthur became a link, both physical and metaphorical, to the universe viewed from the rooftop. The night world known and seen from Rancho de los Burros—the ladder, the sky it climbed into, the moon, and Pedernal—was immortalized in O'Keeffe's painting *Ladder to the Moon*.

O'Keeffe luxuriated in the privacy and silence, but she also wanted to share her new home with selected friends. In the summer of 1937 O'Keeffe began to invite close acquaintances to come to her place on the Piedra Lumbre. Among the first friends invited into O'Keeffe's personal paradise at Rancho de los Burros was Margaret "Peggie" Bok. Peggie Bok had entered O'Keeffe and Stieglitz's Manhattan world in 1935 when she was a thirty-one-year-old divorcée dating David McAlpin. A year later, Bok married filmmaker Henwar Rodakiewicz, who had formerly run the H & M Ranch in Alcalde with his ex-wife Marie Garland. In late July of 1937, Bok wrote to Arthur Pack and inquired about the availability of rooms. Bok learned, as O'Keeffe had several weeks earlier, that Ghost Ranch was full for the summer. When O'Keeffe learned from Pack about Bok's inquiry, she invited Bok and Rodakiewicz, and Bok's three young children, to come and stay with her at the Burros House.

It was a new experience for O'Keeffe—the secluded house under the cliffs suddenly filled with the bustle of parents and children. By her own accounts O'Keeffe enjoyed the social whirlwind of their two-week visit, which included day trips to visit friends in Taos (including writer Aldous Huxley), local sightseeing tours, swimming and sunbathing at the ranch pool, family picnics, and late-night stargazing. Like O'Keeffe, Bok and her familial tribe loved the outdoor life at Ghost Ranch.

O'Keeffe formed a fondness for the Bok boys, Derek and Ben, and their older sister, Wilnuet. The youngest child, Derek, who would grow up to become the president of Harvard, was supposedly O'Keeffe's favorite, although he was too young to remember the ranch or his early relationship with the famous painter. All of the Bok children were treated to private riding lessons with Pete Dozier, who Wilnuet thought "rode as if he were part of his horse."[36]

O'Keeffe was friendly to her houseguests and later wrote to her husband that she had never had a finer time with so many people. But the Bok children understood that their hostess wanted to be left alone to paint. Wilnuet remembered that "Georgia was working, and once in a while went to the store or with us for picnics." But to the Bok children, it was the land of the ranch, not the people, that was the main attraction. "Ghost Ranch was enormous, still, soundless, full of secret life, of danger and beauty. . . . We loved climbing onto the roof at night to look at the stars, so bright there."[37]

Others were invited into O'Keeffe's faraway life at Ghost Ranch that summer—Santa Fe writer Spud Johnson, and Jaconita painter Cady Wells. Haniel Long, a writer who had been a professor of literature at Carnegie-Mellon University and had recently moved to Santa Fe, came for several visits. And British journalist Felix Greene, a cousin of Graham Greene, came to Ghost Ranch to see O'Keeffe, as did first-time visitor to the Southwest, Irish writer Gerald Heard.[38]

When O'Keeffe met Gerald Heard in Taos in August of 1937, he had just arrived in the United States and was the newly appointed chair of historical anthropology at Duke University. Heard had come to New Mexico with his close friend, Aldous Huxley, to visit D. H. Lawrence's widow, Frieda. With Bok and Rodakiewicz, O'Keeffe met Heard at Frieda Lawrence's Lobo Mountain house. O'Keeffe liked Heard immediately and told him that he needed to come and stay a few days at Ghost Ranch.

Heard accepted O'Keeffe's invitation and his stay at Ghost Ranch coincided with a week of bright moonlight. O'Keeffe orchestrated sundown/moonrise activities with Heard and the Bok-Rodakiewicz crowd so that her friends could experience what she loved: they walked into the badlands as the sun turned the cliffs to fire, and then returned to the Ranch of the Burros in the bright light of the rising moon. O'Keeffe wrote Stieglitz, "When we got over to this house—everyone seemed so pleased to be here—it is so still—so alone—so open all around—I love the way they love it—I feel it almost a personal flattery that they like it as I do."[39]

After carrying blankets and fruit juice up the ladder to the roof, the friends huddled together and watched the light of the moon move across the cliffs, buttes, and sand hills. Later, alone in her bedroom, O'Keeffe's attention was again drawn into the night of the wild world that beckoned beyond the window. "When I came into my room with a small lantern Maggie gave me in my hand—it vaguely lighted the white room and through the very big window I could see the cliffs in the moonlight—bright—with the windmill wheel shining bright in front of them—it was wonderful in a weird sort of way—"[40]

Heard began to wander the desert on his own, often following the same cow paths that O'Keeffe frequented. After his departure in August, O'Keeffe found Heard's footprints around the base of a twisted cedar tree that stood alone in the badlands. Heard had also scratched a poem in the sand beneath the cedar.[41]

Do not act as though		Know that you
you were in the	be	are in the presence
		and you will

O'Keeffe had already sketched and painted the gnarled, dead cedar trees of the Piedra Lumbre, but her portraits of the cedar she named "Gerald's Tree" became among her most recognized paintings.

Ansel Adams had become part of the O'Keeffe-Stieglitz art and social circle several years before in New York. During one of Adams's

O'Keeffe painting *Gerald's Tree* in a car at Ghost Ranch.
Photograph by Ansel Adams, 1937.

Manhattan visits, O'Keeffe had introduced the young photographer to friend and fellow Ghost Ranch insider David H. McAlpin. (McAlpin's first wife was the sister of one of O'Keeffe's friends, Esther Johnson.) A lawyer and investment banker by profession, McAlpin's interest in and patronage of photography—McAlpin became a significant benefactor of Ansel Adams's work—enabled Adams and Beaumont Newhall to found the Museum of Modern Art's Department of Photography. An important collector, McAlpin also funded the first chair in the History of Photography program at his alma mater, Princeton University.

In the 1930s, Adams was living in California and had visited Santa Fe and Taos, but he had never seen the Piedra Lumbre or Ghost Ranch. Following glowing recommendations by both O'Keeffe and McAlpin about the natural beauty of the country north of Abiquiú, Adams was introduced to Ghost Ranch in the early fall of 1937 through "a miraculous sequence of circumstances and the kindness of David McAlpin."[42]

Like his friends O'Keeffe and McAlpin before him, Ansel Adams was enamored of Ghost Ranch. In the weeks that Adams was a guest at the ranch he walked, drove, photographed, and soaked up the remarkable land, light, and life of the Piedra Lumbre. O'Keeffe enjoyed the company of the young photographer and was relaxed and good humored during Adams's stay at Ghost Ranch. Adams was allowed to shadow O'Keeffe throughout her workday and took candid photographs of O'Keeffe in her private, faraway world: hiking the red hills, collecting bones in the badlands, and painting in her car. (Adams's visit coincided with O'Keeffe's painting of "Gerald's Tree.")

Adams wrote to Alfred Stieglitz about the remarkable power of Ghost Ranch. "It is all very beautiful and magical here—a quality which cannot be described. You have to live it and breathe it, let the sun bake it into you. The skies and land are so enormous, and the detail so precise and exquisite that wherever you are you are isolated in a glowing world between the macro and the micro, where everything is sidewise under you and over you, and the clocks stopped long ago."[43]

In contrast to O'Keeffe, Ansel Adams "lived and worked amid swarms of people."[44] At Ghost Ranch, when Adams was not out photographing, he could be found in and around ranch headquarters chatting with the ranch guests. Adams knew and admired the work of Phoebe's father, Bill Finley, and Adams and the Packs were friends im-

David McAlpin and William Schuyler "Sky" Thurber leaving Ghost Ranch for a pack trip in the Four Corners Country in October 1936. The woman with the burro is Phoebe Pack.

mediately. After O'Keeffe's chilly attitude toward the summer "dudes," Phoebe Pack was impressed with Adams's all-around affability and community spirit. Pack remembered, "Adams got along with everyone. . . . Adams had no personal prejudices. He was much friendlier than O'Keeffe and was interested in everything. He was a great fellow!"

David McAlpin and his cousin Godfrey Rockefeller were also vacationing at the ranch in late summer and early autumn of 1937. McAlpin was a cheerful, gregarious, energetic extrovert who woke his friends, including O'Keeffe, at dawn for horse and automobile adventures about the valley and high desert. O'Keeffe wrote to Stieglitz about the jovial atmosphere that surrounded McAlpin. "I'm glad Dave drags me out to ride—he is very persistent—and I enjoy it so much, but I can't do much painting at the same time—"[45]

A day later, Adams wrote a letter to Stieglitz describing how "supremely happy" O'Keeffe was: "When she goes out riding with a blue shirt, black vest and black hat, and scampers around against the thunderclouds—I tell you, its something!"[46]

Adams was an accomplished classical pianist, and O'Keeffe told him that the Johnson house harbored a beautiful Steinway grand used by Stokowski during his ranch visits. The Johnsons had closed up—and bolted the doors to—their two-story adobe for the season, but O'Keeffe's desire to hear Adams play wasn't about to be deterred by a locked door. "After supper I got the key to the Johnson house from the housekeeper and we all went there—the sitting room—a good big room covered with a vast piece of unbleached muslin—carpet all covered with newspapers—We dug out the piano—a very good Steinway Grand and Adams played for us—He plays very well—Dave [McAlpin] and [Haniel] Long and I all stretched out on the floor on the newspapers."[47]

In late September McAlpin organized a first-class auto excursion into the outback for himself, O'Keeffe, Adams, and Godfrey Rockefeller to be led by Ghost Ranch guide/driver/mechanic Orville Cox. Cox was among the most respected and experienced guides driving the Southwest, and his twenty years of off-road adventures assured McAlpin's entourage an insider's journey on the roads less traveled across the Colorado Plateau. (Cox is credited with introducing O'Keeffe to what she came to call the Black Place.) O'Keeffe was reluctant to leave her studio, but the irrepressible McAlpin convinced her to go on what would be a memorable adventure.

McAlpin's car camping expedition immersed Adams, O'Keeffe, and the others into the last of the deep wild yet found in the American Southwest. Cox drove the station wagon, packed with people and camping gear, and O'Keeffe herself drove her Ford, filled with painting supplies. Their rugged itinerary included the cliff ruins at Canyon de Chelly, the mountain town of Silverton, Colorado, the San Juan River Canyon and Monument Valley of Utah, and the Grand Canyon on the Colorado River.

The people and the journey were vividly recorded by Adams's three cameras—two view cameras and a 35 mm Contax. Cox knew all of the old traders and also the unmarked roads that connected them across Navajoland. But new roads were cutting through the once-pristine Four Corners, and fences halted cross-country automobile bushwhacking. This autumn excursion was a journey into a place and time that were already vanishing in the American Southwest.

Adams, McAlpin, Rockefeller, and all of the summer guests at Ghost Ranch left by mid-October. But O'Keeffe did not leave the Ranch of the Burros that year until December. "That house was the love of her life," Phoebe Pack later said.

Everyone at Ghost Ranch knew that for O'Keeffe, the ranch was no longer just a place to vacation, to take time out from the real world. Ghost Ranch was the real world, often the only world, and O'Keeffe's time away from the ranch was becoming harder and harder to justify. On the flight back to New York after a long, satisfying summer-fall stay at Ghost Ranch, O'Keeffe wrote a friend, "It is no use to write about any more of the trip. I have left the good country—I must get myself in order for the other kind of life with the dawn—"[48]

Although she would not be able to live year round in the good country until after Stieglitz's death in 1946, in 1940 O'Keeffe became an owner of a small piece of it. After a year's absence from New Mexico, O'Keeffe returned to Ghost Ranch in June—unannounced and unexpected—and planned to stay for six months. The ranch had a spare cottage for O'Keeffe, but Rancho de los Burros was already spoken for. O'Keeffe was furious, although Pack reminded her that the Burros House was his to rent as he pleased. O'Keeffe suggested that in order to keep the peace, Pack sell her the house. Pack agreed, and after rearranging his guests, let O'Keeffe move into her beloved house under the cliffs.

Several months later, on the thirtieth day of October 1940, Rancho de los Burros became the first home owned by Georgia O'Keeffe. She was approaching her fifty-third birthday, and the house and its eight acres on the red and yellow badlands cost O'Keeffe six thousand dollars. It included the house and portal, the Pack family's clay tennis court, the corral and shed once occupied by the baby antelope, and a 360-degree view of the faraway country. The adobe house was a tiny dot in an enormous, uninhabited landscape. To O'Keeffe it was the precise center of paradise. "I have bought a house out here," she wrote her friend Ettie Stettheimer, "the one I have lived in the past three years here—It is for me a nice house and I like being here. I am about 100 miles from the railroad—68 from Santa Fe—95 from Taos—40 miles from town—18 miles from a post office and it is good . . . so far away that no one ever comes—I suppose I am odd but I do like the far away."[49]

Although the Burros House was lacking in creature comforts and seemed to always need repair and structural help from Pack's maintenance staff, it was O'Keeffe's dream home for the rest of her life. She wrote her friend, Maria Chabot, "I can think of no greater luxury than being at the ranch—even if the lights didn't work and the sink wouldn't drain."[50]

O'Keeffe's relationship with Ghost Ranch and New Mexico was now formalized. Inherent to this relationship was O'Keeffe's deeply satisfying commitment to her work, her solitude, and her happiness. Her boundaries were now marked and drawn. Everything she needed and wanted was within her reach, and everyone she did not want was far, far away. O'Keeffe wrote a friend, "I seem to be really most interested in the ranch and nobody."[51]

O'Keeffe had declared her love for Ghost Ranch, but she still loved and returned home to be with her aging husband, Alfred Stieglitz. Dividing her life, and herself, between Ghost Ranch and Manhattan was an arrangement that O'Keeffe and Stieglitz accepted until Stieglitz's death, in 1946. Stieglitz never came to the Southwest, but even from so great a distance, he came to understand through her letters and paintings the intensity of his wife's relationship with the place called Ghost Ranch. In the last month of Stieglitz's life O'Keeffe returned to Ghost Ranch. Stieglitz wrote her, "I greet you on your coming once more to your own country."[52]

Ghost Ranch was O'Keeffe's own country for the remainder of her long life. And even after decades of summers in the house under the shining stone cliffs, O'Keeffe was uncertain she would ever find a better place. "When I think of death," O'Keeffe said when she was in her late seventies, "I only regret that I will not be able to see this beautiful country anymore, unless the Indians are right and my spirit will walk here after I'm gone."[53]

Four War Nearby and Faraway

Lord, these affairs are hard on the heart.—J. ROBERT OPPENHEIMER[1]

In mid-October of 1938, Georgia O'Keeffe stood beside Slim Jarmon and Margaret McKinley and watched the Packs' airplane land on the packed clay landing strip under the cliffs. O'Keeffe and some of the ranch staff had come out to welcome Arthur and Phoebe's first-born child to Ghost Ranch. The Packs had closed the ranch in mid-September to guests—O'Keeffe remained, as did McAlpin and others who now qualified as "family," and so came and went at Ghost Ranch at their leisure—and a very pregnant Phoebe had been driven by Arthur to Denver, where they awaited the birth of their son. Charles Lathrop Pack II was born on September 23, and two weeks later the new family was flown back to New Mexico by Arthur's friend, Albuquerque pilot Bill Cutter.

Although a new road with an oiled surface now connected Española and Abiquiú and was slowly working its way up the Chama Canyon and across the Piedra Lumbre bound for Chama and the state line, medical facilities in northern New Mexico were still few and far away. Hence the Packs had traveled to a Denver hospital for the birth of their baby.

Margaret McKinley was baby Charlie's nurse, a fitting role as her own children were Arthur's legal wards. (Young Henry McKinley, to his father, Jack's, chagrin changed his middle name to Pack.) Ghost Ranch rarely counted an infant, even a baby, amongst its permanent residents, and young Charlie was showered with gifts by the ranch community and was greeted with traditional Spanish blessings and welcomes by local ranchers and their wives. The Pack baby was even treated to a thorough inspection by the grand matriarch of Taos, Mabel Dodge Luhan, who came to Ghost Ranch with her husband, Tony, and their good friend Dorothy Brett. Arthur recalled the threesome's visit. "Mabel, no sooner having heard of the birth of our son Charles, immediately had Tony drive her over to Ghost Ranch and demanded to be taken to the nursery. There she had given the infant a most thorough inspection, and having convinced herself that he was physically normal as well as presumably legitimate, headed straight back for her car and departed."[2]

Phoebe was amused but not surprised by Mabel's inspection of her firstborn—Phoebe had become accustomed to the eccentricities of Mabel Dodge Luhan and her friends at Taos dinner parties. "Mabel came over to see if . . . [Charlie] had both legs and two arms. . . . Because anything that had a story to it was made double by the fact that Mabel turned it into a paper or something!"

In 1938, the first of many annual Christmas letters from the Packs to the extended Ghost Ranch family announced the arrival to the Piedra Lumbre via airplane of baby Charlie. The holiday letter also told the ranch family of the impending arrival of the new highway from Española, oiled as far as Abiquiú. Within months of the New Year, the new roadbed cut across the Piedra Lumbre. It was a mixed blessing: the improved road made food, supplies, and medical support more accessible, but it also shortened the ranch's private road by two miles and diminished the size of the wildness that buffered Ghost Ranch from the outer world.

In the late 1930s, as the country began to recover from the Depression, and visitor traffic began to increase again in the Southwest, the threat to the Piedra Lumbre's wild qualities seemed to be an impending invasion of automobiles and tourists. But in fact, it would be the invasion of Pearl Harbor, and the creation of the secret city of Los Alamos on the Hill, located just over the blue horizon of mountains southeast of Ghost Ranch, that would irrevocably alter the sense of the ranch as a place beyond the reach of time.

As Europe and the Far East were besieged by war, and Americans were discouraged from traveling abroad, the gifts of silence and peace offered at Ghost Ranch became even more treasured by its extended family. In their second Christmas letter, in December 1939, the Packs wrote, "Like 'Shangri La' of 'Lost Horizon' the Ghost Ranch is far removed from wars and rumors of wars, but it has already become a refuge not only for old friends but for new ones, too who hesitate to dodge submarines en route to foreign lands. When the sunlight glows on our llano beneath the ageless silence of old Pedernal, people forget to regret other broken plans and know that here, at least, is still peace and plenty."[3]

Throughout 1939 and 1940, the Packs and Ghost Ranch functioned much as they had in the past decade. But the outside world spiraled deeper into the dark chaos brought on by the Nazis and Japanese. The tourism industry was tentative in New Mexico, and in June of 1940, the Packs thought their summer guest business would be "blitzkrieged out of existence." But by midsummer, the ranch's casitas were filled with a "sudden rush of old friends and new" seeking a momentary respite from the harsh realities of a world at war in the primordial silence found under the Cliffs of Shining Stone. The Packs wrote to their friends: "From Ghost Ranch, below the sheer bastioned cliffs of ever changing red and gold, we look out across the llano toward ancient Pedernal, and the feeling creeps over us that these things alone are permanent and real while the troubles of the world outside must be some mad illusion. . . . We can only hope that Time, which brought at last so perfect a peace to the rocks and desert under the limitless sky, will do as much for men."[4]

It was, of course, no mad illusion, and there would be no Christmas letter sent from Ghost Ranch in December of 1941. Following the invasion of Pearl Harbor, New Mexico, like states far more modern and industrialized, was instantly thrown into the maelstrom of the world conflict.

The war became an intimate affair to Santa Fe and surrounding rural northern New Mexican villages with General MacArthur's defeat on the Bataan Peninsula in the Philippines in early spring of 1942. New Mexico's National Guard became the 200th Coast Artillery, and then the 515th Coast Artillery, under General MacArthur, that the Japanese overwhelmed at Bataan. The men not killed were taken prisoner, and those soldiers that survived the horrific Bataan Death March suffered more than three years in Japanese prisoner-of-war camps. Barely half of the eighteen hundred Hispanic, Native American, and Anglo New Mexicans who had been at Bataan returned home.

By mid-1942, tourist traffic to New Mexico had dropped by a third, and by 1943, the tourist industry that was the backbone of the state's economy was less than half of what it had been prior to Pearl Harbor.

Gas rationing and tire conservation began in the spring of 1942, and, in a region where distances between people and their jobs and loved ones, between villages and even small urban centers, was, by national standards, extreme, the travel-suppressing sanctions were especially difficult and life altering. The effect of rationing on locals, along with the loss of some $80 million a year from the defunct tourist business, moved New Mexico's society back into the horse-and-buggy days. Only now the horse-and-buggy days were not indicative of the simple life and simple pleasures. On September 12, 1942, an editorial in the *Santa Fe New Mexican* summed up the New Mexican psyche: "Rationing would strike New Mexico harder than anything since Bataan."

Ghost Ranch had to become a completely self-sufficient entity on the high desert. The closest mercantile/grocery store was Bode's on the old plaza of Abiquiú, fifteen miles away. Española and the nearest telegraph and railroad station were some forty miles. Santa Fe and the necessities and amenities found in apparel shops and hardware and electrical stores might as well have been in another country, nearly seventy miles away. Arthur Pack was assigned to the Española Ration Board, and, even with B rationing that gave the ranch agricultural status, motor trips in Ghost Ranch vehicles down the valley were few and far between.

Like all of their neighbors on the Piedra Lumbre, the Packs and their staff rose to the challenges brought on by world war. The ranch already generated its own electricity, but during the war, there was little or no use of anything electric after dark. Kerosene lamps and candles returned to tables and windowsills, and even these primitive sources of light were used sparingly. The Packs' old Pierce Arrow "struggle buggy" was retired to a shed beside the bunkhouse, and a team of horses and a wagon was brought into active daily service. Phoebe and Arthur began to ride horseback together each morning out to the mailbox at the ranch gate on the highway; again in the late afternoons, one or both climbed back on their horse and carried the mailbag out to be picked up by the southbound mail truck.

With no dudes to wrangle and guide, Ghost Ranch cowboys and wranglers—most too old to enlist—left the ranch, and often New Mexico, to work in various war-related industries. Henry Peabody, builder Ted Peabody's son, left for Colorado and then Gallup in 1942. Slim Jarmon went to California.

By late 1942, Archie Galbraith, the gardener, and his wife, housekeeper and cook LaVerna, had also left the Piedra Lumbre. A new foreman, Herman Hall, came to the ranch with his wife, Jimmie, and their daughter, Yvonne. Hall handled the heavy maintenance and mechanical work, but Arthur and Phoebe, with their "adopted" children Barbara, Henry, and Wayne McKinley, assumed the garden-poultry-dairy chores. "Gardener, carpenter, plumber, electrician, I smashed my thumbs at each type of enterprise, but I learned something about them all," Pack wrote after the war. "I would not trade the experience of those half-dozen years of manual labor for anything. Nor would I now choose to repeat them."[5]

In the years before the war, the ranch dairy needs had been supplemented by milk and cream brought up each day from Bode's store in Abiquiú. But with gas rationing limiting trips to Abiquiú, Ghost Ranch had to buy its own milk cow. Initially, Bessie was Arthur's responsibility, although he "had never handled one of nature's bovine spigots."[6] Eventually the ranch dairy shed counted three milk cows, at which time Arthur, tired of rising alone before dawn on cold winter mornings, taught teenager Henry McKinley the finer points of milking. The ranch community had plenty of milk and cream, and throughout the war years Phoebe Pack and Jimmie Hall churned several pounds of butter two to three times each week.

Prior to the war, the splendid remoteness of the ranch had forced the Packs to become proficient in the basic skills and duties necessary to raise their own meat, poultry, and vegetables in the arid sand lands. Although their contact with friends and family in other parts of the country was diminished, and their mobility greatly reduced, during the war Ghost Ranch residents ate very well. Charles Lathrop Pack I would have been proud of his Ivy-educated but self-reliant gentleman rancher grandson, and of the Packs' World War II victory garden in the middle of an isolated yet sustainable community on the high desert of Ghost Ranch.

Even after the departure of master gardener Archie Galbraith and his three nephews, who worked as his assistants, the Ghost Ranch war garden was an impressive plot. Along with every conceivable "common" vegetable—Phoebe's personal favorites were celery and asparagus—the garden boasted a variety of melons and four kinds of berries. The orchard produced cherries, apples, apricots, and plums. There was always plenty of water flowing down the Yeso Canyon stream, and regardless of the region's rainfall, the ranch garden was always spectacular. Every morning throughout the summer, Phoebe and the McKinley boys labored over the vegetables. And in late summer and early fall, every year throughout the war, Phoebe Pack and Jimmie Hall put up twelve hundred quarts of the ranch's fruits and berries for the coming winter.

There was cold storage for beef in a subterranean room dug in the hillside under the Packs' house. Pack later recalled,

> Then there were the hogs and chickens, the hundreds of hams and pork tenderloins that we cured, the eggs which were either too plentiful, so that we had to put them down in preservatives, or too few to go around. . . .
>
> We . . . certainly lived on the fat of the land, but as a result, both [Phoebe and I] learned to prefer oleomargarine and the white fluid out of a cardboard container, rather than all the tribulations involved in getting it direct from the source.[7]

The spectacular garden at ranch headquarters was a source of both comfort and concern for Georgia O'Keeffe, who, in spite of personal and war-related obstacles, made an annual pilgrimage to the Piedra Lumbre throughout World War II. O'Keeffe realized that she was completely dependent upon the Pack operation if she were to live even part-time at Rancho de los Burros. The obtaining of fresh, even adequate, food was going to be O'Keeffe's number-one issue at Ghost Ranch. Gas rationing would limit her mobility, but if she could get to New Mexico, could reach her beloved adobe house on the vast desert below Pedernal, O'Keeffe could happily survive with just food and water.

For years, O'Keeffe had relied upon Arthur's staff to keep her life at Ghost Ranch hassle and trouble free: Orville Cox served as O'Keeffe's driver and was also a fixer of wells, generators, and automobiles. Ted Peabody was called in to fix the Burros House's chimneys, leaky roofs, stuck windows, and creaky doors. O'Keeffe also called upon the ranch kitchen staff to prepare food when she had company, and she hired Phoebe's maid for housecleaning duties. And O'Keeffe had always taken for granted the availability of superb fresh produce grown in the Ghost Ranch garden near headquarters.

But the war changed everything. With their own staff drastically reduced, and with rationing impacting their own ability to get to town for supplies, the Packs' manpower and food supplies were suddenly finite. When O'Keeffe returned to Ghost Ranch in the summer of 1942, she could no longer assume that her basic needs could be met by the ranch staff.

In the fall of 1940, O'Keeffe had met a young woman named Maria Chabot at Mary Wheelwright's ranch in Alcalde. Chabot was a twenty-six-year-old cousin of Wheelwright's who had come from Texas to New Mexico in the 1930s to work as a photographer on Works Progress Administration (WPA) projects. An aspiring writer, Chabot had offered to manage O'Keeffe's Ghost Ranch summer household in exchange for room, board, and some time to pursue her own creative work. Thus, beginning in the spring of 1941, Chabot had become the seasonal manager of Rancho de los Burros, a role she would fill for several months of each year until the late 1940s.

Chabot opened, cleaned, and oversaw the repair work at the Burros House each spring and then closed up the house after O'Keeffe left in late fall. When O'Keeffe was in New York, Chabot often served as O'Keeffe's go-between with the ranch staff—a position for which Chabot was not particularly skilled. Chabot assumed an adversarial position with Pack during her first spring at the ranch and was confrontational with all members of the Ghost Ranch community from the start. Her admiration for O'Keeffe was enormous, and Chabot felt the Packs and the Ghost Ranch community ought to serve someone of O'Keeffe's stature like royalty, which O'Keeffe was, in the world of art. Instead, Chabot found out in her first season at the Burros House that the Packs maintained a respectful but casual attitude toward their famous neighbor, and their lack of awe for O'Keeffe infuriated Chabot.

Chabot's demands on the ranch staff began the moment she stepped into the Burros House each spring. The generator and water heater needed the immediate attention of Orville Cox, and the roof, windows, and doors often needed Ted Peabody's carpentry skills. When workers did not appear at first summons, Chabot berated them in her letters to O'Keeffe. With the escalating shortfalls and strains of the war, it was a time in the life of Ghost Ranch when O'Keeffe should have been asking the Packs for less rather than more. O'Keeffe understood this, but Chabot did not, and misunderstandings and miscommunications between the Burros House and Ghost Ranch resulted in several years of very cool relations between the Packs and O'Keeffe.

Electrical generators on the Piedra Lumbre were high-maintenance affairs, and Pack's staff had their hands full with Ghost Ranch's system housed in the bunkhouse. With rationing, and in response to the Burros House's seemingly endless need for assistance to keep its generator up and running, Pack suggested to Chabot in late 1941 that O'Keeffe's residence would benefit from its own Wind Charger—a twenty-dollar item available from Montgomery Ward. Chabot knew that it would be prudent to generate electricity with wind power at the Burros House, but her letter to O'Keeffe, following Pack's suggestion that they immediately pursue this step toward self-sufficiency, portrayed Pack and his staff as heartless villains. "Is a prime necessity to be independent of Arthur's man coming once a month to charge your batteries. Don't, don't be dependent upon that outfit, Georgia. It stinks: They don't love you."[8]

When Arthur and Phoebe visited O'Keeffe in New York in March of 1942, they assured her that come summer, she could have all the vegetables she wanted from their ranch garden. O'Keeffe's kitchen was stocked with fresh produce from the Packs' garden throughout the summer of 1942, but with no end to the war in sight, O'Keeffe realized that she needed to find property near Abiquiú that had ample water and good soil for her own garden.

That fall, after O'Keeffe departed for New York, Chabot remained in New Mexico and looked for land and a second house for O'Keeffe. But Abiquiú and its satellite communities along the Chama River offered few properties with clear title and with the irrigation rights O'Keeffe needed for a garden.

In April of 1943, with no prospect of a garden near Abiquiú, with the war escalating and rationing an indefinite hardship, O'Keeffe was ambivalent about her future at Ghost Ranch. "I believe one must learn to eat in a new way to live up there," she wrote Chabot from New York. "Maybe I'll not be able to live there—but I intend to try another year at it."[9]

Chabot consulted with Orville Cox and the Galbraiths about gardening at Rancho de los Burros, but everyone's advice was against even trying to grow anything in such clay-laden soil as that found out under the cliffs. There was a water spigot near the old antelope corral, and Chabot thought that with manure added to the clay and sand, and with mesh fencing to keep out the rabbits, this might prove the best place for a garden. But the local logic finally persuaded even Chabot that gardening would be impossible at the Burros House, and nothing was planted. She wrote O'Keeffe.

> It's going to be difficult this year—much more difficult than you in New York understand. . . . Even with a B ration we can make only one trip a week to Abiquiu for water and nowhere else can we go in that car. Trips to Espanola and Santa Fe are practically out. And when you get to Espanola there is so little you can buy under the stamp system. . . . Archie and Laverna are here. You might make up with Mr. Pack and go eat out of his garden. That's really the simplest way for you to live out here—just pay for it. . . . As for chickens: that's a good idea, but you have to kill them. As for planting in the patio: the reason why nothing grows there is—the wretched adobe soil—and the lack of adequate sun. Vegetables need eight hours a day. The patio doesn't have it.[10]

O'Keeffe did "make up" with the Packs and accepted their help with food and water during the summer of 1943. But O'Keeffe was realizing that life at the Burros House, with and without the rationing imposed by a world war, would always be a challenge, especially the longer she stayed into the fall. And winters would be impossible. With Stieglitz nearing eighty years of age, O'Keeffe was beginning to think ahead to the time when she would move to New Mexico as a full-time resident.

After years of looking around the Chama Valley, O'Keeffe and Chabot finally found a promising property near the Abiquiú plaza with irrigation rights, a fine view, and the skeleton of what was once a fine adobe house. In 1945, after years of negotiations with the property's owner, the Archdiocese of Santa Fe, O'Keeffe bought the crumbling adobe hacienda that had once served as the home of General Jose Maria Chavez. It would take four years, but once rebuilt, this adobe house and compound would give O'Keeffe the closer-to-town headquarters she needed and the water rights and good soil for the grand garden she wanted. But to O'Keeffe, the Abiquiú house was always just a house. The difficulties of life at el Rancho de los Burros never overshadowed O'Keeffe's intense love of the dwelling on the Piedra Lumbre. The house at Ghost Ranch was forever O'Keeffe's home. "I store my belongings, sleep, and work in Abiquiu," O'Keeffe later explained, "but I do my living at my ranch."[11]

Martin Bode, the German-born owner of Bode's store in Abiquiú, did everything he could to help his Piedra Lumbre neighbors obtain supplies and food through the war years. His daughter, Elizabeth, was a small girl during the war, and she remembered "soft spoken, considerate and sensitive" Mr. Pack coming into her father's mercantile on the plaza to discuss business, the life of the valley, and the war faraway and nearby. Bode was also friends with O'Keeffe and invited the painter to the Bode home for dinner and animated discussions. Elizabeth recalled, "My father and O'Keeffe [and] . . . I'd sit at the dinner table and I'd hear these things—they disagreed on politics, they disagreed on the neighbor down the street, they disagreed on everything and had a wonderful conversation about it!

"And I remember dad, during the war, when things were hard to get—food—he could get steaks and things. O'Keeffe always got the finest—he made sure she got them!"

For all her complaints about Arthur Pack, even Chabot grew to appreciate Pack's quiet reliability. Chabot was especially grateful for Pack's intervention and legal advice when Chabot's cousin, Mary Wheelwright, included Chabot in her will in late 1944. "Arthur came by, and in a very business-like manner advised me to call upon Mary's lawyer in order that he might legally confirm what she has done—in order to protect me, which was good of him—and I am grateful for it!"[12]

Until O'Keeffe moved to New Mexico to stay, in 1949, her annual departure from Ghost Ranch was always a difficult and even dreaded time. Chabot, too, fell in love with the house and life at Ghost Ranch and, after the war, confessed that "the Piedra Lumbre is the best thing I've ever known in New Mexico—the closest thing to God, I guess."[13]

The landscape and house under the shining cliffs cast their famous spell on Chabot, just as they did on everyone else who came to stay for a week, a month, or for half a lifetime. "This is my last night at the

Ranch," Chabot wrote O'Keeffe on the eve of her departure in November of 1943. "I am sad. . . . You are the only one who can really know how I feel about that. . . . Each time I leave here it is like a Death, and each time that I return it is a Birth."[14]

The events of World War II transpired a world away from Ghost Ranch, but when a pine-covered mesa on the Pajarito Plateau above the Rio Grande was chosen to be the site for the Manhattan Project and the secret city of Los Alamos, northern New Mexico was suddenly and intimately a part of the most profound events in the story of the war, if not in the story of mankind. Although the specifics of the secret behind Los Alamos were not fully understood by residents of northern New Mexico until August 6, 1945, and the dropping of the atomic bomb on Hiroshima, Japan, the presence of an ultraimportant, top-secret, war-related project on the Hill was common knowledge. In such a rural, unpopulated region, it was impossible for the U.S. military to camouflage the enormous influx of civilian and armored vehicles, building equipment, fencing, watchtowers, barbed wire, gates, and what grew to include several thousand people onto the Pajarito Plateau.

To the outside world, Los Alamos was a well-kept secret, but among northern New Mexicans, it was a secret of specifics and details only. The community on the Hill that did not have a name or an address doubled in size every nine months from 1943 until the end of the war. Hundreds of local New Mexicans were employed at Los Alamos, and, although talk about the place and the project was forbidden, everyone from Santa Fe to Tierra Amarilla speculated about the secret city. Popular theories about the Hill included that it was a home for pregnant WACS, a nudist colony, or a secret base for submarines. The shallowness of the Rio Grande made the last theory the least accepted, although there was further speculation that the plateau might harbor a production plant for submarine windshield wipers.

The federal government was not amused by the local newspaper editors' attempts to give the mystery a humorous cloak, and Washington officials confiscated issues with editorials that openly speculated about New Mexico's veiled involvement in the war effort. New Mexicans were, however, amused by Washington's confused ideas about the state's topography and populace. Arthur Pack remembered several federal war directives misdirected at New Mexico.

> There was the occasion when our local draft board almost resigned in a huff upon receipt of a directive to start drafting some of the many "cattle guards" Washington had heard about. Washington simply did not know that a cattle guard was not a man. . . . Again, when local sheepmen requested more kerosene to warm their lambing tents in early spring, Washington directed them to "change the lambing season." The sheep reproduction cycle remained unmoved by bureaucracy.[15]

The Manhattan Project was placed on the Pajarito Plateau within a few canyons of the old Ramon Vigil Ranch, where thirty years earlier Carol Stanley and Natalie Curtis had envisioned a museum and cultural center that would share the remarkable world of the ancients with the world of the moderns. The very qualities of isolation and distance that had drawn Stanley and Curtis to the plateau made it valuable to the Manhattan Project team, headed by General Leslie R. Groves and J. Robert Oppenheimer.

Oppenheimer was considered among the best theoretical physicists in the country and in 1941 had left his teaching positions at Berkeley and Cal Tech to join and then head the $2 billion dollar project that would build the first atomic bomb. "My two great loves are physics and New Mexico," Robert Oppenheimer told a friend several years before the secret project in the secret city was conceived and born. "It's a pity they can't be combined."[16]

Oppenheimer's two great loves *were* combined in October of 1942 at the Los Alamos Boys' Ranch School. Oppenheimer had visited the school and the Pajarito Plateau in the 1920s before he began undergraduate work at Harvard. The magic of New Mexico had cast its spell on Oppenheimer those summers, but his work and career took him far away from the land of enchantment for nearly two decades. Then, in 1942, when Groves laid out the government's location criteria for the Manhattan Project—isolation, controlled access, little or no local population, adequate water, moderate climate, west of the Mississippi, and at least two hundred miles from an international border or the Pacific Ocean—Oppenheimer remembered the Pajarito Plateau in northern New Mexico.

The seizure of the Boys' School by the federal government and the birth of the city of Los Alamos irrevocably changed the Pajarito Plateau. The arrival of the Manhattan Project would also change the red and yellow sand lands of the Piedra Lumbre. Site Y, the secret city of Los Alamos, was a mere thirty miles as the ravens fly over the mountains southeast of Pedernal. The isolated paradise of Ghost Ranch was about to enter a new and incongruous era in its story.

The Manhattan Project came to Ghost Ranch in 1942 in the form of several "curious strangers" who came not as sightseers or visitors but as interrogators of ranch staff, residents, and guests. Phoebe Pack recalled that the suited, serious men who arrived one morning on their front porch asked everyone at Ghost Ranch "where you were born, what did you do, where did you go to college, what have you done since?"

Like everyone else in Rio Arriba County, the Packs knew that there was a supersecret project cloaked in the cover of the high pines of the Jemez Mountains. The Packs were old friends with the Los Alamos Boys' School's founder, Ashley Pond, and in prewar summers, many of the Boys' School's families had come to Ghost Ranch for vacations. The Packs knew of the sudden closure of the school on the Pajarito Plateau, and of the forced and unhappy departure of its teachers and students. And Arthur, like all pilots military and non-, had been told that any aircraft flown within several miles of the Los Alamos plateau country would be shot down without warning or explanation.

The Packs cheerfully, and a bit apprehensively, endured the "G-Men's" inspections and interrogations of the Ghost Ranch community and were not surprised when shortly after their departure a "polite but positive summons" came instructing them to meet with Dorothy McKibben (the Manhattan Project's office manager) at 109 East Palace Avenue in Santa Fe. In Dorothy McKibben's Sena Plaza office the Packs finally learned the reason behind the strangers' formal visits and invasive, blunt questions: the federal government needed a retreat for some of its top personnel to use for weekend getaways.

Like the Boys' Ranch School before it, the place called Ghost Ranch had passed federal inspection. Unlike the ranch at Los Alamos, the Packs and their staff could remain in residence. Ghost Ranch had, and did not have, exactly what the government wanted. With only one entrance, surrounded by a natural barrier of cliffs and mountains, buffered by a wilderness of deep sand and difficult canyons, miles from pavement and the eyes of the outside world, the ranch could serve as a safe haven for top-secret government employees.

In Dorothy McKibben's office, the Packs were asked if they were amenable to having their guest ranch used by government personnel on a regular basis. The Packs were amenable, and, beginning in the summer of 1943, their contribution to the war effort involved handing over the Ghost Ranch reservation book to the U.S. government. O'Keeffe could still come and go as she pleased, as could the Bennetts, the Johnsons (although they sold their house to Pack in 1939), and their friends and staff. The Packs could still invite personal friends and members of their family onto Ghost Ranch, but not in large numbers.

Outwardly, Ghost Ranch looked and functioned as it always had. There were no obvious security measures—the Ghost Ranch gate remained unlocked, as did all of the ranch cottages. At Ghost Ranch, the Hill guests and their families were given a respite from the heavy security measures that befuddled every other aspect of their lives during the war. If there were guards watching the comings and goings of people on the Piedra Lumbre, they were hidden, even from the Packs. (Several of the more important men from Los Alamos were shadowed by Counter Intelligence Corps agents, fondly nicknamed the creeps by project personnel. The Packs called these government guards Junior G-men and were grateful that their presence was kept to a minimum at the ranch.)

To the visitors from Los Alamos, the contrast between the atmosphere of the Hill and Ghost Ranch was profound: the barbed-wired, gated, and guarded compound of austere barracks and prefab buildings of the Manhattan Project's Site Y were temporarily replaced by mud-plastered adobe casitas nestled under cliffs on the edge of the wide, unfenced, unfettered open spaces of the Piedra Lumbre.

The government's visitors were treated like all guests at Ghost Ranch: they became part of the Packs' extended family. Each morning, weather permitting, saddled horses awaited riders, trails beckoned hikers into the wild places of the cliff country, and the cool stream-fed pool welcomed swimmers anytime of the day or night. Late afternoon all guests were invited for mint juleps and conversation on the Packs' supper porch, where dinner was served family style at the small Mexican leather-topped tables. Every seat had a fine view of Pedernal and the variegated sands of the Piedra Lumbre, and dessert and coffee were always served in tandem with the sun's final slide into the horizon of mountains.

Arthur and Phoebe had been instructed by McKibben that they were not to ask their government guests anything remotely personal or professional. Even their names and details about their childhoods were off limits. The Packs quickly identified acceptable conversational topics and became adept, as did their guests, at sustaining lively and even challenging dinner dialogues centered on the weather, the landscape, their valley neighbors, oft-seen wildlife, the menu, and the daily happenings around the ranch. The visitors still spoke to one another in coded sentences, and there were lists of words that were *never* spoken —physics, fission, atom, bomb. But at Ghost Ranch there was a temporary return to a world without war and death and secrets so powerful that divulging them to the wrong person could bring swift personal punishment, and possibly horrifying global consequences.

In spite of the lopsided quality of social interaction, the relationships that developed between the Packs and the men they later learned included the top scientists in the world were extremely enjoyable. They said nothing, but the Packs recognized Oppenheimer early on from photographs and knew enough about his work at Berkeley to suspect that his circle of highly educated colleagues were somehow involved in physics research at the burgeoning but invisible community across the mountains. With all-American names like Nicholas Baker and Eugene Farmer, but with decidedly non-American accents, Pack and all of the ranch staff guessed that these men and their families were from Europe and Scandinavia, Hungary, Russia, Italy, and the Balkans. After the war the Packs were able to put names to now-familiar faces—Enrico Fermi, Niels Bohr, George Kistiakowsky, Richard Feynman, Edward Teller, Robert Oppenheimer, and many others.

Just prior to the war, in early summer of 1941, Arthur's cousin, Roger White, a junior at Stanford, visited the ranch en route home to Ohio with his brother. The White brothers had stayed at Ghost Ranch as Arthur's guests in 1936, following the death of their father. During their weeklong stay in 1941, Roger met and fell head over heels in love with a young ranch guest, a nursing student from New York named Kitty Barnes. Kitty and Roger completed their degrees on opposite coasts in the next year and then married in 1942, and Arthur and Phoebe invited them to spend their honeymoon at Ghost Ranch.

The new Mr. and Mrs. Roger White returned in August to the magical place where they had fallen in love. Kitty and Roger hardly noticed the other guests at the ranch that week, but the newlyweds—and the fact that Kitty was a registered nurse and Roger a mechanical engineer—were noticed by their neighbors in the casitas behind Ghost House. At the end of their honeymoon, the Whites departed Ghost Ranch for Santa Fe, where they were approached on the street by a woman they had never seen before. Roger White remembered that fateful encounter that would change their lives. "We were standing there on the corner at La Fonda waiting for the bus [to the train station at Lamy] to show up and this perfectly strange woman walks up to me and says, 'Are you Roger White?' And I said, 'Yeah.' And she says, 'Dr. Bainbridge has come in to interview you.' And I said, 'I don't know what you're talking about.' She said, 'I think you better come with me.' She had me by the arm by that time, and Kitty said, 'Go ahead, this sounds real exciting. . . . I'll go over to the La Fonda and have a drink.'"

The strange woman was Dorothy McKibben, who, after seeing a car with the Ghost Ranch logo on its door drive past her Palace Avenue patio, had run out onto the Santa Fe plaza and hunted down the newlyweds. McKibben had been alerted to the couple in a phone call from the woman—who was an assistant to the Los Alamos personnel manager—staying in the casita next to the Whites' at Ghost Ranch. The Whites were perfect candidates for the fledgling project at Los Alamos—an engineer and a nurse, just married, with no jobs, no ties, no children, and already in love with New Mexico.

Roger was taken into a back office at 109 East Palace Avenue and interviewed by Dr. Kenneth Bainbridge. Bainbridge was destined to become the technical director of the Trinity test of the first atomic bomb, which Bainbridge would witness six miles from ground zero, shoulder to shoulder with Kistiakowsky and Oppenheimer three years down the road.

"Dr. Bainbridge was trying to find out what I was good for without telling me what the job was," Roger White recalled of that remarkable meeting in the fall of 1942.

That same day, Roger and Kitty White accepted the job offers on a project no one could explain in a place with no name. After a quick trip by train back to Cleveland, where their friends and family had been drilled by the FBI, the Whites "vanished from the outside world into the secret behind the well-guarded gates of 'The Hill.'"[17]

The Whites were among the first brought into the Project and were given a little attic room in Fuller Lodge—one of the original log buildings of the former Los Alamos Boys' Ranch School. "We were put to work right away," Roger White later recalled. "It was pioneering. And you don't get to do that much anymore . . . building a new town right from scratch. And all in secret. The whole atmosphere was just full of excitement and challenges here and there."

During the war, Roger and Kitty White were allowed to return to Cleveland and New York to visit their families. But they could not leave the continental United States, and they could never talk about where they lived and what their work was involved with. The birth certificates of the Whites' two children, like all children born on the Hill during the war, reflected the federally mandated fiction that there was no place called Los Alamos: their official place of birth was a post office box—1663 in Santa Fe.

Visits to Cousin Arthur and Phoebe Pack at Ghost Ranch were among the highlights of the Whites' war years in New Mexico. The Whites shared the Packs' supper porch meals with Kitty and Robert Oppenheimer, Enrico Fermi, Niels Bohr, Richard Feynman, and George Kistiakowsky. Other guests staying at the ranch ate their meals at the same time as the Los Alamos visitors, and Roger remembered that Arthur politely and often humorously deflected their questions about the mysterious hill. "Arthur made a lot of jokes . . . like that they were making orange crates, or it was a submarine base for the Rio Grande Navy. . . . He knew that something important was going on. Arthur had a lot of contacts."

In spite of security regulations to the contrary, the scientists did continue lab-related discussions at the ranch. Roger remembered how "the scientists were all constantly together, talking physics. . . . 'How are we going to cope with this problem?' . . . and I remember thinking, we're all here for a little r'n'r, why are we talking shop so much? . . . It was just the stress of this constant drive to get the thing done."

The thing was done and tested on July 16, 1945, at the Trinity test site near Alamogordo, New Mexico. Northern New Mexico residents who were outside tending to their morning chores at 5:29 that dawn saw the light from Trinity flash in the sky over the mountains; many in their beds were awakened by the shock wave that passed through their homes like an earthquake. Windows were blown from their frames in buildings in Gallup, New Mexico, 235 miles northwest of Trinity, and people on the Arizona-New Mexico state line, 150 miles from ground zero, saw "the sun come up and go down again."[18]

The secret of Los Alamos was a secret for only a few more weeks. On August 6, 1945, "Fat Man," a twin of the bomb tested at Trinity, was dropped on Hiroshima. Three days later, a second atomic bomb was dropped on Nagasaki. On August 14, V-J Day, the citizens of the previously invisible city of Los Alamos set off every siren and horn that could be found in the town and lit a small arsenal of explosives in celebration of the end of the war, and the end of their secret lives.

After the war, the Packs and their desert sanctuary under Pedernal were revisited by many of the same men and women who had previously come to the ranch veiled in secrecy. They joined the Packs for dinner on the supper porch with real names and very real concerns about their work and its implications for the future of mankind. Arthur Pack wrote, "After the surrender of Japan, our atomic energy friends could talk a little more freely and philosophically about the future of the world. Here, on a Ghost Ranch evening, the utter incompatibilities and terrible contrasts inherent in man's warring natures stood out as starkly as did mountain, cliff and sky. The Hiroshima destruction, which one or two had actually witnessed, was a nightmare they might vainly wish undreamed."[19]

By 1946, Robert Oppenheimer and Niels Bohr had brought together a sizable group of their Los Alamos colleagues to form the Federation of American Scientists, which lobbied Washington to place the bomb and all atomic research under some form of international control. Their ultimate goal was to have no more secret cities with secret projects.

Pack did not disclose the names of his Los Alamos friends, even after the war. But he did write about one acquaintance who returned to Ghost Ranch and "became one of the organizers of that group of scientists who fought long and hard for world-wide agreement to outlaw atomic war and lock up forever the Pandora's box they had helped to open. Perhaps this scientist's frequent days at Ghost Ranch had served to shape his world view for peace."[20]

In 1941, Arthur and Phoebe had begun a small hotel business in Tucson, the Ghost Ranch Lodge, where they planned to eventually spend each winter and then the school year when young Charlie began elementary school. The war had changed the Packs' plans: gas rationing had ended their prospects for winter visitors to the new lodge in Tucson and had also limited their ability to come and go between Abiquiú and southern Arizona. So for the duration of the war, the Packs placed the sixteen brick cottages into active duty and offered the housing at cut-to-the-bone prices to Tucson's new population of Air Force officers and cadets.

All of the Ghost Ranch Lodge apartments were fully occupied for the next few years by grateful servicemen and their brides. The Packs' philanthropy paid off after the war, when their now civilian lodgers became permanent neighbors and friends whose praise for the Packs' generosity and facilities became the foundation of a bustling year-round business. In the late 1940s, the Ghost Ranch Lodge expanded around its park-sized lawn of orange trees, flowering cactus, palms, and flowers until it included eighty units, a swimming pool, restaurant, and even a service station. The Ghost Ranch Lodge was on the main highway northwest of Tucson and was among the first independent motels to join the organization that became the successful and powerful national chain called Best Western Motels.

Arthur and Phoebe's second child, Phoebe Irene Pack, called Pip or Pipper, was born in Santa Fe in early January of 1944. War-imposed travel limitations meant the Packs could not fly or drive to a Denver hospital, and so Phoebe birthed their daughter in St. Vincent's Hospital in Santa Fe. It was a difficult seventy-mile drive from Ghost Ranch, and the Santa Fe hospital was an old facility, overcrowded and understaffed. Phoebe Pack remembered,

> While I was there, the woman in the next room was having some trouble and facing a Caesarian section. I listened to [this woman] and she had no nurse. . . . She couldn't afford it. . . . So this woman got my nurse.
>
> At this time the thought was born in my mind, "Where are the

Arthur and Phoebe Pack with Charlie and Pipper at Ghost Ranch in the 1940s.

hospitals in Rio Arriba County?" They don't exist. . . . There was nothing north of Santa Fe.[21]

Within a few months of baby Phoebe's birth, the Packs were visited by old Princeton friends of Arthur's who had never seen Ghost Ranch. In late spring Charles and Anne Morrow Lindbergh came into the ranch office and asked Phoebe if Arthur Pack might be around. Phoebe Pack had never met the Lindberghs, and although she could not immediately place the famous couple in front of the ranch office, she knew the deeply tanned and somehow familiar-looking people asking for Arthur were famous or important, or both. "The Lindberghs came to see us more than once," Phoebe Pack recalled. "They'd drive out from Santa Fe. . . . Arthur was quite able to talk to Mr. Lindbergh. I just sat and listened with my mouth open because a lot of what they talked about was very technical. Mrs. Lindbergh wanted to see the children in our nursery. And she loved them from here on up! She loved children."

Phoebe Pack was understandably in awe of Lindbergh, but she was not as ignorant of aviation as she claimed. Although she was afraid of flying, Phoebe traveled all over the country by airplane with Arthur. In 1947, determined to overcome her fear, Phoebe Pack took Arthur's advice and earned her own pilot's license.

As her children grew, Phoebe Pack continued to voice her concern about the lack of medical facilities in Rio Arriba County. With Arthur's help, Phoebe began to look for solutions. Española seemed to be the obvious location for a new hospital, but two issues had to be resolved before building a hospital could be successfully undertaken: money to build it and someone to run it. For years, the children from Ghost Ranch had attended school in Española at McCurdy, a mission school of the United Brethren Church. The school had successfully educated hundreds of Hispanic, Native American, and Anglo children since the early 1900s. Pack approached the United Brethren about undertaking the administration of a new hospital in the same community on the Rio Grande. The church accepted the proposition to run the hospital, but they were in no position to fund such a facility.

The Packs could contribute some of the money personally—they had already funded the building of a school in the Piedra Lumbre community of Coyote—but it was clear from the outset that their donation would be a "drop in the bucket," and the community's contributions would be meager at best. The sizable Charles Lathrop Pack Foundation could give nothing toward the half million needed, as its sole purpose was to support projects that promoted conservation.

Decades earlier, when Arthur's brother, Randolph, was struggling with hemophilia back in New Jersey, Charles Pack I had begun stamp collecting with his bedridden son. After Randolph's death, Charles Pack Sr. continued to collect stamps, perhaps to honor and remember his departed child. By the time of his death, Charles Pack had acquired several valuable and specialized collections that were exhibited all over the world. The stamp collection was eventually given to Arthur, who placed it in a New York City safe-deposit box and all but forgot about it.

In 1946, the Pack stamp collection was pulled out, dusted off, appraised, and put up for private auction. The collection caused a small sensation among stamp enthusiasts. (One part of the collection, a rare twopence stamp of Queen Victoria forged by hand in Australia, was sold to the British Crown.) When the auction was complete, the stamp collection begun on the deathbed of Arthur's frail and beloved brother netted a half million dollars, and the Española Hospital was born.

Santa Fe architect John Gaw Meem was an old friend of the Packs, and Meem agreed to donate his time and offered his firm's expertise at cost until the thirty-bed hospital was completed. The hospital's layout was based on a design recommended by Dr. Sam Ziegler, who was the hospital's first chief of staff. Although the hospital floor plan was laid out in the form of a cross—a design characteristically found in many of Meem's more famous buildings, including the Church of Santo Tomas on the plaza of Abiquiú—the final structure was more institutional than "Santa Fe" in style.

Twelve acres of land with a view of the Truchas Peaks and the Sangre de Cristo Mountains were donated by the Bond Willard Mercantile in Española. Ted Peabody, the builder of the casitas, headquarters, Bennett house, Johnson house, and Rancho de los Burros at Ghost Ranch, became the foreman of the hospital construction crew. By late 1947, the building was completed, and by May of 1948 the new hospital was equipped, staffed, and opened to great local fanfare and celebration. Ziegler and his staff quickly earned a reputation for excellent and personable care, and the little hospital on the road to Abiquiú drew patients from rural communities in northern New Mexico and southern Colorado, and even from Santa Fe and Los Alamos.

Alfred Stieglitz died in July of 1946. O'Keeffe was in New Mexico—shopping in Santa Fe—when she received the news that her husband of twenty-two years had suffered a massive stroke. Without returning to retrieve her things from Ghost Ranch, O'Keeffe hopped onto a nonstop flight from Albuquerque to New York and was with Stieglitz when he died on July 13. Following cremation of Stieglitz's body, O'Keeffe called David McAlpin and asked him to drive her with Stieglitz's ashes to Lake George—Stieglitz's beloved place—where his ashes were scattered in the ground below a tree near the lake. O'Keeffe then climbed on an airplane and flew back to her own beloved corner of the world, Ghost Ranch, where she spent the remainder of the summer soaking up the healing silence of the Piedra Lumbre.

It took O'Keeffe three years to organize and distribute Stieglitz's art collection. When it was done, in the spring of 1949, O'Keeffe packed and left New York for New Mexico for the last time. It was a bittersweet time of endings and beginnings. The years of living with her divided self were over. Stieglitz and their life together were finished. The house on the Abiquiú mesa was renovated and ready for winter-spring occupancy. And the House of the Burros on the glorious summer land of the Piedra Lumbre awaited O'Keeffe's return. At sixty-two years of age, O'Keeffe permanently moved her physical life to the place where her heart and soul had lived for decades. "This is my kind of world," she explained to a journalist visiting her at Ghost Ranch years later. "The kind of things one sees in cities . . . well, you know, it's better to look out the window at the sage."[22]

Five Bones of Serendipity

Perhaps it was a matter of fate; if I had been an ancient Roman I might have thought that the gods had decided I shall go to Ghost Ranch with my companions, there to make the discovery that would profoundly affect the course of my life.—EDWIN H. COLBERT[1]

June 14, 1947, was a gloriously bright, hot, wide, and wonderful almost-summer day in northern New Mexico. Far across the Piedra Lumbre from Ghost Ranch a jeep carrying three men slowly worked its way along the road that meandered across the basin toward the Cliffs of Shining Stone. A painted sign on the jeep's dashboard said *American Museum of Natural History*. Edwin H. Colbert, Thomas Ierardi, and George O. Whitaker watched the band of cliffs broaden and take on detail and color as they crossed the Chama River and began to look for the gate with the famous skull that marked the road to Ghost Ranch. They were vaguely familiar with O'Keeffe's paintings of the Chinle badlands and rock spires below Pedernal, but it was not the beauty of the place that had brought them thousands of miles. Theirs was a scientific, not aesthetic, pilgrimage.

Ned Colbert was curator of vertebrate paleontology at the American Museum of Natural History in New York, and in June of 1947 he came to the Piedra Lumbre carrying the field notes and locality data of a colleague who had dug for Triassic fossils in these badlands nearly two decades before. There had been numerous fossil finds in the Piedra Lumbre's red hills—the Chinle—in the decades before 1947. But Colbert and his two assistants—Dr. Thomas Ierardi, a professor at the City College of New York, and George Whitaker, a fossil preparer and field assistant at the Museum of Natural History—were only passing

Edwin H. Colbert and crew at the Johnson House in the summer of 1947.

through northern New Mexico en route to their real summer bone excavation destination—the Petrified Forest of Arizona.

Dr. Colbert had never been to Ghost Ranch, but he easily found the skull-capped gatepost and drove the jeep onto the dirt road across the badlands to the guest ranch where the three men hoped to camp for a few days. "As we pulled up in front of the headquarters building we were greeted by a slightly built, sandy-haired man who welcomed us with a smile. He was Arthur Pack. Arthur was not in the least disconcerted by our abrupt, unannounced arrival. . . . Without further ado he invited us into the headquarters for lunch."[2]

During lunch with the Pack family, Colbert and his crew were delighted to find that Arthur Pack was an educated and devoted land owner, "dedicated to the conservation of all wild things, botanical and zoological, and to the advancement of knowledge about life on the earth, past and present."[3] Paleontology, an important but little-known science among nonpractitioners in the 1940s, "fit" Pack's philosophy toward life and the preservation of all things wild and wonderful. Pack had been fascinated by the work of previous Piedra Lumbre fossil hunters from the University of California and the University of Chicago in the early 1930s and, by the end of the lunch hour, had invited Colbert and his crew to camp on the ranch as his guests for as long as their schedule permitted.

Colbert's summer work permit with the Department of the Interior dictated a travel schedule that permitted only a few nights at Ghost Ranch before the three would have to depart for the Petrified Forest. But Colbert, Ierardi, and Whitaker's casual stopover at Ghost Ranch was about to become *the* textbook example of the role of serendipity in paleontological research. Ned Colbert would later liken himself and his two companions to the *Three Princes of Serendip*, "the heroes of which were always making discoveries, by accidents and sagacity, of things they were not in quest of."[4]

The three heroes' story that was about to begin at Ghost Ranch in June of 1947 is inextricably linked in history to the twists and turns of several stories that predate their appearance on the Piedra Lumbre. And when all of these stories are said, done, and told, they reveal that they have been one story all along.

During the war, gas rationing and the general difficulties associated with travel and the funding of scientific pursuit halted fossil fieldwork at all major institutions. In the summer of 1945 Ned Colbert gladly accepted the opportunity to leave his office at the American Museum of Natural History in New York to teach for a few months at the University of California, Berkeley. While at Berkeley, Colbert, whose primary career work had been with Paleozoic mammals, studied the fossils held in the university's collection, particularly its impressive collection of Mesozoic reptiles, which included twelve phytosaur skulls from a place called Ghost Ranch. The phytosaur quarry unearthed in the red badlands of the Piedra Lumbre by Charles L. Camp was famous among paleontologists as the discoveries made here offered a remarkable look at this crocodile-like Triassic reptile.

Dr. Camp was a gregarious and energetic professor and scientist who, incidentally, had studied and worked with Colbert's father-in-law, the prominent paleontologist William Diller Mathew. During Colbert's summer at Berkeley in 1945, the older Camp encouraged the younger Colbert to study the fossils Camp had found in the Chinle strata of northern New Mexico years before. The world of science was still very much puzzling the origins of the dinosaurs, and Colbert, like Camp,

Dr. Charles Camp at the Canjilon Quarry at Ghost Ranch at 1933.

recognized there were new clues to the mysteries of the past held in the Triassic bone fragments found in New Mexico.

Colbert finished his work at Berkeley and returned to the American Museum of Natural History that fall with a renewed interest in the paleontology of the Triassic. Colbert also returned to New York with Charles Camp's personal field notes and locality data from his summers at a site called the Canjilon Quarry at a place called Ghost Ranch. Camp's field notebooks contained everything Camp and his crew had found and studied during four summers on the Piedra Lumbre, beginning in 1928. When Camp handed his data and field journals to Colbert, he was in symbol and in fact handing the quest for clues about the origin of the dinosaurs yet held in the Triassic of New Mexico to his younger but equally adept colleague.

Colbert came to Ghost Ranch well versed in the fossil record unearthed here by previous paleontologists, and his arrival at Ghost Ranch that June day in 1947 was the continuation of a scientific journey on the Piedra Lumbre begun by Charles Camp and *his* predecessors decades before.

But how and why had Dr. Camp of Berkeley come to set up a fossil-hunting expedition under the Cliffs of Shining Stone in the first place? The climate of Ghost Ranch, like all of the Colorado Plateau, is perfect for fossil preservation and excavation. The Southwest is rich in locations boasting what fossil diggers the world over fondly call the "Triassic red." Paleontologists questing for Triassic reptile and amphibian fossils frequent landscapes defined by delicately shaded red badlands and colorful painted sand lands: the Bay of Fundy in Nova Scotia; the Maleri beds of India; the Buntsandstein of southern Germany; the red beds of the Karroo Desert in South Africa; the Santa Maria Formation of southern Brazil; and the high desert of the Piedra Lumbre of northern New Mexico. These red deserts of the Chinle Formation and a dozen more like them attract Triassic fossil hunters the way a flame attracts moths.

The Chinle Formation is widely exposed in New Mexico and Arizona. It is at its geologic best along the eastern border of Arizona in an extensive series of multihued outcroppings called the Painted Desert. The Piedra Lumbre basin is a small but blue-blooded cousin and contains miles of red rock badlands and canyons that catch an educated bone hunter's eye. The Cliffs of Shining Stone that rise from the floor of the Chinle sand land offer a dramatic glimpse into the three periods of the Mesozoic era—the Triassic, Jurassic, and Cretaceous—in clearly defined, multihued geologic bands. Time is preserved here in layers of three-dimensional space. On the Piedra Lumbre, fossils aren't necessarily underfoot but can be found at eye level, embedded in a sandstone ledge or partially exposed in a wall of an arroyo. Geologic information is above ground at Ghost Ranch, and the exact age of the fossil-bearing strata easily identified. To a fossil hunter, this combination of visual information and surface accessibility is rare and wonderful.

In 1928, the field of paleontology was relatively new. There were dozens of undug sites in the American West awaiting the attention of a serious Triassic bone hunter, of which there were only a few. But one of the most prominent, Charles Camp, came to Ghost Ranch. Camp was following the scraps of the Piedra Lumbre bone story preserved in a drawer at Yale. This handful of bone fragments called *Coelophysis bauri* and held at the Yale Peabody Museum had been the source of much discussion and speculation among paleontologists since their discovery at two different sites in northern New Mexico in the winter of 1881. The bones were tiny and hollow, but even missing a skull or feet, early scientists believed they belonged to a Triassic dinosaur that

The red Triassic badlands at Ghost Ranch—fossil hunters' country since the 1800s.

would prove to be the basic patent for all the giant dinosaurs that later evolved in the Jurassic age.

From the fragments of bone found on the Piedra Lumbre and at a second site near Gallina, New Mexico, *Coelophysis bauri* was formally recognized and named by Edward Drinker Cope in Philadelphia in 1889. Nothing more was found or known about the little dinosaur's tenure on earth for the next half century. The cup full of bone fragments mailed in two parcels from the Abiquiú post office waited in near oblivion for some modern bone hunter to revisit the sites that had offered the first clues and unearth the rest of their story.

David Baldwin, the sender of the sacks of bone fragments to Cope in 1881, was a loner who preferred the company of his burro to that of humans. Baldwin had been introduced to New Mexico when he accompanied the Wheeler Mapping Expedition into the Southwest in 1875. (Cope was also on that expedition, during which he discovered a new fossil animal he named *Typothorax*.) Baldwin was a mountain man, not a scientist, and after he completed work as a field assistant with Wheeler's geological survey crew, which worked its way through Abiquiú and northern New Mexico, he returned to the remote high desert basin and set up a permanent camp.

The tiny adobe post office on the plaza of Abiquiú was Baldwin's "home" address in the late 1870s and 1880s, but Baldwin was rarely in residence at the old pueblo. Baldwin lived out of his tent pitched in the Chama Valley wilderness, even in winter, and made a small living collecting fossils for the Big Two: the aforementioned Cope of Philadelphia, and his rival, the calculating and exploitative Othniel Charles Marsh of Yale. Baldwin was never formally trained in geology or paleontology, but he had an eye for detail, was a tenacious seeker, and was a valuable fossil hunter for whoever employed him.

Because there was snow for water, Baldwin preferred to fossil hunt during the winter. In February of 1881, while collecting for the kindly, appreciative, and well-paying Cope, Baldwin established a campsite under the Cliffs of Shining Stone. From this unmarked base camp, and with all his worldly possessions carried on the back of his burro, Baldwin hunted fossils in the red hills and badlands near the Arroyo Seco on what is now Ghost Ranch. It was fortuitous for science that the Archuleta brothers had not yet begun their nefarious operation at the mouth of Yeso Canyon. Had Los Animales been his neighbors, Baldwin might not have remained long near the Arroyo Seco; or if he had, he may not have lived long enough to share with Cope what he had found.

Baldwin's most important fossil find that winter on the Arroyo Seco were tiny, "small and tender . . . almost microscopic" bones that he tied together in a sack and shipped east in a box to Cope.[5] There were no feet, no skulls, and only one tooth in the scraps.

Later that same year, Baldwin found similar bone fragments near the mountain village of Gallina, New Mexico, some twenty-five miles across the mountains from the Arroyo Seco site. Baldwin sent the fragments back to Cope, and in the next several years, Cope's study of these tiny, incomplete bone fragments resulted in Cope's creation and naming of the new genus *Coelophysis*, meaning "hollow form."

Cope's conclusions about this Triassic dinosaur were published in the *American Naturalist* in 1889, and *Coelophysis* and its birdlike bone fragments gained recognition among paleontologists. But the little dinosaur still had no head and no feet, and most everything in between was missing also. *Coelophysis*'s bones were tucked away in a drawer in Cope's Philadelphia home and later moved with his entire collection to the American Museum of Natural History in 1895.

The assorted bones of *Coelophysis* remained in a dark drawer another sixteen years, at which time they were briefly pulled out into the light of day in 1911 by a German paleontologist, Friedrich von Huene, of Tubingen University. When von Huene visited the United States, he traveled throughout New Mexico, and, although he did not stop at the Piedra Lumbre, he did camp near Baldwin's Gallina site. Intrigued by the little dinosaur, von Huene arranged to have the American Museum of Natural History's *Coelophysis* fragments sent to him for closer study back in Germany. After a lengthy paper that included thirty-seven illustrations by von Huene describing and illustrating *Coelophysis*, the bones were returned to their drawer in the American Museum of Natural History, where *Coelophysis* remained an important but mysterious ancestor of the great dinosaurs.

When Charles Camp came from Berkeley to dig for bones on the Piedra Lumbre in mid-October of 1928, he knew all about von Huene's *Coelophysis* research. He also knew that no one had dug in these Chinle badlands under the Cliffs of Shining Stone since the 1880s, and Camp set up his autumn field headquarters in the same locale near the Arroyo Seco (also known, in the 1920s, as the Canjilon Arroyo) between the two chimneys as Baldwin had forty years before. The land was owned by the Salazar family, who lived across the basin. Juan de Dios Gallegos was at the Vadito de Chicos Ranch a few miles to the southeast on the Chama River, but in 1928, no one lived at the Yeso homestead on the red and yellow sand land plateau under the cliffs.

Within three days of their arrival on the Piedra Lumbre, Camp and his fellow digger, a graduate student named Vertress Lawrence Van der Hoof, found bones from the rare Triassic quadrupedal reptile, *Typothorax*—the same armored thecodont found by Cope in the 1870s when he passed through New Mexico with the Wheeler Expedition. It was an auspicious beginning, and within the week, Camp unearthed numerous crocodile-like skulls of another Triassic thecodont reptile, phytosaur. The sandy bench above the Canjilon Arroyo, soon to be the backyard of Pack's Rancho de los Burros house, was rich with the fossils of these Triassic reptiles, and Camp christened it the Canjilon site. Before leaving New Mexico in late October, Camp and Van, as Camp called his assistant, shipped more than eight hundred pounds of Triassic bones back to Berkeley from the post office in Española.

Camp returned in 1930 with three graduate assistants and set up camp on the same Chinle sand lands under the magnificent cliffs on the northern edge of the Piedra Lumbre. They retraced Cope's and Baldwin's trails along Canjilon Creek, hoping to find bone fragments of *Coelophysis*. They did not find *Coelophysis*, but they did unearth an eight-foot-long *Typothorax* skeleton, this one graced by a skull.

The discovery of the complete *Typothorax* brought the Canjilon Quarry under the cliffs the kind of acclaim that allowed Camp to secure funding for a prolonged season of digging. In late May of 1933, Camp returned in his ten-year-old, seven-passenger Cadillac, loaded bumper to bumper with gear for an entire summer on the Piedra Lumbre badlands. On this expedition Camp brought his wife, Jessie, their son, Chuck, and five graduate assistants—four men and one woman. The 1933 Canjilon Quarry base camp was larger than the previous camps and was placed one hundred yards from the dig site in the shade of cottonwoods that grew along the arroyo. The campsite had its own hand-dug well. There were canvas tents with cots for sleeping, and an elaborate outdoor kitchen was built in the juniper trees with its own cabinet, counter, cooler box (made by tacking burlap over a tight packing case), and table, all protected from the sun and rain by a canvas canopy. Dr. Camp and his helpers built a sturdy rock-and-mud, wood-fired cook stove with a sizable tin cooking surface. A wooden sign nailed to one of the tarp's support poles proclaimed Camp's field school rules: "No Fossils—No Jam."[6]

During his visit in 1930, Camp had been told that the Salazar family had sold their interest in the Piedra Lumbre Land Grant to some Texas millionaire. But upon his arrival to the Canjilon Quarry in 1933, Camp learned that the new owner of the fossil-rich land under the cliffs was in fact a woman named Caroline B. Stanley, who was neither a millionaire nor a Texan.

Camp promptly paid a visit to the new proprietress at her rustic living quarters in the old homestead under the infamous hanging trees near Yeso Canyon. Construction was underway on what was to be a new dude ranch. Stanley and her foreman, Lloyd Miller, were overseeing an adobe-making crew, and hundreds of adobe bricks—about an acre's worth—were drying in the hot sun of early summer. Camp introduced himself and explained to Stanley why he was camped on her land. Stanley was glad to have the Berkeley diggers as neighbors, and, during that first meeting, she and Camp struck a deal: Camp needed the use of a team of Stanley's horses and plow, and Stanley needed Camp's crew's hands to move and stack dried adobes. Camp's crew would stack adobes for a morning in return for the use of Stanley's team, plow, and wagon.

Thus began a neighborly relationship between Charles Camp and Carol Stanley that lasted several summers. The summer of 1933 was one of historic beginnings and discoveries: while the first casitas and the headquarters of the new Ghost Ranch emerged adobe by adobe, less than a mile away, Camp and his crew uncovered a vast cemetery of 210-million-year-old *Typothorax* and phytosaur bones. In early June, graduate assistant Natasha Smith "struck oil"—an enormous *Typothorax* that proved to be larger than Camp's eight-foot specimen found there in 1930. This singular corner of the site eventually yielded numerous phytosaur bones tangled near and below the *Typothorax*. The Canjilon Quarry and its fossil riches kept the crew busy for the next two months, and the summer bone treasure even included several small scraps of vertebrae, skin plates, and ribs of the Piedra Lumbre's celebrated ghost dinosaur, *Coelophysis*.

Carol Stanley invited Charles and Jessie Camp, their son, and all of the crew over for many fine meals and informal gatherings that summer. Gathered about her table in the old homestead called Ghost House, Stanley told Camp the legends behind Ghost Ranch's name and reputation and informed him that their campsite was in a place the locals called Spooky Gulch. Witches and ghosts were of little concern to Camp, but all of the fossil hunters were plagued by what came to feel like a haunting of their desert campsite by rattlesnakes. Before the summer was over, they had to kill nine in camp alone, and there were numerous additional rattlesnake encounters during their hikes on the badlands.

It was a summer of extreme weather, with intensely hot mornings followed by torrential rains in the afternoons, even in early summer, when the Piedra Lumbre is usually dry. Stanley was praying for rain to help her newly planted vegetable garden, and Camp was praying for clear skies for the duration of his excavations. By late June, Camp declared in his field notebook that Stanley had won: "It rained all night."[7] The New Mexican monsoon season arrived two months early in 1933 and, with lengthy daily downpours, the main roads became impassable bogs, making the weekly journey to Española for supplies and bone shipments an all-day chore and sightseeing trips to Santa Fe unpleasant ordeals.

Camp sat under the kitchen tarp one thunderous June afternoon and watched the water level in the arroyo beside their camp rise an alarming five feet in five minutes and then undercut and carry away a huge juniper tree. The diggers' well was completely inundated and washed out on several occasions, as was their makeshift bridge over the Arroyo Seco. During these deluges, Camp and the crew nervously watched the dry cliffs become waterfalls for the raging river of floodwater that gathered in the upper mesa country. Funneled into a roaring torrent, the rock- and debris-filled water plunged off the stone ledges to the Piedra Lumbre basin down the front face of the five-hundred-foot walls.

Samuel Welles, one of Camp's 1934 assistants from Berkeley, dubbed Carol Stanley the crew's "guardian angel." Welles's field notes record Stanley's many kindnesses to the alternately drenched and muddied or scorched and thirsty diggers. Stanley appeared in her car or on horseback at their dig site at high noon with lunch baskets that held home-made goodies—cookies, cakes, and cooled avocado and grapefruit salads. On one occasion Stanley sent the Berkeley campers four gallons of cold milk—an unheard-of luxury among desert bone hunters.

Stanley had her own personal and professional struggles surrounding the end of her marriage, the recent closure of San Gabriel, and the building of her new guest ranch. But Stanley was delighted to have Camp and his Berkeley grad-student crew as neighbors and, during the summers of 1933 and 1934, brought the bone hunters over to her Ghost House for candlelight suppers and music. Stanley drove out onto the desert (often in the company of her foreman and future husband, Lloyd Miller) for late-into-the-night games of hearts beside the fossil hunters' campfire.

Stanley's modest dining table was frequented those summers by local and national notables who made the long and dusty journey to Ghost Ranch for stimulating conversation amidst some of New Mexico's most spectacular scenery. In late June of 1933, Camp and his wife were invited to a dinner at Ghost House that included Stanley's summer guests—Arthur Pack and his wife, Brownie, and their travel companion, a young man from Princeton named Frank Hibben. The next morning the three from Princeton visited the quarry along with Martin Bode and his Abiquiú neighbor, Mr. Chavez, grandson of Abiquiú's brigadier general, José Maria Chavez. On a Sunday evening in mid-July, Stanley included Dr. Camp at a dinner party with several of her oldest Santa Fe friends: Mr. and Mrs. Jesse Nusbaum, writer Anna V. Huey, and a Mr. and Mrs. Johnston. (Camp does not give the name, but says that he believed Mr. Johnston was the editor of the Santa Fe newspaper. E. Dana Johnson was editor of the *Santa Fe New Mexican*, and was most likely at Stanley's supper table that July night.) The Ghost House dinner party also included Mr. and Mrs. Ted Cabot of Harvard, several Harvard geology students, and two honeymooners, the Lowensteins.

Jesse Nusbaum was the director of the newly opened Laboratory of Anthropology in Santa Fe, and as the former superintendent of Mesa Verde National Park, knew as much if not more than anyone in the Southwest about the archaeology and geology of the Four Corners. Camp and Nusbaum had a lot in common and were fast friends, and several days later Camp took a day off from the digging and, with his family, braved the rutted and soggy roads to see Nusbaum at the Laboratory of Anthropology. Nusbaum gave Camp a tour of yet-undisplayed archaeological treasures and shared little-known reports of fossil finds in various parts of New Mexico.

That same day, the Camps went to tea at the Huey residence. Anna V. Huey was active in the Santa Fe literary and theater circle and had invited her friend, writer Mary Austin, to meet Charles Camp. After an hour at Anna Huey's, Austin insisted the Camps come and visit her new home, Casa Querida—Beloved House—on Camino del Monte Sol. The Camps went immediately to Austin's house, where they continued the friendly conversation begun at Anna Huey's. Camp told Austin the legends and stories surrounding Ghost Ranch, the Piedra Lumbre, and the fossil quarry. Austin did not have a ghost story but shared with Camp how angels had transported her to safety in the midst of a life-threatening avalanche years before on Mt. Whitney.[8]

The Berkeley summer field expedition on the Piedra Lumbre came to a close in late July when the last of the twenty-one boxes containing fifty-six hundred pounds of bones was shipped from Santa Fe to Berkeley. The worst storm ever witnessed by the local ranchers hit the Chama Valley that same week, on July 24. The road through the Chama Canyon above Abiquiú was cut side to side by a six-foot-deep ditch and was blocked by four-foot-high piles of stone and debris from muddy rockslides down the steep mesas. Dr. Camp was returning from Santa Fe and, with assistance from local men who were out attempting to repair the roads, managed to laboriously nudge his Cadillac the last ten miles to Ghost Ranch.

At a last supper at Stanley's, Camp shared his recent visit to the prehistoric watchtowers located near Gallina, New Mexico, the same ruins that Cope had visited and written about before 1900. Camp does not say who the other dinner guests were at this goodbye gathering, but within the next few years, Frank Hibben would publish an archaeological report about the same Gallina watchtowers that would bring him considerable fame and notoriety.

Camp and his family, including his young daughter, Nancy, Sam Welles and his wife, Harriet, and three graduate students returned to the ranch again in July of 1934 to excavate more of the Canjilon Quarry. Drought was beginning to parch the land of New Mexico, but there were still several torrential storms that slowed work. In spite of days that brought both intense heat and flash floods, the crew persevered and had a second season of prodigious fossil finds. In early August, the crew set out to Santa Fe with a load of bones ready for shipment. After getting their crates off at the post office, Camp and the Berkeley crew celebrated the end of another successful season by heading off for the corn dances at Santo Domingo Pueblo. But their car broke down, and they missed the dances because they had to perform a lengthy roadside mechanical repair. However, upon their late-night return to Ghost Ranch the frustrated crew "had a delightful supper at Mrs. Stanley's that more than compensated for missing the dance."[9]

That summer Camp again reciprocated Stanley's generosity toward his family and crew and hosted fireside suppers for her and Lloyd Miller. Ghost Ranch guests often joined the festivities at the Arroyo Seco camp: Mr. and Mrs. Ted Cabot came for supper at the fossil hunters' outdoor kitchen, and Mary Driscoll, a young Santa Fean who loved riding horseback in the high country of Ghost Ranch, frequently passed up her comfortable bed in one of the ranch casitas for a night in her bedroll under the stars at the fossil camp. The Driscoll family had a fine house near the old Santa Fe Plaza, and Camp's crew gladly accepted Mary Driscoll's invitation to spend a weekend in civilization at the elegant Driscoll home in the capital.

The Packs now lived at Rancho de los Burros, an easy walk across the sand hills from the Arroyo Seco campsite, and many a fine summer evening was spent at the Packs' or Stanley's, or fireside at the diggers' camp playing cards. "Mrs. Stanley came over this evening, accompanied by Arthur and Mrs. Pack, Miss Seymour, Frank Hibben, and Lloyd," Sam Welles wrote in his field journal on the summer solstice in 1934. "We played hearts and bridge and had a fine time."[10]

Later that fall, after Camp and his crew had left for California, a paleo crew from the University of Chicago came to Ghost Ranch. They knew all about Dr. Camp's bone-abundant Canjilon Quarry and wanted to do some fossil prospecting of their own on the Piedra Lumbre. Pack and Stanley knew of the widely honored fossil diggers' credo that said bone hunters do not hunt bone in another hunter's site, and they suggested the Chicago diggers do their prospecting in the Triassic badlands to the east of the ranch headquarters, on the sand lands at the base of Orphan Mesa, a good mile or more from the Canjilon site. Pack wrote, "I recalled the old superstition about a 'Vivaron' having been seen near what the natives called the Mesa Huerfano (Orphan Mesa).

Descriptions of this supposedly twenty to thirty foot long snake-like creature given by badly scared sheepherders had suggested that there really must have been something unusual to have occasioned a fright of such degree, and I half jokingly proposed that these young paleontologists might go over there to look around."[11]

Several hours later, the Chicago diggers returned to Pack's house under the cliffs and excitedly urged him to come and see what they had found. Pack returned with them on horseback to the sandy arroyo under Mesa Huerfano and saw that they had, indeed, found Vivaron. Pack recalled, "It was a hot summer day when direct rays from the sun reflected from the bare ground in shimmering waves. . . . A coiled skeleton, perhaps twenty feet long, uncovered by the vagaries of wind and storm suddenly appeared on the opposite slope."[12]

It took several days for the fossil hunters to wrap the enormous phytosaur skeleton in plaster and wood and prepare it for shipment to Chicago. And in that one week in the fall of 1934, the ancient myth of Vivaron merged with the prehistoric story of phytosaur, and the giant serpent of the Piedra Lumbre took its rightful place in the high desert's fossil record.

It would be more than a decade before the Piedra Lumbre would again be the focus of the fossil-hunting world. And then it would be so by accident. Ned Colbert had an educated hunch that the Chinle badlands at Ghost Ranch yet held fossil remains, but he did not foresee a fossil find that would eclipse Camp's already formidable discoveries.

Ned Colbert's visit to Ghost Ranch in 1947 was as much in homage to his mentor and friend Dr. Charles Camp as it was to see for himself the famous Triassic beds of the Piedra Lumbre. Colbert later wrote about his first visit.

> I was completely unprepared for that first stupendous view of the Ghost Ranch cliffs. Charles Camp and his associates had been quite matter of fact when we talked about Ghost Ranch; I suppose because our conversations were along paleontological lines it never occurred to them to mention that Ghost Ranch is a place that almost rivals Zion Canyon in the beauty of its setting.[13]

Several days after their initial luncheon with Arthur Pack and his family, Colbert, Whitaker, and Ierardi returned for a week's stay at

Ghost Ranch. After setting up their campsite in the cottonwood and juniper trees on a flat ridge above the Arroyo del Yeso, about half a mile from headquarters, the three men set out for a morning of prospecting up one of the side canyons. They found a nice phytosaur skull within the first hour and spent the next three days chiseling the bone free of the surrounding rock and then encasing it in plaster for transportation.

With the phytosaur protected and ready for shipment, the three resumed their survey of the Chinle badlands under the cliffs to the east of the ranch's headquarters. (Camp's Canjilon Quarry was to the west.) They split up, Colbert and Ierardi walking in one direction, Whitaker in another. It was June 22. Several months later Colbert wrote an account of that day for a national magazine.

> All morning we had climbed up and down and back and forth, searching along the foot of the cliffs and up the talus slopes for fragments of fossil bones. It was hot and tiring work and for the most part unrewarding. We had found only a few scraps of fossils, none of them very promising. . . . Our main consolation for several hours of tramping and climbing was a certain amount of geology and a powerful lot of colorful scenery.[14]

At high noon, Colbert and Ierardi were ready for lunch and an hour out of the searing sun. They walked back to the jeep and found Whitaker waiting for them. He pulled from his pocket a small handful of bone fragments—several pieces of vertebrae and a few sections of limb bones. Colbert recalls that moment at the jeep.

> One of the pieces, no bigger than the end of your finger, was to determine our entire season's work. . . . This piece could only be the articular end of a compressed claw belonging to one of the earliest and smallest dinosaurs. . . .
>
> As I looked at it, I felt the excitement that comes to one who glimpses treasures in the earth. For years we had hoped to find traces of these primitive little dinosaurs, and the features shown by these fossils could not be mistaken.[15]

Ned Colbert had spent hours at the Museum of Natural History studying the *Coelophysis* fragments found by David Baldwin nearly three-quarters of a century before somewhere in these same sand lands. Colbert knew their color, their consistency, their size and weight. Colbert knew *immediately*: the fossils in Whitaker's palm belonged to *Coelophysis*, the shadowy, partially known Triassic dinosaur that held in its yet-untold singular story important clues about the evolution of the Great Age of Dinosaurs.

The heat of high noon and all thoughts of lunch were temporarily forgotten; Colbert wanted to visit the site immediately. It was a short but arduous hike across the sand hills back to the talus slope where Whitaker had found the bone fragments. The three men climbed about the hillside and immediately found more pieces of the small, hollow fossils in moderate but confirming abundance. When they finally quit for lunch, Colbert knew: the June solstice of 1947 had ushered in not only summer, but also a season of unimaginable scientific opportunity.

The high noon lunch and accompanying siesta at the campsite were much abbreviated that day. The bone hunters quickly returned to the site, which was on the side of a steeply sloping sand hill, and spent the remainder of the afternoon clearing away the loose sand, dirt, and rock. "At first, the bones were not very apparent, but as we brushed away the loose, weathered dirt, the fossils began to appear. The more we brushed, the more of them we saw. It was evident that this was more than a sporadic occurrence of isolated fossil bones."[16]

Colbert, Ierardi, and Whitaker spent the next two days digging and probing the fossil deposit in the steeply sloped hillside. They continued to uncover an extensive deposit of skeletons—not just fragments and odd pieces of bone, but complete backbones and legs, a jaw and skull, and finally, completely articulated skeletons. Not just several skeletons, but dozens, layers upon layers of them. It became clear to Colbert and to his colleagues working in the red sand beneath the towering stone cliffs that this was a rare and wondrous site with an unusual, staggering, perhaps record-setting concentration of dinosaur bones. But what to do?

From his office in the American Museum of Natural History, Colbert had pursued miles of red tape across dozens of bureaucratic desks to obtain a permit from the Department of the Interior that granted Colbert a summer of digging at the Petrified Forest in Arizona. It was not an opportunity easily passed up, and there could be professional repercussions for Colbert and the Museum of Natural History.

Colbert called his friend and colleague, George Gaylord Simpson, for advice and counsel. Simpson was working across the mountains on a fossil site near Lindrith, New Mexico—the same region where Baldwin had found *Coelophysis* scraps in the 1870s. Simpson was Colbert's immediate superior at the Museum of Natural History and was widely regarded as one of the greatest paleontologists working anywhere in the world. Simpson drove over to Ghost Ranch a few days later and followed Colbert to the site under the gypsum-capped mesa east of ranch headquarters. After surveying the ledge and the dozens of exposed skeletons, Simpson turned to Colbert and in one simple sentence confirmed Colbert's opinion that he should remain the summer at Ghost Ranch. The tiny bones emerging in fantastic profusion from the hillside before them were, in Simpson's words, "the greatest find ever made in the Triassic of North America."[17]

Simpson and Colbert sat down on the ground in the shade of a lone juniper and devised an agenda for the development of the Ghost Ranch site. With the Packs' permission, Colbert, Ierardi, and Whitaker would stay the entire summer at Ghost Ranch. Colbert would go to Española and telegraph the museum in New York to send its senior preparator, Carl Sorensen, to assist with the excavation and preparation of the fossils for shipment. Before they even left the site, Simpson and Colbert identified the additional funding that might be required and agreed that this excavation would require at least two summers of fieldwork. They then agreed that the site should be closed to further excavation until the material pulled out could be studied.

Arthur and Phoebe were delighted and privileged to have Colbert and his crew remain the summer at Ghost Ranch. Carl Sorenson arrived in record time, and the summer of work at the quarry became the first priority for both the Museum of Natural History and for Ghost Ranch. Although Colbert's field camp was initially set up within sight of the much-appreciated swimming pool, Arthur and Phoebe both knew the rigors of working in the wilderness and offered the fossil hunters the spacious and comfortable house built by the Johnson brothers. Colbert and the crew gleefully moved into the two-story adobe near ranch headquarters. "No longer would there be the alternating cycles of dust and mud inherent in tent life," Colbert wrote, "no longer would I face the ordeal every night of working up field notes under the light of a hot lantern, with moths and other insects banging into my face and eyes and down my neck. . . . Camping out is great for a summer vacation of a week or two, but as a steady thing, week in and week out, month after month, it gets to be pretty tiresome."[18]

Colbert's Piedra Lumbre "camp" was much envied by other fossil hunters—especially by Simpson and his crew across the mountains in a remote camp near Lindrith. Not only was Colbert's field camp bolstered by the high energy that surrounds a big fossil find, but their bone quarry was located within walking distance of a first-class guest ranch, not to mention a swimming pool. The pleasant accommodations built by the Johnson brothers, complete with a modern kitchen, two full bathrooms, several large bedrooms, and a lounging and reading area with shelves of books, also came with evening dining and entertainment offered by the Packs. "For us," Colbert remembered, "it was fossil collecting *deluxe*."[19]

Everyone living at Ghost Ranch was drawn into the excitement surrounding the discovery, although why such tiny, visually unremarkable bone fragments could cause such a sensation among scientists was a mystery to most. Dorthy Burnham was working on the Packs' garden when the crew drove up in the jeep to the ranch headquarters with their huge discovery—a handful of what looked to her to be ordinary red rocks. "George [Whitaker] kept saying 'I found it! I found it!' Colbert knew immediately the importance of what George had found . . . long before the digging began . . . Colbert *knew*. A few days later, the Packs held a big celebration party for everyone at the ranch. It was a very exciting time."

The discovery of the *Coelophysis* quarry was not immediately revealed to the public, or even to the scientific community. The American Museum of Natural History did not announce the discovery for three weeks, until the middle of July. At that time, the Ghost Ranch bone quarry made front-page headlines in papers across the country. On July 14, 1947, the *New York Times* banner headline announced, "Museum finds dinosaur 200 million years old." The front page–center story mistakenly placed the quarry at Simpson's comparatively unspectacular site near Lindrith, but it did accurately report the excitement in the paleontological world surrounding the discovery of not just one complete *Coelophysis* skeleton but *dozens*. Few fossil sites yield even one complete dinosaur skeleton; the quarry at Ghost Ranch boasted, as Colbert said again and again, "an embarrassment of riches."[20]

Betty Chapman was a young journalist living that summer in Santa Fe, where she was working as "stringer for a stringer." Always on the lookout for a good story, Betty often ended her workday chatting up the locals in La Fonda bar on the old plaza. One afternoon in late June of 1947, Betty watched a particularly attractive young cowboy enter the lobby of La Fonda, where he checked his saddle and his chaps at the front desk before coming into the bar for a drink. Betty started up a conversation with the tanned and friendly Alfred Colbert and learned that he was on his way to a place called Ghost Ranch to visit his Uncle Ned. It all seemed like pretty regular stuff, except that Alfred was noticeably reluctant to say much about Uncle Ned's activities at Ghost Ranch. Alfred departed the bar, promising to call Betty one day soon.

Alfred Colbert did call Betty and, several weeks later, invited her to go to Ghost Ranch and visit Uncle Ned with him. By now, Alfred knew Betty was an aspiring journalist, and he also knew that Uncle Ned Colbert's fossil site was about to make national headlines. At Ghost Ranch, Betty was introduced to Colbert and the crew and was allowed to ask questions and take notes about the *Coelophysis* discovery. Betty returned to Santa Fe with first-hand facts about one of the biggest scientific stories of the century in her notebook, but she dutifully handed her findings over to her boss. With Betty's notes and additional information from the Museum of Natural History, a salaried staff writer wrote the lengthy and well-illustrated article that was featured the very next month in the August 11 issue of *Life* magazine.

Although Betty was passed over for a story she very much wanted to author, she did get to know more about Colbert and to spend many more days at Ghost Ranch, as she married Alfred H. Colbert and became Ned's niece-in-law in 1948.

Numerous other periodicals and newspapers carried the story by midsummer, and the hillside in the Triassic badlands under the Cliffs of Shining Stone became the unlikely destination for dozens of journalists, photographers, and scientists from all over the globe. Arthur Pack was amused by the tribulations of the urban press corps as they struggled to work in the desert outback. Seasoned journalists were sent by metropolitan newspapers to get the *Coelophysis* story, but were shocked and befuddled to find the story was in the middle of nowhere, and that all accommodations were in adobe casitas at a ranch forty-five miles from a telephone. The photographer dispatched to the quarry by *Life* magazine was particularly out of his element at Ghost Ranch. Pack wrote:

> *Life* magazine flew in their nearest cameraman, who happened to be in Hollywood specializing on movie actresses. . . . The young and shapely legs he was used to photographing were one thing, but small leg bones a million years old were something else again, especially when they lay embedded in red clay and the hillside was always sliding and filling the photographer's handsome sport shoes."[21]

Another visiting writer, Santa Fean W. Thetford LeViness, thoroughly enjoyed his time at the ranch and had a gourmet luncheon on the Packs' supper porch while interviewing Colbert. LeViness knew the camp life endured by most fossil hunters and described for his *New Mexico Magazine* readers the unusually luxurious field headquarters given the expedition at Ghost Ranch. In fact, LeViness found the whole situation at Ghost Ranch exceptional, especially since the land of the quarry was owned by a prominent naturalist who placed his considerable resources at their service. LeViness wrote, "Fate, which had preserved these fossils for countless ages, had kindness left over for the fossil hunters."[22]

In spite of her intense desire for privacy and dislike for mobs of people in general, and inquisitive journalists in particular, O'Keeffe became a regular visitor to the dinosaur quarry. O'Keeffe's first visit to the *Coelophysis* site was in the company of a jeepful of nuns who were teaching school in the village of Abiquiú. On subsequent summer mornings before the heat became prohibitive, O'Keeffe drove her car as far up the rugged road toward the site as she could and then walked cross-country to the steep slope containing the quarry. In Ned Colbert O'Keeffe found an articulate, committed scientist and a humble genius. O'Keeffe watched the fossil excavation work for hours at a time and quizzed the always-friendly Colbert about what they were doing and why. Colbert and O'Keeffe became good friends that summer, and the fossil crew was invited to Rancho de los Burros for informal dinners with O'Keeffe. Colbert fondly remembered those summer days.

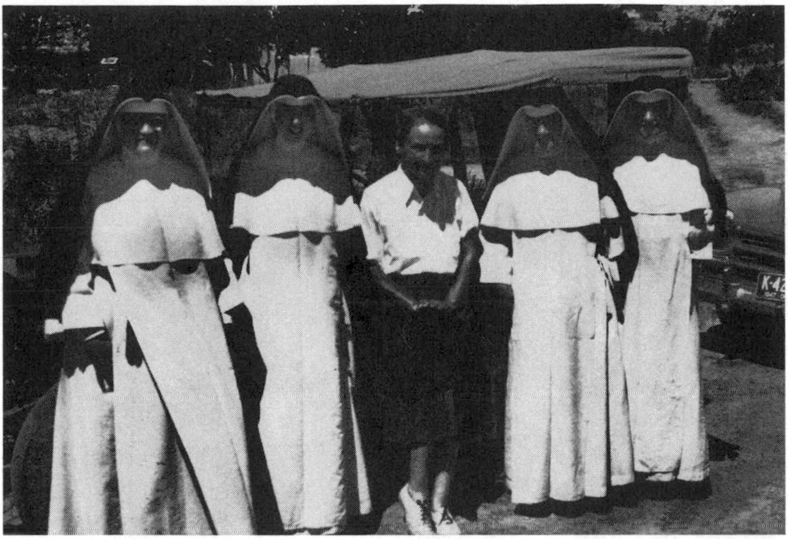

Georgia O'Keeffe and nuns from Abiquiú visiting Edwin Colbert and the fossil quarry in the summer of 1947.

> O'Keeffe would come over from her house to visit the quarry, and we would on occasion visit her at her home. She and I became good friends, I suppose in part because we were both fascinated by bones. Although the bones she liked were recent and the ones I liked were very old, still they were bones—and that gave us common interests. Also, she had me describe to her what life was like millions of years ago, when Ghost Ranch was a tropical environment.[23]

Pack placed his ranch foreman, Herman Hall, all of the ranch's heavy equipment, and a second jeep that Arthur had bought for his own use after the war, at Colbert's disposal. Hall spent two days cutting a road across the desert to the quarry site, and, although extremely rough and only passable by a jeep and the bulldozer itself, the road allowed the diggers to come and go with large amounts of equipment with relative ease.

Roger and Kitty White continued to live and work at Los Alamos after the war and continued to visit the Packs and Ghost Ranch on weekends. When the quarry was discovered, Roger made additional

Ghost Ranch foreman Herman Hall (on the bulldozer) removing blocks of fossils from the *Coelophysis* quarry that summer.

trips to the ranch and spent many hours out under the hot sun watching the fossil hunters. By the middle of the summer, White's connections at Los Alamos were beneficial to Colbert's cause on at least one occasion. White wrote,

> Every time we came to the ranch, we'd head right up there to see what was going on [at the quarry]. One time they were trying to chisel out a big chunk of rock with bones in it. And they didn't have what they needed—a long chisel. And Ned said, 'God, I wish we had one of those . . . *things*! And you can't buy one of those *things*!' I said, 'Well, I can probably get you one.' So I went back to the lab where, at that time, you could go any place and do anything in the laboratory. I got hold of some scrap tool steel, and made a couple of these chisels and brought them back to Colbert. He was just elated!

Early on in the first summer of work, sections of the quarry were covered by a tarp and a wood platform that protected the bones as well as the diggers from exposure to the intense sun and the equally intense rains. Once the fossil layer was exposed, Colbert determined that

Plastering *Coelophysis* bones at the quarry in 1947.

they could not remove the delicate skeletons bone by bone but would have to cut them out in large blocks. The exposed *Coelophysis* bones were shellacked and hardened, covered with Japanese rice paper, and then encased in plaster buttressed with wood splints. The position of each and every bone in each of the blocks was carefully charted. Although this was a proven method for safely removing and transporting dinosaur bones, the concentration of fossils found in the sands of the quarry at Ghost Ranch posed problems for even the best of methods. Colbert wrote about one such problem in his first published description of the quarry.

> The problem was to cut channels through the bone layer and thus separate it into blocks of a size convenient to handle. And here we were faced with a decision reminiscent of Solomon's. Wherever we placed our line, we would cut right though the creatures to get them. . . .
>
> As we cut down into the deposit, we found there were not merely skeletons on the top but more of them underneath, layer after layer. We would start a channel at a likely looking place, only to find a valuable skull or pelvis underneath.[24]

Every test hole, every half foot that cut deeper down into the ledge, produced more bones: piles of bones, layers of bones, bones jumbled into one another, bones perfectly laid down in the death pose of the little dinosaur who died here 220 million years ago. Dozens of bones turned into hundreds of bones; hundreds became an estimated thousand. And the thousand eventually excavated prompted Colbert's educated estimate that some ten thousand more lay buried in the hillside.

By the end of the summer of 1947, seven massive, plaster-encased blocks of bones had been lifted from the sands of Ghost Ranch. The story of the *Coelophysis* dinosaur could now be investigated through what would become at least one hundred complete, articulated skeletons. Within the seven blocks excavated in 1947 (the largest, block V, measured eight by four by three feet in size and weighed more than two tons *before* the plaster jacket was added) were *Coelophysis* specimens of all ages and sizes. The seven blocks from 1947, and an additional six removed from the quarry in 1948, were shipped by truck to the American Museum of Natural History, the Yale Peabody Museum, the Museum of Comparative Zoology at Harvard, the Connecticut State Park Museum, the Cleveland Museum, and the University of Texas.

Coelophysis was among the earliest dinosaurs and carried the "basic patent" for the coming giant dinosaurs of the Jurassic age. Understanding *Coelophysis*'s evolution opened the doors to new understandings of the great dinosaurs whose ancestry can be directly traced to Triassic dinosaurs like *Coelophysis*.

The *Coelophysis* story reconstructed from the bones discovered at Ghost Ranch unfolded 225 million years ago. Among paleontologists, theirs is a story that can be retold with a detail almost unheard of in the annals of dinosaurs. The Ghost Ranch quarry offered a population sample of an entire herd—newly hatched infants, juveniles, young adults, full-grown adults, elderly adults—all piled together where they all died and were immediately buried in one sudden, local catastrophe.

Coelophysis was slightly built and quick moving and was a very active, aggressive, and successful predator. It stood four to six feet tall and walked and ran in a semierect position on hind legs that were very strong and very fast. *Coelophysis*'s agility and speed on land gave it the necessary edge to survive the dominant carnivores of its time, especially the phytosaur. Itself a carnivore with sharp teeth in its jaws,

Coelophysis had long claws on its hands and feet and had a long, slender tail.

The instantaneous mass burial of the Ghost Ranch *Coelophysis* herd preserved their skeletons. Perfectly and beautifully articulated, the Ghost Ranch *Coelophysis* herd retained their exact death poses for 220 million years in the red sand hillside at the foot of a great cliff on the northern edge of the Piedra Lumbre basin. Thus, the Ghost Ranch dinosaur mausoleum, as Colbert called it, was the ultimate buried treasure that awaited fate, luck, and destiny to bring scientists to stumble upon its final resting place.

Although their story belongs to Ghost Ranch, when the little dinosaurs actually walked and ran across this landscape it was not this place at all. Two hundred and twenty million years ago, *this* place—the high desert plateau of Ghost Ranch and all of northern New Mexico that sits thirty-five degrees north of the equator—occupied *another* place—a moist, humid summer land that lay just ten degrees north of the equator. The world of the little dinosaurs was a tropical land of streams, rivers, lakes, and ponds with swampy, rolling terrain in between. The rivers and lakes were bordered by great coniferous forests with thick undergrowths of ferns. There were hills and flatlands, but the geographic and climatic characteristics of the high desert and mountain country of the Colorado Plateau did not yet exist and were yet eons away in the future. And on a continent yet unformed.

The story of *Coelophysis* at Ghost Ranch is truly a global story that Colbert would spend the rest of his career researching and connecting. Although unearthed on the Piedra Lumbre, *Coelophysis*'s narrative is "much more than a local tale of life and death some 200 million years ago," Colbert wrote. "The contemplation of these earliest dinosaurs brings us to a consideration of why they were so close to dinosaurs that lived on the other side of the world. . . . The key to the puzzle is our new-found knowledge of plate tectonics."[25]

Coelophysis's closest relative is the dinosaur *Syntarsus*, which was found in present-day Zimbabwe. Until the theory of an ancient supercontinent, Pangaea, and its breakup into the continents known today (which began in the transition from the Triassic to the Jurassic time and was complete by the Cretaceous period) began to evolve in the scientific community, Colbert could not understand how *Syntarsus* could be so closely related to the older, and half a world away, *Coelophysis*. After years of excavating and studying the fossil evidence for continental drift and plate tectonics that took him to Antarctica, Colbert came to the conclusion that the two dinosaurs had once walked the same continent. Theirs was a closely connected story that unfolded in a *shared* place, and their "migration" to separate continents on nearly opposite sides of the planet was a chapter of their story that was written *after* the dinosaurs had vanished from the face of the earth.

The *Coelophysis* quarry preserved in the red Triassic badlands of Ghost Ranch actually tells an ancient story that belongs to another place: a story of a herd of dinosaurs that lived and died in a place that once existed thousands of miles from this canyon cemetery. Colbert wrote,

> The natural tombs of these various fossils were transported, like the remains of Viking warriors in their funeral ships, to resting places far removed from the places where they had lived.
>
> The story of Coelophysis is more than a local story, restricted to Ghost Ranch; it pertains to the vast stretches of ancient continents.[26]

In the next half-century, Edwin H. Colbert became among the most influential and respected paleontologists in the world. The serendipitous discovery of the *Coelophysis* quarry at Ghost Ranch precipitated Colbert's lifelong study of Triassic dinosaurs all over the earth. The Ghost Ranch discovery also brought the friendly and humble Uncle Ned Colbert a certain amount of fame in the scientific community. Upon meeting Charles Camp again, in 1949, by which time Colbert's luck and destiny at Ghost Ranch were well known among many appreciative but also envious colleagues, Camp had just one question for Colbert: what made him fossil hunt near the mouth of Yeso Canyon in the first place? Fossil hunters rarely went up canyons, and never searched hillsides, and Baldwin's field notes did not ever mention the talus slopes east of the ranch.

Colbert had no good answer. It was a just a hunch, he told Camp, and a bit of luck.

Ned Colbert remained with the American Museum of Natural History for forty years and then went to the Museum of Northern Arizona for another twenty. He spent the polar summer of 1969 in Antarctica excavating the Triassic bones that greatly contributed to the modern theory of continental drift. Over the years, Uncle Ned became known as "Mr. Dinosaur" because of his prolific discoveries and for his many books on dinosaurs that made his work, and the work of all paleontologists, accessible to a wide audience.

In 1990, the definitive reference for modern paleontology, *The Dinosauria*, was published. The mammoth publication's twenty-nine chapters offer comprehensive coverage of every major discovery and theory in the world of paleontology. *The Dinosauria* was dedicated to two scientists: Richard Owen, the English anatomist "who started it all" when he formally recognized and named the dinosaurs in 1841, and Edwin H. Colbert, the serendipitous hero of Ghost Ranch "who lit so many candles."

Six A Theology of Place

The desert will lead you to your heart where I will speak.—HOSEA 2:14

At the close of what would always be remembered as the summer of the grand fossil find, after Colbert and his crew had packed and shipped the last block of *Coelophysis* bones, Arthur and Phoebe packed up young Charlie and little Pip and headed for Arizona. The expansion of the Ghost Ranch Lodge, along with the children's need for closer schooling, had prompted the Packs' decision to hand over management of Ghost Ranch so that they could spend the school year at their lodge on the outskirts of Tucson.

Arthur was fifty-four years old and tired of the demands that the daily management of a twenty-plus-thousand-acre ranch placed on his mind and body. Arthur and Phoebe wanted to return each summer to their little adobe house at the foot of the mesa, but they did not want to oversee the ranch the rest of the year. So the Packs leased Ghost Ranch to a friend, Earl Vance, who had already managed Bishop's Lodge—the same guest ranch that Carol Stanley's husband Roy Pfaffle had managed with a young Jack Lambert when it first opened after World War I.

Margaret McKinley and her three children accompanied the Packs to Tucson, where the boys enrolled at the university. Ranch foreman Herman Hall, his wife Jimmie, and their teenage daughter, Yvonne, agreed to remain. Vance promoted Ghost Ranch in regional and national magazine articles and hired Santa Fe–based photographer Laura Gilpin to photograph the ranch's scenery, facilities, and semiannual cattle roundups. Twenty years after his first visit, Oliver La Farge was still visiting the cowboys at Ghost Ranch, and La Farge featured the ranch in a lengthy article about New Mexico in *Holiday* magazine in

A Plymouth advertisement photographed at Ghost Ranch by Laura Gilpin in 1951. Jody McDonald, left; Earl Vance, right.

1952. The *Holiday* story included a photograph of one of Ghost Ranch's more recognizable dudes, actor Cary Grant, who came with his wife, Betsy Drake. Grant knew Vance from visits to Bishop's Lodge and came to Ghost Ranch over three summers, staying for two to three weeks at a time in Center House.

Cary Grant was not the first Big Movie Star to grace the Ghost Ranch dining room after World War II. John Wayne came in the early 1950s to scout for a film location for a new western. Yvonne Hall was serving coffee to lunch guests when the tall, broad-shouldered Wayne, "who looked and talked just like he did in the movies," sauntered into the ranch dining room and sat down. Yvonne was speechless, but managed to ask Wayne if he wanted some coffee. He did, and Yvonne claimed Wayne's was the hardest cup she ever poured, but she did it without spilling a drop.

Much to Yvonne's and all of the ranch staff's disappointment, after a long talk with Wayne and his producer, Arthur Pack decided against Ghost Ranch being the location for their next movie because he feared

Cary Grant and his wife, Betsy Drake, in the Ghost Ranch dining hall, also in 1951.

the production would cause too much devastation to the ranch's landscape.

When Grant came to Ghost Ranch in the summer of 1951, he and his second wife, Drake, had just completed their film *Room for One More*. Fittingly, the Grants came to Ghost Ranch with Grant's former stepson, Lance Reventlow. Lance was the only son of Grant's first wife, Barbara Hutton, the Woolworth heiress. Born in Denmark—Lance's father was a Danish nobleman—the towheaded sixteen-year-old brought to Ghost Ranch his French governess, Chrissie, his registered horse, and plenty of unbridled, high-spirited energy and blue-blooded orneriness.

Although the Grant party arrived in a fancy, fit-for-a-film-star Oldsmobile convertible with a leather interior that seemed doomed to ruin under the scalding sun, Grant turned out to be an extremely affable, low-maintenance, easygoing guest. The ranch staff felt comfortable around the handsome movie star, who seemed happy to shed the tailored suits and bright lights of Hollywood for jeans, plaid shirts, and the quiet night life under the sparkling stars found each evening on the Piedra Lumbre.

Grant, Drake, and young Lance swam in the pool kept refreshingly cold by the Yeso stream and sunbathed on the deck with the panoramic view of Pedernal. The McKinley brothers, Wayne and Henry, returned to the ranch each summer and in 1951 accompanied Reventlow and his horse on long rides under the cliffs and into the high country above Yeso Canyon.

Grant and Drake could stay only two to three weeks at a time, but Vance agreed to let young Lance and his governess remain at Ghost Ranch for several months during three consecutive summers. Lance was considered a handful by the staff, especially the wranglers like the McKinley brothers who, along with Yvonne Hall, were asked to keep him out of trouble.

During one summer stay, Grant engaged his stepson in the making of a home movie at Ghost Ranch. The film took about a week to make and was produced, directed, and shot by Grant. It starred Betsy Drake, the McKinley brothers, and Reventlow in some sort of farcical mystery. Henry McKinley played the "good guy," and brother Wayne the "bad guy." No one remembers many details about the narrative except that someone had stolen something that everyone was looking for—

Lance Reventlow, son of Barbara Hutton, came to Ghost Ranch with his former stepfather, Cary Grant, in 1951. Photograph by Laura Gilpin.

perhaps the plot was loosely based on the Archuleta brothers' lost olla of gold? Grant carried the completed film back to California, where it never enjoyed a wide audience and was eventually forgotten somewhere in the Hollywood Hills.

The ranch staff followed Grant's and Drake's film career and marriage in the news over the next decade (they divorced in 1962) and also kept up with the life of Lance Reventlow. Reventlow became a professional race car driver and was briefly married to actress Jill St. John. Reventlow found what the ranch staff thought a worthy outlet for his unbridled energy, and for his mother's money, in Formula 1 racing cars. In 1960, the twenty-four-year-old Reventlow bankrolled the ambitious but flawed Scarab sports car that he himself drove in its debut race in Monaco. Reventlow's life was fast and furious and tragically ended at thirty-six years of age, when the single-engine Cessna that he was a passenger in crashed into the Rocky Mountains in Colorado in July of 1972.

Handing the management of Ghost Ranch over to Earl Vance worked well for the Packs. But as their family grew into adulthood—Arthur's daughters, Peggy and Norrie, were now married, Vernon was a schoolteacher, and the McKinley children were through college and beginning careers and families of their own—Arthur realized that he had to actively develop a plan to ensure protection of the ranch's land.

Pack considered giving Ghost Ranch to all of his children—five of his own from both marriages and the McKinley three he had adopted—but none of the children could realistically afford to come and live at the ranch as managers. In the mid-1940s, Pack had discussed with the McKinley boys the possibility of their operating the ranch as a cattle and horse operation. But by the early 1950s, Pack realized that the cost of maintaining Ghost Ranch in even a good year—which meant the casitas full from late spring until well into the fall, and with good rainfall providing ample grass on the rangeland—was always going to be prohibitive to all but the wealthiest private owner. And Ghost Ranch would never have the rangeland necessary to be a viable cattle or horse ranch. Ghost Ranch was an expensive enterprise, and left as an undeveloped wilderness, as was Pack's wish, was ultimately unprofitable.

In spite of its unprofitability, Ghost Ranch was coveted by several investors, who made inquiries through local bankers and realtors. Most of these were wealthy Texans looking for summer vacation ranches in the high country of northern New Mexico. The Packs could have made a small fortune by selling Ghost Ranch—at least a quarter of a million in the early 1950s—but relinquishing "the most beautiful and spectacular piece of privately owned real estate in the Southwest" for any sum of money represented in the Packs' minds a breach of trust between themselves and the land.[1]

After twenty years as owners/stewards of Ghost Ranch, the Packs had come to believe that the extraordinary place of badlands, spires, buttes, llanos, river bosque, and canyon country below the Cliffs of Shining Stone was something to be simultaneously protected and shared. People who lived for any length of time at Ghost Ranch knew that they were at a special place, a magic place. For most of its historic life, the ranch had been the private paradise of a handful of wealthy and/or influential people and their select circle of friends. The Packs believed it was time to open the ranch gate to people of all economic and social backgrounds. The challenge was to find a way to share the ranch with a broader constituency without overwhelming its wondrous, fragile landscape and ruining the very qualities that were the heart and soul of its character.

The Packs began to actively search for an individual or organization that shared their vision of Ghost Ranch as a great place worthy of great care. Pack had informal conversations about Ghost Ranch with the national YMCA, the Boy Scouts of America, the Archdiocese of Santa Fe, and the United Brethren Church. The Y had a large camp in Colorado, and the Boy Scouts were developing their 130,000-acre Philmont Scout Ranch near Cimarron, New Mexico. And for the Roman Catholics and the United Brethren, the property out under the great shining cliffs fifteen miles above Abiquiú appeared to offer too few amenities in the midst of too much wildness to be economically feasible.

It was the Presbyterians who responded with the enthusiasm, creative spirit, and sense of mission that the Packs were looking to find in the ranch's next *patrón*. Tucson pastor and friend, Dave Sholin, who vacationed at Ghost Ranch with his family in the early 1950s, suggested the Packs offer Ghost Ranch to the national Presbyterian Church. Pack liked the idea; he had been raised a Presbyterian, and before he had left Princeton Pack had been active in the extremely intellectual and forward-looking Presbyterian community that included his longtime friend David McAlpin. So in early 1955, Pack sat down at his desk in Tucson and wrote in longhand a letter to Dr. Paul Calvin Payne, the general secretary of the Presbyterian Board of Christian Education in Philadelphia. Pack's letter outlined his offer of the twenty-one-thousand-acre Ghost Ranch to the Presbyterian Church. Payne was interested, but skeptical. "We occasionally had received offers of property," he remembered, "usually on terms more advantageous to the donor than to the Board . . . but [I] felt I must send George Renneisen, our Treasurer, and Jim Gailey, head of our field service, to look over the property. They returned full of enthusiasm."[2]

The letter from Arthur Pack circulated the Witherspoon Building—national headquarters of the Presbyterian Church—with a recent issue of *National Geographic* that showcased Ghost Ranch's phenomenal natural beauty. Even Presbyterians who had never been west of the Mississippi recognized something very special about this place in New Mexico.

The postwar era for the Presbyterians was one of rising membership and a swelling treasury. The phenomenal success of the Board of Christian Education's "Faith and Life Curriculum" had produced a wealth unparalleled in the Presbyterian denomination. Developed under Dr. Paul Calvin Payne, this curriculum was used by 90 percent of all Presbyterian churches—it was also used by eleven hundred non-Presbyterian churches nationwide—and by 1955, the annual budget for the Board of Christian Education had increased from $740,000 to $4 million, and its staff had jumped from a mere eighteen individuals to over one hundred executives across the United States.

The church was not looking for a large piece of property in the middle of the high desert, but the Presbyterians were in a position financially and socially that enabled them to ponder the hows and whys of assuming the care of such a place as Ghost Ranch. Pack wanted it to be used as some kind of educational facility. The Presbyterians agreed, but there were virtually no models within their own organization—the church had dozens of successful colleges, and there were regional synod camps and small educational facilities affiliated with congregations around the country. But none of these came close to Ghost Ranch in raw space and natural potential. Payne was the first to admit that Ghost Ranch presented a lot of nothingness to most board members back in Philadelphia. The Presbyterians had mission schools and hospitals on the desert. But no one on the board had any expertise with the creation of a national study center in a remote wilderness—Ghost Ranch was still functioning without telephone service—and Payne made it his highest priority to ask for help.

Before Payne and the board actually accepted what they suspected was a gift of immeasurable value, a committee of men and women from the national headquarters, and from churches in the Southwest, was assembled to meet at Ghost Ranch and look the place over. A young pastor from Hobbs, New Mexico, James Wallace Hall, was one of two New Mexicans asked to serve on the advisory committee. Hall had great respect from the get-go for Payne and the Board of Christian Education. "I have great affection for that board," Hall said decades later. "They were good and smart. . . . Being creative and responsible people, they really asked what they would do with 20,000 plus acres out in New Mexico? It was a real honest to God question for them. They weren't going to take [Ghost Ranch] if there wasn't any use for it."

The first discussions were held in the ranch dining room, and Arthur Pack was always involved. Jim Hall and other visitors asked for personal tours of the ranch's acreage, and Herman Hall drove them in the old jeep to de Dios's abandoned River Ranch (Pack purchased it in 1940), out to the east pasture and the Burnham homestead (Pack bought the underground house and outbuildings in 1940), across the sand lands under the cliffs to the *Coelophysis* quarry, and west across Antelope Flats to the edge of the Chama Canyon. The question was always in their minds: what could Ghost Ranch become that would not ruin the place?

It was a newcomer to the Southwest, Paul Calvin Payne, who had the strongest conviction that Ghost Ranch could evolve into a first-class study center. After numerous visits and consultations with his advisory board, Payne convinced the Board of Christian Education in Philadelphia that at the spectacular place called Ghost Ranch they could create something of lasting value to the church and to the society it was part of.

The official announcement that the dude ranch was to become a Presbyterian educational facility was made in local and national newspapers on November 18, 1955. The change in Ghost Ranch's ownership caused only minor commentary and small ripples of response in the greater world. But on the ranch itself, Pack's gift of el Rancho de los Brujos to the Presbyterians ignited a spirited reaction from its resident

Dale Brubaker (in the driver's seat), George Carson (standing), and other Presbyterians looking over Ghost Ranch in 1956.

artist, Georgia O'Keeffe. O'Keeffe's home and seven-plus acres were not affected by the transfer of ownership, and Payne and the board had been coached by the Packs about O'Keeffe's ferociously guarded privacy. What the board did not know, however, was that O'Keeffe had always hoped that Pack would sell her Ghost Ranch—or at least a goodly chunk of the desert sand lands—so that she could further insulate herself and Rancho de los Burros from the ordinary folks coming and going over at headquarters.

Pack apparently never mentioned it to his friends and did not include it in his published memoir of Ghost Ranch, but O'Keeffe later claimed that she had at one time secured the right of first refusal from Pack.[3] It is doubtful that O'Keeffe wanted to own and maintain Ghost Ranch, but she certainly wanted to purchase more of the badlands she considered her backyard.

Knowing her as he did by 1955, Pack might have done himself, and the Board of Christian Education, a favor and forewarned O'Keeffe in private about his plans for the ranch. But he did not, and O'Keeffe learned of his plans after the advisory committee had arrived at Ghost Ranch. To say that O'Keeffe was upset about Pack's gift to the Presbyterians would be a colossal understatement. O'Keeffe was *furious*.

Dave Sholin was among those sitting in the Packs' living room when O'Keeffe drove up and brought her car to a stop in a cloud of dust at the foot of the hill below headquarters. From the house, Sholin and his colleagues watched the famous painter, then in her midsixties, stride quickly up the front steps and, without bothering to knock, burst into the Packs' home, where she angrily confronted Arthur and Phoebe. "O'Keeffe was downright mean," Dave Sholin remembered. "She said, 'Arthur, what's this I hear about your giving the ranch away?! If you were going to do that, why didn't you give it to me?!'"

Pack attempted to introduce O'Keeffe to the people sitting like mortified statues about his living room, but O'Keeffe ignored them. Ghost Ranch was her home, and the Packs had just gone and given it away to strangers—ordinary, common people who wanted to bring hundreds more ordinary, common people to the Piedra Lumbre. O'Keeffe's emotional diatribe lasted for several minutes. Pack stood his ground but did not interrupt her. It was not the first time in their twenty-year relationship that O'Keeffe had verbally assaulted Pack. "O'Keeffe was very, *very* angry with Arthur," Sholin remembered. "She really *believed* he should have given her the ranch."

After proclaiming her dislike for Presbyterians (exclusive of her good friend Dave McAlpin) and everyone else who might come along with them to spoil Ghost Ranch, O'Keeffe departed the Packs' house in a huff. Phoebe Pack went after her and managed to have an at least civil conversation with O'Keeffe before she drove back to her home under the cliffs. Arthur and Phoebe Pack patched up their relationship with O'Keeffe as they had many times before, and they remained friends with her until the end of their lives. But it would take years before O'Keeffe would come to like even a select handful of Presbyterians, and even then she never let them forget what Pack had taken from her.

Ghost Ranch had functioned extremely well as a small guest ranch for twenty guests plus staff. The Presbyterians wanted it to function just as well as an educational center for one hundred and fifty guests. In early 1956, there were more visits by various experts to determine exactly what needed to be added to the ranch's facilities to increase its guest capacity. Pack remained an advisor after the transfer by fee simple to the Presbyterians (the only stipulation in the deed transfer was that the Packs could live in their home behind the headquarters for as long as they chose), and Paul Calvin Payne agreed to spend his last year before retirement as acting director of the new desert conference center.

Payne and his wife, Edna, moved into the former Bennett house. Casa Monte Rojo had been sold by the Bennetts during the war to Chicago friends, the Van Berghs. Mr. Van Bergh, an attorney, died shortly after, and the house at Ghost Ranch was rarely used by his widow. She died shortly before the Packs' gift to the Presbyterians, and when the house under the cliffs and its two hundred acres was put up for sale, the Presbyterians bought it for twenty thousand dollars. The Paynes renamed the Bennett house Casa del Sol, House of the Sun.[4]

It was important to Pack that the Presbyterians design and place their new guest quarters and meeting facilities in such a way as to have a minimal impact on the landscape. Payne went looking for examples of successful wilderness retreats. The Boy Scouts of America had been successfully running the Philmont Scout Ranch at Cimarron, New Mexico, since 1941. Philmont could easily accommodate two thousand scouts and masters at one time on its 138,000-acre ranch in the mountains, and Payne was soon making frequent trips up the Rio Grande and over the Sangre de Cristos to study the Boy Scouts' facility. Payne liked the Scouts' idea of cottage units clustered about a shared bath facility, but cut the number of campers sharing one toilet area in half—from 100 people per restroom, which was the Scout way, to fifty.

Ghost Ranch needed new facilities, but it also needed major renovations of the older buildings. The bunkhouse built by Stanley for her wranglers and guides needed a complete overhaul, as did the headquarters kitchen and dining room. The ranch also needed a meeting room of some kind and several more housing units like the adobe casitas near Ghost House.

Arthur Pack was in agreement with the proposed expansion but was concerned about the where and how of it all. The ranch seemed in danger of becoming a cluttered and chaotic camp. Pack's fears echoed Payne's concerns that Ghost Ranch not be subjugated to an urban concept of an educational center. "This is not going to be a conventional summer camp," Dr. Payne told a magazine writer during his first year at Ghost Ranch. "It will be a research laboratory for Christian activities. . . . There is going to be no ornamentation. We are not going to 'beautify' the ranch; God already has done that."[5]

Several preliminary architectural plans considered placing major ranch facilities somewhere other than the main headquarters of Stanley's guest ranch. After it was learned that the only potable water was in the old homestead area, planning for the study center remained focused at the mouth of Yeso Canyon.

Before any buildings were even drawn on paper, Payne went looking for someone with both the naturalist's vision and the hands-on building experience to guide the design and placement of the new facilities. Following the recommendation of Jim Hall, who was made chairman of the architecture and development committee, Payne met with W. T.—Will—Harris, a tall, lanky, energetic, good-humored, and enormously farsighted young architect out of Hobbs, New Mexico. Immediately after the ranch was given to the Presbyterians, Harris came to the ranch with his pastor and friend, Jim Hall. Harris loved everything about Ghost Ranch, especially its rustic ambience and lack of telephone service! With Payne and Hall, Harris began to create an architectural template that would be used for the next half-century at Ghost Ranch. "The design philosophy for the Ghost Ranch development was established rather early," Harris later reminisced, "and I think the result is apparent to most people when they come to the ranch. Simply stated . . . because the beauty of nature at Ghost Ranch is so overwhelming man does well to take a low profile."[6]

With Harris's sensitive eye and careful guidance, the new buildings did take a low profile. Harris's designs were simple, modest structures that blended in form and color into the mesas and hillsides. Payne, Hall, and Harris implemented a site plan that split the ranch's housing onto two levels, with most of the new guest units located on the mesa above the Pack and Johnson houses. The advantage to this plan was that more than one hundred people could live on the mesa and be completely invisible to those living in the casitas below. The mesa housing meant a hefty hike up a steep trail, but Harris, Payne, and Hall agreed from the outset that Ghost Ranch was not going to become a luxury retreat center. Ghost Ranch was to be a study center in the middle of the wilderness, and the wilderness would remain front and center of whatever else was being studied. "When Arthur Pack gave [Ghost Ranch] to the Church, he gave it freely with no conditions and no reversionary clauses," Hall explained. "But, out of his own history and out of his own personal statement there was conveyed the concern that this tract of land which is surrounded on three sides by national forest, be held in the kind of trust that would prevent it from becoming a new sub-development or an over-used wasteland."[7]

Besides, the view from what would be very modest housing units on the mesa was spectacular—wider than from the casitas below and completely unfettered by gardens and bushes, shade trees, or even sand hills—and boasted a panoramic perspective of the entire Piedra Lumbre, with Pedernal visible through every room's door or window. It was ranch living at its best. Guests learned to live with the rhythm of the landscape: sunrise and sunset were personal events, storms could be seen approaching from miles across the basin, and the movements of the stars and the moon could be followed from any doorstep throughout the night.

The budget was modest, and Harris's firm broke even on its first year of work at Ghost Ranch. (In subsequent years, Harris donated his services.) Over the next few years, Harris designed and oversaw construction of the first large meeting room that was soon called Convocation Hall and the new dining room set on top of Pack's old airplane hangar at the east end of the alfalfa field. Harris also reconfigured the headquarters into offices and a trading post and renovated the rooms in the bunkhouse, renamed Corral Block. The mesa eventually had eleven housing units and small classrooms. Harris also supervised the building of two larger meeting rooms, Upper Pavilion, on the mesa, and Lower Pavilion, near Corral Block.

The famously frigid swimming pool near the mouth of Yeso Canyon was replaced by two modern—and heated—pools near the new dining hall, in 1957. The swimming pools (one for adults, one for children) were the gift of Margaret Weyerhaeuser Driscoll, who not only built the pools but subsidized their maintenance and heating for the next twenty-five years. Peggy Driscoll was the granddaughter of the founder of Weyerhaeuser lumber. Like Arthur Pack, Driscoll had inherited a substantial fortune from her family's lumber empire. And also like Pack, Driscoll was an educated (a Vassar grad), personable, and committed philanthropist. Driscoll was the first woman president of St. John's College, and she volunteered her time and energy to numerous boards across the United States, including Macalester College in St. Paul and the Santa Fe Chamber Music Association.

Driscoll was a member of the Presbyterian Board of Christian Education in 1955 when Ghost Ranch was offered to the Presbyterians. Unlike most of her colleagues in Philadelphia, Driscoll already had some personal knowledge of the ranch and its spectacular gifts. Her late husband, Walter Driscoll, had a family home in Santa Fe. Walter's younger sister, Mary Driscoll, was the young woman who two decades before had slept out under the Piedra Lumbre stars at Dr. Camp's expedition campsite, and who invited the Berkeley bone diggers into Santa Fe for weekend visits at the Driscoll home near the old plaza.

Peggy Driscoll's personal and financial involvement with Ghost Ranch began with its new role as a study center and continued for the next several decades. Driscoll's commitment to the place and its mission would become as legendary as it was crucial, as she "rescued" the ranch in many an economic crisis during its years of rebirth as a study center. Driscoll's care for the people and the place of Ghost Ranch earned her the reputation of the "ranch's angel" years before her untimely death in an automobile accident in 1981.[8]

From the beginning of Ghost Ranch's life as a conference center, Jim Hall was involved with all decisions and discussions about the ranch. Quite simply, everyone in Philadelphia and everyone in the Southwest, Presbyterian and not, seemed to intuit early on that Hall was the person to steer Ghost Ranch into its future. This opinion was not based on personal or professional alliances. Ghost Ranch presented a complex and even perplexing opportunity for the Presbyterians, and the place needed a person equipped with more than just energy, imagination, a divinity degree, and an unwavering Christian faith: Ghost Ranch needed someone with hands-on experience of what happens when ordinary folks are plunked down in the middle of God's wilderness. And that person was James Wallace Hall.

Gazing back over half a century, it is impossible to imagine what Ghost Ranch would have become if Jim Hall had not sauntered onto the ranch and hitched his star to its story in the mid-1950s. Anglo, Hispanic, and Native American friends and colleagues in and out of the church pretty much agree that modern Ghost Ranch is a testament to the vision and energy of Jim W. Hall. The gifts of the person were tailor-made to serve the gifts of the place.

Hall was born in the great stretch of nothingness that is the cattle country of west Texas. Although Hall left the rural Southwest life for the urban intellectual life found at Macalester College in Minnesota, and then McCormick and San Anselmo seminaries, he was always a cowboy at heart. In the mid-1930s, Hall was the only student on the Macalester campus who owned, much less wore, cowboy boots. But it was Hall's experiences as the son of the Southwest's most famous and beloved in-the-saddle cowboy preacher, Ralph J. Hall, that ultimately made Jim Hall a natural for Ghost Ranch.

Ralph Hall was raised on a Texas cattle ranch and left home at eighteen to answer his calling as a lay missionary in what he called "the Lord's outfit." As a circuit rider in the early 1900s, Hall lived under the open sky with his Bible in his saddlebag and a bedroll and camping gear on his packhorse. Hall rode the narrowest trails to the farthest-flung cow camps and ranch hamlets twelve months of the year, spreading the Gospel and lending a helping hand, although not necessarily in that order. In 1916, a special dispensation by the Presbyterian Board of Home Missions ordained Ralph Hall as a minister, although poor eyesight had prevented him from completing college or attending seminary.

Formal recognition of Hall's mission work did not change his circuit rider style or place boundaries on his ministry. Long before he was ordained, the hardworking, often desperately lonely cowboys, miners, timber men, farmers, ranchers, and homesteaders were Ralph Hall's wilderness congregation. Hall's mounted ministry eventually became the largest parish, geographically, in the United States. "I have never been able to travel over the western range country," Hall wrote, "whether by car or horseback, and see a dim road or trail turning off without feeling a longing in my heart to follow that trail and see where it will lead me. I have followed a great many of them . . . to people . . . and to unexpected and rich experiences where I could be of service."[9]

Brother Hall met people on their own turf, which was usually the sage- and cactus-adorned rangelands occupied by the ranchers of the Southwest. Sometimes Hall's trail took him to the middle-of-nowhere home of a single family, but more often his "destination" was the chuck wagon or campfire ring of cowboys following a herd across the plains of southern New Mexico or west Texas.

Hall's style was not like most conventional preachers: he didn't preach down from a pulpit, but rather, he moved into the herd of weathered men and worked alongside them branding, rounding up, or just keeping the cattle moving toward a distant destination. He was an expert camp cook and could whip up the morning pancakes or the eve-

The cowboy preacher Ralph Hall packing up his horses in the early 1940s.

ning cornbread, and through all he could tell stories—godly and not—with the best of them. A magazine writer who rode with Hall wrote: "The Rev. Dr. Ralph J. Hall can rope a steer in near record time and he can ride a bucking horse with the best riders the Southwest has produced. He reads trail signs like an Indian, and spends more nights in a bed-roll than he does under a roof."[10]

Hall married Lillie Bess Owens in 1917, and his first son, James Wallace, was born in Weatherford, Texas, a year later. Ralph Hall's love of the great outdoors, and of the people living close to the land, in community and alone, was passed on to his son Jim. Young Jim accompanied his father on horseback, in his Model T, and later in his pickup truck, into the outback each summer. Before he started school, Jim Hall was an adept rider and camper, cowboy, and cook, and like his dad, completely at home under the stars.

Ralph Hall understood how lonely and isolated teenagers living on the range felt, having been one himself and, in the 1930s, when Jim Hall was a teenager, began organizing weeklong church camps in the mountains for teenagers from ranch hamlets and homesteads and logging, mining, and timber camps. By 1940, Hall expanded these under-the-stars social and prayer gatherings to include adults. The first Ranchman's Cowboy Camp Meeting was held on Nogal Mesa, New Mexico, a beautiful high pine mountain site "where," Ralph Hall wrote, "I just have to take off my hat every time I ride by it."[11] Hall hoped the camp meeting would attract one hundred participants from neighboring ranches, but seven hundred showed up with their camping gear and Bibles. The Ranchman's Cowboy Camp Meeting became an annual event on Nogal Mesa near Carrizozo, New Mexico. Attendees were Protestants and Catholics, and neither. There was no charge—a hat was passed, and there were always enough donations to break even on food and supplies.

These cowboy camp meetings were so successful in New Mexico that the word spread all over the West: soon Ralph Hall was organizing the same Christian get-togethers under the stars in remote locations in Arizona, Colorado, Wyoming, Nevada, Nebraska, and the Dakotas. There were eventually eleven locations attended by thousands of rural folks, who planned all winter for the upcoming summer's "camp-meetin' week," and the return of Preacher Hall, who was fast becoming legendary.

A Ranchman's Cowboy Camp Meeting at Magdalena, New Mexico, in 1956. Many of these men became directly involved with the development of Ghost Ranch into an educational center of the Presbyterian church. Will Harris, an architect based in Hobbs, New Mexico, is second from left; Jim Hall, the future director of Ghost Ranch, is third from left; Ralph Hall is at the far right; and Ralph Hall Jr. is third from the right.

Like all things Southwestern and cowboy, Ralph Hall's camp meetings caught the imagination of folks back east. By the late 1940s, there were two films about Hall's circuit riding and camp meetings. Features in *Time* magazine and the *Saturday Evening Post* brought national attention to Ralph Hall's cowboy ministry and heightened the mystique surrounding his wilderness prayer meetings among Presbyterians.

In the summer of 1940, Ralph Hall, accompanied by his son, Jim, home from studies at Macalester, began traveling seminars to accommodate the many folks back east who wanted to experience for themselves a piece of Preacher Hall's Southwest. Also called the Cowboy Bedroll Seminars, the event was more of an expedition than a tour, and paying participants slept out under the open sky in the old-fashioned, canvas-covered mattress bedrolls favored by Ralph and all honest-to-God cowboys. With twelve to eighteen vehicles hauling up to one hundred people and their food, their fifty-pound-a-piece bedrolls, work tables, and "prefab" canvas-and-pipe privies, Hall led the caravan of eastern dudes on a two-thousand-mile tour of the Southwestern backcountry.

The Cowboy Bedroll Seminars followed the old trails known by Orville Cox and other guides across reservations and into pueblos, and to numerous Presbyterian mission schools, clinics, and outposts in New Mexico and Arizona. Participants climbed off the train in Raton or Lamy dressed in suits and ties, dresses and heels. It was the first time most had slept out under the stars, and the first time that they had seen the desert and canyon country and the high pine mountains, except in movies. The caravan of trucks and automobiles stopped at least once, in the 1940s, on the ridgeline mesa above Ghost Ranch and set up their night camp with Pedernal to the south and the Cliffs of Shining Stone to the north. Jim Hall had marveled at the beauty of this landscape of stone pinnacles and red badlands as a boy, when he came through the Piedra Lumbre with his dad in the 1930s. But the name Ghost Ranch meant nothing to him, and Jim Hall's second trip across the badlands was as much remembered for a broken axle on the semi he was driving, and the hours spent loading and reloading those fifty-pound bedrolls, as for the space and light of the remarkable place that surrounded him.

Exactly what made Jim Hall precisely the sort of preacher-director that Ghost Ranch needed to move into its next incarnation as a study center was a combination of his father's can-do cowboy know-how and frontier missionary self-reliance and Hall's worldly, inquisitive, intellectual savvy acquired during his years away from the Southwest. By the mid-1950s, when the Presbyterians were looking for someone to take Ghost Ranch, Jim Hall had graduated from Macalester, had attended McCormick Seminary (although he had not completed his studies), had held a pastorship in Ketchikan, Alaska (where he also worked as a fisherman), had completed seminary at San Anselmo, California, and had served pastorates in the small copper mining community of Morenci, Arizona, and in the oil boomtown of Hobbs, New Mexico.

Although Hall was officially called in to serve as counsel to Payne and the board, his first mark on the ranch came in the form of a group of volunteers from his Hobbs, New Mexico, church. Hall's congregation at the Presbyterian Church in Hobbs included the community's oil barons, but it also included a large constituency of men who worked as skilled laborers in the oil fields and local ranchers and farmers. Hobbs was an independent, spirited community of Southwesterners who had come into their own using their wits and their hands. In Jim Hall, the Hobbs Presbyterian community had an educated, energetic pastor who led them spiritually, met them socially, and was known to match any mechanic, cowboy, or farmhand skill for skill around a truck, tractor, horse, or cow. Hall was gentle-spoken and charismatic and enormously respected for his ability to engage in meaningful conversation with an Ivy League seminarian, a local banker, a diesel mechanic, or the foreman from one of the local cattle ranches. Hall read Greek and Latin and spoke passable French, and later, Spanish; he was also an excellent marksman and possessed his father's ability to make everyone feel valued and welcomed. And Hall never forgot a name.

In 1955, as Hall was drawn into the development of Ghost Ranch, so was the Presbyterian community in Hobbs, New Mexico, some four hundred miles south. Already proficient at rallying volunteers for local community projects, Hall extended his congregation's volunteerism efforts to the high desert of the Piedra Lumbre. The Hobbs work crews in the 1950s gave new meaning to the word "volunteer" and raised forever the ranch standard concerning the kind of work a volunteer crew could be expected to successfully take on. Not only did Hall bring a sizable number of able-bodied, skilled men to Ghost Ranch for a week or more of hard, manual labor on buildings, roads, and mechanical facili-

Jim Hall (standing) and Hobbs volunteers completing the Padre Jim Bridge at Ghost Ranch in 1957.

ties; Hall also used his considerable negotiating skills to secure whatever heavy machinery and big budget materials he needed for a particular Ghost Ranch task. Will Harris, who often accompanied Hall on those long overnight hauls between Hobbs and Ghost Ranch, remembered, "It's a whale of a long way to come . . . seven hours of reasonably fast driving. . . . Jim would con the oil companies, or truck companies, into loaning him a truck, flatbed or wench truck, or whatever other equipment that he wanted. He'd go over and work on the trucks as a mechanic, you know, get friendly with them and as a result they'd say well, you can take that flatbed truck . . . but, you know, I can't remember any truck that he ever borrowed where the tail lights worked."

Hall drove the heavily loaded—and often overloaded—flatbed truck many times between Hobbs and Ghost Ranch, carrying bridge beams and lumber, steel, pipe, even a water tank. He favored night driving on back roads without weigh stations, although Reverend Hall was known to talk his way past state troopers on several occasions.

Once at the ranch, the mighty Hobbs volunteer force went to work like professionals, which they were, and between 1956 and 1960 undertook countless small projects—laying the tile floor in Convocation Hall, doing a dozen electrical and plumbing jobs, and pouring concrete sidewalks around the dining hall. The Hobbs volunteers are best remembered for their completion of two large projects—the erection of the eight-thousand-gallon water tank at the mouth of Yeso Canyon and the building of the bridge across the Arroyo Seco near Dr. Charles Camp's former fossil site. The bridge was christened the Padre Jim Bridge, and it gave Ghost Ranch its first all-weather entrance—O'Keeffe soon used it exclusively, as it afforded a shorter drive between her home under the cliffs and the paved highway. The bridge's name honored the construction crew's pastor and foreman, Jim Hall, but it also, with almost divine prescience, foretold the influence and weight that Padre Jim the person would carry at Ghost Ranch for the next thirty years.

With those first work groups from Hobbs, Hall introduced to Ghost Ranch the basic template of the frontier Christian community embodied by the ministry of his father for half a century. People traveled hundreds of miles to participate in a mission at Ghost Ranch that served themselves and others. They came together as a community of faith, and they shared hard work and long days under the hot sun. There was fellowship and there was solitude within a landscape that was blessed, magical, and at once universal and deeply personal. A week at Ghost Ranch, like at Nogal Mesa and at every other cowboy camp meeting that gathered folks together to talk, sing, and pray in the pristine places of the West, transformed people.

By 1958, Payne and the Board of Christian Education knew that Jim Hall was the person they wanted to be director of Ghost Ranch. But Hall was leaving Hobbs to assume the pastorship of a church in Arlington, Texas. Hall told Payne that he had to give the Arlington congregation three years before he could come to the ranch. Payne knew Jim Hall was worth waiting for. It was never discussed in public, but the board in Philadelphia and Hall in Arlington understood that in 1961 Jim and his wife, Ruth, would move to Ghost Ranch, and Ghost Ranch would become his official calling.

Paul Payne retired in late 1957, and the Rev. W. H. Vernon Smith served as interim, off-site (he remained in Philadelphia) director until May of 1961, when Jim Hall finally arrived to stay. (Hall had returned to the ranch every year with his volunteer force that now included people

Jim Hall, c. 1975.

from both Hobbs and the new church in Arlington.) Jim came with his wife, Ruth, and they moved into Casa del Sol with their three sons, Jim and Tim, who were in college, and ten-year-old Jon.

Hall accepted the job as director with two stipulations: first, he wanted to be in charge of everything, from range management to program development. The Board of Christian Education would act as his consulting/clearing committee, but Ghost Ranch decisions would be driven by and through Hall's office at Ghost Ranch, not through an office in the Witherspoon Building in Philadelphia. Second, Hall asked the Board of Christian Education to relax its bureaucratic modus operandi in regard to Ghost Ranch.

> [Our] staff was too small for the [Board's] outrageous bureaucratic structure! We had a ranch manager, an assistant ranch manager, maintenance man, land man, kitchen person . . . papers everywhere! They just snowed us with paper! I said, "that's not acceptable." They said "okay." I said, "I don't want to be program director, but director, responsible for everything. I'll set up structure." They said "okay." We forgot the titles. People stayed. We had to make a budget . . . early on, we made the budget together.

The Hall era coincided with the completion of new housing units and meeting facilities, including the expansion of the old Johnson house into a library renamed Cottonwood. The new dining hall, built on Pack's old hangar site, could seat three hundred at one meal. In the late 1950s, Teepee Village, composed of traditional Plains Indian lodges, had been erected on Colbert's 1947 campsite near the old swimming pool above the Yeso stream. During Hall's first summer, a cluster of traditional Navajo hogans was built in this same area below the cliffs by a volunteer work group of Navajo clergymen and lay people who came to Ghost Ranch from the Presbyterian missions in Ganado and Chinle.

The conference center now had a variety of housing options: the quaint, private, and comfortable adobe cottages built by Stanley in the 1930s; dormitory-style rooms that opened on portals and shared bathroom facilities, including the renovated bunkhouse now called Corral Block; eight units that totaled nearly fifty rooms up on the mesa; and teepees and hogans. Hall wanted all of the buildings at Ghost Ranch to be simple, even stark, emphasizing the outdoors instead of the indoors. Reverend Dale Brubaker, one of the Presbyterian Church's first consultants, understood Hall's concept immediately: "What happens to the spirit here transcends the buildings."

Hall also insisted that, with the exception of the teepees and hogans, the ranch charge one rate for all accommodations, be it a bunk in one of the no-frills mesa dormitory rooms or a carved-wood bed in the quaintly attractive Ghost House. People would be housed where their seminar was housed, including leaders. Hall wanted the ranch to reflect a community of equality, and he defended this decision many times over the next few decades, especially to visiting Presbyterian dignitaries.

> This ruffled a few feathers. The Board of Christian Education staff was used to living out here in luxury, and now they were living on the mesa and had to trek to the shower. But my reasons were clear: I didn't want distinction between leader and group; involvement after hours around seminars was helpful. I thought it was a sound educational approach. Put the leaders with the people they were involved with. It also made it very clear that money does not carry any clout at Ghost Ranch.

By 1961, there had already been several summers of seminars that imitated and sometimes enlarged upon the educational programs of the church found in other parts of the country—synod camps, Bible study and leadership training, National Mariners gatherings. The difference at Ghost Ranch, from the beginning, was that *families* were welcomed: there were staffed facilities—morning activities for the children, lifeguards at the swimming pools, and evening campfires chaperoned by counselors—that offered women with children an unprecedented opportunity to attend classes. Pack had been very specific about the ranch fostering youth activities, but Hall wanted to expand this to include families, and Ghost Ranch was early on promoted as an adult study center opened to people of all races, creeds, religions, and ethnic backgrounds.

The preeminent trailblazer in modern psychiatry, Dr. Karl Menninger, of the Menninger Foundation in Topeka, Kansas, was a personal friend of Arthur Pack's. Introductions were made, and Dr. Karl, as he was called, agreed to come to Ghost Ranch in the winter of 1957 and lead a seminar for clergymen on the link between religion and psychiatry. Twenty-nine pastors from twenty-nine churches representing congregations from New York to California attended. The event was extremely successful and foreshadowed the scope and quality of seminars Ghost Ranch could sponsor.

A college work-study program was initiated in 1957 through the national Presbyterian Church's Volunteers in Mission (VIM) office. In a manner reminiscent of the summer staff found at the Packs' guest ranch in the 1930s, college students came to Ghost Ranch for several months of hard work, little pay, and the priceless gift of one glorious summer in a community plunked down in the very center of one of the most magnificent places on earth.

With an advisory committee of board members and friends that met formally in Philadelphia, but also very informally in the Halls' living room or fireside on the patio at Casa del Sol (board meetings were always planned around the full moon), an early blueprint for Ghost Ranch as an educational center was sketched out. The summer seminars were set up as weeklong classes, with afternoons left unscheduled so that participants could explore the country of the ranch. Time alone and/or with family and friends spent hiking, gazing, wandering, and simply being was encouraged by the morning-evening class schedule, and many a first-time participant remarked on the amount of exterior and interior *space* they discovered at Ghost Ranch. One participant and teacher, Dietre Hessel, wrote: "Deliberately, Ghost Ranch was *de*scheduled just enough to allow time to unwind and marvel in a setting that occasions too many snapshots, but must be savored in order to unplug participants from technocultural captivity."[12]

Hall firmly believed that Ghost Ranch was among the most beautiful and special places on earth, and its classes and leaders should reflect and enhance the power found in the landscape. A great place was worthy of great programs. Over the next decades, there was no one too important, too influential, too famous or accomplished for consideration as a seminar leader. Hall and his program committee aimed high and ninety percent of the time secured the best and the brightest teachers in any field.

With his wife, Ruth, Hall led one of the most popular annual seminars at the ranch, the High Country Trail Ride. For this seminar, Hall was able to use every skill in and out of the saddle learned from his father, Ralph. The event was in the high mountains of the Pecos Wilderness, and every participant was on horseback. People of all ages and all professions and religious preferences enlisted for the weeklong adventure—one summer the seminar included a blind man Hall agreed to take on horseback into the wilderness. The camp kitchen duties and daily menu were overseen by Hall himself, and most of the cooking was done in his father's camp meeting cast-iron fry pans and Dutch ovens. There was always a long waiting list for this authentic cowboy trail ride, although it demanded a lot from participants, physically and psychologically.

Ghost Ranch and Jim Hall had a way of making believers out of everyone who came there. Not believers in the traditional Christian sense, although spiritual transformation happened with regularity, but believers that there was something rare and wonderful found in the Ghost Ranch environment of land and people. Famous and common folks claimed the ranch as their own and found themselves members of a common tribe united by place. A supper table in the ranch dining room could include a clergyman and his family of four from Oklahoma breaking bread with a major television network's White House correspondent and his wife. On any given day in the summer, a presidential candidate could be sitting under the portal with several Midwestern college students, and a best-selling author could be found standing in the hash line discussing the local bird population with an astrophysicist from Berkeley. Ghost Ranch's—and to a great extent, Jim Hall's—mystique crossed all boundaries and made devotees out of people from every conceivable social, educational, economic, and religious background.

Ned Colbert had maintained a relationship with the Packs and the ranch throughout the 1950s. When Colbert passed through the Southwest with his family, which now included five sons, he always made a point of returning to Ghost Ranch for a night or two in Ghost House. In 1965, Colbert and his wife, Margaret, were touring the Southwest with A. W. "Fuzz" Crompton, director of the Peabody Museum at Yale, and two other professors of paleontology, from Brazil and Israel. Colbert wanted to take his paleo pals to see the *Coelophysis* quarry at Ghost Ranch and stopped in to meet Jim Hall.

Colbert's and Hall's introductory chat in the front office spilled over into dinner and an evening at the Halls' house, and then an invitation for the Colberts and their three traveling companions to spend the night in the sprawling hacienda under the cliffs. Hall was intrigued by Colbert's and his colleagues' pursuits, and he also wanted to have a better understanding of Ghost Ranch's *Coelophysis* quarry and its importance in the world of paleontology. Colbert and his companions were just as intrigued by Hall's intellectual-cowboy style and the educational and spiritual environment he was creating with the Presbyterians at Ghost Ranch. Before Colbert and his international fossil hunters departed the ranch, Doctors Colbert and Crompton had committed to return and teach a paleo seminar the following summer.

Beginning in 1966, the weeklong paleontology seminar at Ghost Ranch became a popular annual event often led by Colbert and Crompton. The first summer classes and field trips were attended by Ruth Hall, and what began as a casual interest in the bones of Ghost Ranch was soon to become Ruth Hall's passionate hobby.

Ruth Clark Hall was raised in the same ranch country of west Texas as Jim, and when Jim Hall and Ruth Clark were born on the exact same day in May of 1918, there were greetings and congratulations passed across the dusty miles between their family ranches. Ruth Hall was petite and small boned and spoke with a soft Texas accent. She was comfortable around horses, cattle, and, by the time she came to Ghost Ranch and had been a minister's wife for several decades, all manner of people. She thought nothing of being alone on an isolated desert basin where her nearest neighbor was an artist-hermit who in the early years kept a wide boundary between herself and Ruth's family.

Ruth Hall's fossil interest began within a year of her move to Ghost Ranch. In 1962, Robert Hunt, the college-aged son of one of the first field directors sent to Ghost Ranch by the Board of Christian Education, took Ruth Hall along on several fossil-finding jaunts in the sand lands. Hunt had come to visit the ranch with his dad in the 1950s. Ned Colbert was there that week, and after Uncle Ned showed Bob Hunt a phytosaur vertebrae he had found in the badlands, Hunt was hooked on fossils. Hunt was a graduate student in paleontology at the University of New Mexico when he showed Ruth Hall the various bone quarries near her home under the cliffs. On one of their summer expeditions into the badlands across from O'Keeffe's home, Hunt and Hall found a six-foot phytosaur skeleton that was eventually bandaged,

Ruth Hall showing children dinosaur fossil sites on the Painted Desert at Ghost Ranch in 1976.

excavated, and prepared for exhibition. After finding that phytosaur, Ruth Hall, like Hunt before her, was hooked on fossils.

In the fall of 1963, Hunt returned again to Ghost Ranch to fossil hunt. While roaming the Chinle west of Mesa Huerfano, several miles from ranch headquarters, Hunt found a second, larger phytosaur skeleton. Hunt took Ruth and Jim Hall out to the new site, and, after much discussion, they decided to leave this magnificent specimen where it had been for 150 million years.

Two years later, when Colbert and Crompton stopped in at Ghost Ranch in the summer of 1965, the Halls took them to see "Old Phytie," as the Mesa Huerfano skeleton was soon called. The two professionals were impressed with the find and decided the specimen—obviously a relative of Vivaron—was worthy of excavation. Fuzz Crompton himself directed the extraction of Old Phytie, and the beautifully articulated skeleton—missing only its skull—was moved to Ruth Hall's garage, where it awaited preparation.

After Old Phytie became a resident of the Casa del Sol garage, Colbert and Crompton urged Ruth to take formal training in field technique and bone preparation that would enable her to work on the phytosaur. After much discussion, Ruth accepted Crompton's offer to spend a month in the Comparative Zoology lab at Harvard, where he was now teaching, to study bone preparation. When Ruth returned to Ghost Ranch she began what would be years of enormously satisfying work on Old Phytie's mud- and stone-encased skeleton.

Ruth Hall became a very proficient and respected bone hunter. She followed Colbert about the badlands every summer he came to Ghost Ranch, but even after training with Crompton, arguably among the world's top paleontologists, Ruth Hall remained modest about her skills. And she always reminded visitors to Old Phytie's garage lab that she was only an amateur. However, Crompton and Colbert both admired Ruth's scouting abilities and valued her observations, and her devotion to the fossil record of the Piedra Lumbre earned her honorary membership in the Society of Vertebrate Paleontology.

In the early 1980s, Colbert asked Jim Hall to allow him to reopen the *Coelophysis* quarry, a Natural Historic Site since 1976, to remove more specimens. Hall agreed, and with ranch equipment and personnel assistance, the quarry was reopened in 1981 and 1982. The quarry, again, yielded an incredible number of skeletons in a joint excavation by the

Carnegie Museum, the New Mexico Museum of Natural History, the Museum of Northern Arizona, and the Yale Peabody Museum.

With Colbert, Jim Hall had begun to develop plans for a museum at Ghost Ranch to showcase and honor the paleontology of the Piedra Lumbre. In the fall of 1985, before construction began, a gargantuan, eight-ton block of plaster-encased *Coelophysis* fossils excavated three years before was removed from the quarry. The block was hoisted by crane onto a flatbed truck that laboriously transported the fossils from the quarry site in the steep sand hills near Yeso Canyon down several rough miles to the newly poured foundation of the museum near Corral Block. After the colossal block was set down onto its prepared footing, construction of the Ghost Ranch paleo museum began around it.

The new museum housed the stories of a banner list of internationally known fossil hunters, and when it came time to name the museum, Ned Colbert's name was an obvious early choice. But Colbert believed that the museum should be named for the ranch's resident amateur, who over twenty-five years had tirelessly shared her enthusiasm for the Piedra Lumbre's fossil story with hundreds of children and adults. And so the new building was christened the Ruth Hall Museum of Paleontology.

"But it's not my story," Ruth Hall would say again and again. "It's their story—the fossils that have been found here, the evolution that has been pieced together—and all the people over many years who have hunted and dug this land with hope that what they found would further the understanding of life that was here long before man."

Ned Colbert finally found the time to sit down and write the long-awaited and definitive text on the *Coelophysis* quarry at Ghost Ranch in the early 1990s. The book, *The Little Dinosaurs of Ghost Ranch*, was published in 1995, when Colbert was ninety years of age! The book was dedicated to Arthur and Phoebe Pack, and to Jim and Ruth Hall, "whose generous support of dinosaur hunters made Ghost Ranch internationally renowned in the annals of dinosaur research."[13]

In early summer of 1968, on the heels of Colbert and Crompton's inaugural seminars and what was becoming a very successful paleontology program at Ghost Ranch, Florence Hawley Ellis stepped onto the ranch, bringing with her the best of the world of Southwestern archaeology. Ellis's field school from the University of New Mexico was about to spend the summer excavating the prehistoric pueblo ruin of

Sapawe, near the neighboring village of El Rito. Dr. Ellis was looking for a place to set up camp for her thirty-five field students and had heard about Ghost Ranch. She was wary of the ranch's Presbyterian ownership but decided to stop by and look around anyway.

Ellis remembered that she was surprised by two separate encounters that initial afternoon at Ghost Ranch: the first was with an enormous deer, a buck with antlers reminiscent of an O'Keeffe painting, standing in the middle of the ranch road. "I braked my car with a spurt of pebbles. . . . Looking, listening, dreaming in dignity—. He was not mine to disturb, and I sat as if sewn into the upholstery until he finally took his way down into the wash."[14]

The second encounter was with Jim Hall, with whom, although he was a reverend and a Presbyterian both, Ellis felt an immediate camaraderie. Hall asked Ellis about her summer plans and then offered her field school the use of Teepee Village. After a quick tour of the canvas-and-pole quarters clustered under the sheer stone walls of Yeso Canyon, Ellis and her students moved in for a six-week stay.

Ellis and the UNM field school, which came to include forty-six students from all over the United States, spent three consecutive summers at Ghost Ranch. In spite of her criticisms of the Presbyterians and their mission work with the Native Americans of the Southwest, Ellis came to admire the people and program at the ranch. Ellis found the Reverend Hall open and receptive to her vast knowledge of Pueblo culture and religion. "Florence came and brought all we wanted to absorb in terms of cultural anthropology," Jim Hall remembered of those first summers. "She was quite intrigued by the fact that she could come down pretty heavily on the Presbyterian Church and all missionaries to the Indians who did the same things—superimposed a culture and religion—and this group [at Ghost Ranch] didn't get exceedingly defensive and withdraw and get angry. But said, 'yeah, you're right.'"

Ellis was an elegant, vigorous, world-renowned anthropologist in her early sixties when she stepped onto Ghost Ranch and into its story in 1968. She was one of the first women to receive a Ph.D. in anthropology (from the University of Chicago, in 1934) and was also a member of the first class (which counted four students) to graduate with an M.A. in archaeology from the University of Arizona, in 1928. Ellis began her fieldwork in 1929 at Chetro Ketl in Chaco Canyon, where she worked for eleven seasons, and she was an energetic, popular, and challenging professor at the University of New Mexico, where she began to teach cultural anthropology in 1934.[15]

After the three summers on the Piedra Lumbre with her field classes, Ellis had become very fond of Ghost Ranch. Dr. Ellis was approaching retirement—she officially retired from the University of New Mexico in 1971—but when Hall asked her to teach a class at the ranch in the summer of 1970, Ellis agreed, and the Ghost Ranch archaeology program was begun under her exceedingly experienced guidance.

Ellis did not initially envision a field school–type seminar program, but the Piedra Lumbre's fate, luck, and destiny spirits intervened, and Ghost Ranch was to become the home of significant Ellis-led archaeological expeditions begun after her "retirement" from university life.

At the close of Ellis's second week of teaching at Ghost Ranch, in 1971—a class studying the ethnology and anthropology of the northern New Mexican pueblos, with tours of local pueblos that included very personalized visits to the homes of Ellis's Native American friends—John Hayden, a local forest ranger and friend of Jim Hall's, invited Ellis to take a look at what he believed to be a site of the prehistoric Gallina people in the national forest above Ghost Ranch. Hayden's description of the artifacts he had found in lava beds and caves, called Turkey Springs, piqued Ellis's interest, and an expedition was planned. On the last day of Ellis's stay at the ranch, Hayden, Ellis, Jim and Ruth Hall, and a vanload of sworn-to-silence seminar participants (Forest Service sites were kept secret to avoid pot looting) drove several miles north of the ranch into the Canjilon Mountains. They stopped and parked near a forest lava bed on one of the highest mountains in the Chama drainage. The class fanned out across the lava bed, and almost immediately there were sherds found from Gallina culture cooking jars. Ellis knew the Gallina people had been in the vicinity seven hundred years before, but discovering pieces of their broken pottery wasn't all that illuminating to their story.

While the adults picked over the lava field on top of the ridge, two young brothers, Pete and Larry Johnson, wandered down into the scramble of automobile-sized boulders below the ridge. They began to climb about the large boulders and peer into deep crevices. "We said, well, maybe the Indians go into these caves?" Pete Johnson recalled of their exploration into the boulder field. "It started to have the look like some of these were spaces that a person could get down into. It just had that feel that somebody might have lived here. . . . You know, we were just kids!"

The Johnson boys climbed down into the cavelike hollows in the lava bed and after twenty minutes found a "room" that had a floor made of flagstone. They knew it was not natural. "We were on our hands and knees," Larry Johnson remembered, "and Pete was ahead of me and all of a sudden he goes 'A Pot!' And of course, we didn't know The Rules. . . . We grabbed that thing! Just picked it up and climbed back up to the top of the rock. All we had to do was emerge on top of the rock pile and say, 'hey, we found a pot' and a swarm of middle-aged to older women and men began pouring across the surface of the rocks! From that moment on it was just a frenzy of searching!"

The terrain was extremely difficult to walk across, but the middle- to older-aged seminar participants, including Dr. Ellis and the Halls, after seeing the Johnson brothers' cave and pot, which was replaced into its niche in the cave for photographing and note taking, fanned out into the boulder field with youthful agility.

Another fifteen ceramic jars were found that afternoon and also the skull of a young girl. The Halls, Hayden, Ellis, and others returned the next day, and, after two days at Turkey Springs, more than thirty pots had been collected. The canteens and cooking vessels were brought back and set out on tables at Ghost House, where Dr. Ellis assured everyone that what had just happened—the finding of so many entire ceramic pots hidden in a lava field—never happens. It was a remarkable site to have stumbled upon, even for someone with fifty years in the field.

Before Ellis left for the summer, it was decided that Ghost Ranch, with Forest Service permission, would sponsor archaeological fieldwork the following summer at Turkey Springs. The Ghost Ranch archaeology seminar under Ellis's direction was expanded to two weeks, and participants worked at Turkey Springs for four seasons. The results gathered by amateur crews, and Ellis's interpretation of the Gallina people, were eventually published by Ellis in her book *From Drought to Drought*.

For nineteen years Ellis oversaw Ghost Ranch archaeology digs and trained hundreds of volunteer diggers. In 1980, Ellis became the founding director of the Ghost Ranch anthropology museum named for her, and ten years later "retired" from teaching and fieldwork for a second and final time.

For twenty-five years, Ghost Ranch lived on cowboy time—Hall did not adjust the ranch clocks with daylight saving time each spring. The hour difference between the time on one side of the ranch gate and time on the other added to the ranch's mystique as a faraway place disconnected from ordinary life and society. During the summer months, it meant employees who lived off the ranch had to keep a foot in two time zones, and ranch staff had to constantly remind off-ranch friends that they operated on Ranch Time, and to schedule accordingly. Hall wanted the ranch community to get up with the sun and go to sleep with the stars. And like all good cowboy outfits, there was a declared siesta hour every day after lunch. Except for chores that could not be postponed, everything on the ranch came to a halt under the sizzling midday sun—the office was closed to campers, the pool was closed to swimmers, the trading post was closed to shoppers, and leaders, parents, and even reluctant children closed their eyes for a much-appreciated nap.

Remarkably, Ghost Ranch maintained its edge-of-the-outback ambience even as the facilities at the mouth of Yeso Canyon expanded to accommodate more than five hundred folks a week during the summer. Everyone on the ranch was invited to a weekly gathering at Casa del Sol, and campers aged nine to ninety eagerly made the trek by car and sometimes on foot across the badlands for a few hours of conversation under the stars on the old house's patio. The Halls presided over the camp meeting–style open house, which centered around a roaring campfire that kept the evening chill away. These gatherings could include a dozen or boast more than one hundred people—"no bother," Jim Hall would say—and could last far into the night, with clusters of folks from all walks of life from all parts of the country, the world, absorbed in conversation. Sometimes the rugs in the living room were rolled aside and the Halls led dancing until the wee hours of the morning. "Party time at Ghost Ranch is partying at its best," one leader, Lora Morgan Wermuth, remarked, "with all ages, all faiths, all races blending."[16]

The headquarters area sustained a marked increase in buildings, people, and use after the Presbyterians arrived, but the twenty-one thousand acres of Ghost Ranch rangeland was given a decade of rest following the Packs' gift. "[The land] was at the end of a drought period," Jim Hall remembered of the fall of 1955. "It had a history of being overgrazed for 100 years or more. It was pretty sad, and when you looked out across the country you could see some grass, but you could stand and throw your hat on the ground and not hit grass seven times out of ten."[17]

For nine years only the jackrabbits and antelope grazed on the ranch's limited grasses. Before Hall arrived, Paul Payne had sought advice from the U.S. Forest Service (USFS) as to how the rangeland might be reclaimed. The Forest Service studied Ghost Ranch and then proposed a multiyear restoration plan that was basically a reseeding and a water conservation program. The land was contoured so that the water would not run off so quickly, and pockets were punctured into the soil to catch water. The cost was about sixty thousand dollars and was funded by the Pack Foundation. Within the first year of the program, and with help from a banner amount of rainfall, the llanos of the Piedra Lumbre were green with a thick grass crop.

The cultivated and wild lands of Ghost Ranch were placed, in 1957, under the supervision of a twenty-four-year-old missionary named James Shibley. Shibley was working as a Presbyterian volunteer in Puerto Rico when he met Vernon Smith and learned about the big new ranch the church now owned in New Mexico. Shibley had been raised on a ranch in Oregon and had studied agriculture in college, and Smith asked him to take a look at Ghost Ranch when his term finished in Puerto Rico. Shibley stopped at the ranch on his way back to Oregon in early September and, after a tour that included the barns, corrals, pasturelands under conservation, and the newly completed Padre Jim Bridge, accepted the job.

"Back east they play golf on weekends," Shibley was told by the new ranch business manager, Heil Waters. "Out here we play cowboys."

Some of the staff played cowboy on weekends, but Jim Shibley's job was to be the head cowboy seven days a week. His duties as cowboy/ranch manager did not fit easily into a job description back in the Presbyterian personnel office in Philadelphia, and the first title given to Shibley by Paul Payne seemed burdensome and lofty—Superintendent of Roads, Grounds, and Soil Conservation. It was eventually shortened to Ranchlands Supervisor, and Shibley held the job for thirty-five years.

There were horses and burros kept at the ranch barn and corrals near headquarters, and, after nearly a decade of reseeding and rest, cattle were returned to the rangeland in very limited and closely monitored numbers. Shibley was a progressive, open-minded rancher and, with advice and counsel from experts from the Soil Conservation Service and New Mexico State University, implemented a New Age type of range management for Ghost Ranch. But Shibley's responsibilities would come to involve far more than land and animals. Because land is a highly emotional and political commodity in northern New Mexico, Shibley's position at Ghost Ranch—and Ghost Ranch's position as one of the last great undivided ranches in the area—would place him and the ranch center stage in some of the most volatile and complex socioeconomic issues in the region in the twentieth century.

Shibley's arrival at the ranch coincided with the Army Corps of Engineers' seizure of the Chama River on the Piedra Lumbre. The Corps' stated purpose was to build an earth-fill dam across the river at the mouth of the Chama Canyon that would control sediment deposit and flooding of the river. The Abiquiú Dam, soon renamed the Damn Dam by Hall and his staff, although not built upon ranch land, and located far across the llanos and mesa country so as to be invisible from Ghost Ranch, was to have an irreversible impact on the physical and emotional landscape of the Piedra Lumbre.

In 1957, the federal government began condemnation procedures that claimed hundreds of acres of privately held land along the river. The Chama crossed the ranch for two miles and was its southern boundary for another six miles. Condemnation forced Ghost Ranch to sell 161 acres at ten dollars an acre to be inundated by the proposed permanent pool. But the acreage needed for the reservoir was only the beginning: like all local landowners behind the proposed dam, the ranch was forced to sell thousands more acres to the federal government for flood easement rights at the undervalued price of two dollars and fifty cents an acre. Outraged that they had to sell any of Ghost Ranch, and unable to reverse the forced sale, the Presbyterians went to court and sued. They asked that the Corps pay all landowners an amount closer to the appraised value of seven dollars per acre. Ghost Ranch lost the case and was forced to sell 5,148 acres for a pittance of its worth.

After the dam's completion in 1963, Abiquiú Reservoir began to rise. The water flooded the ancient bosque of trees, Juan de Dios's River

Ranch, and two thousand Ghost Ranch acres of sand, sage, and hard-won gamma grass. The real headaches began for Shibley when cattle and horses became mired in the mud and had to be rescued before they drowned. Beaver that had lived along the Chama successfully for thousands of years began to wander up dry arroyos looking in vain for suitable home sites. And the rising and falling of the reservoir itself destroyed the ecological balance of the high desert and replaced the llano grasses and cactus with Russian thistle, knapweed, cockleburs, and a whole host of inedible or poisonous nonnative interlopers.

This pattern would be repeated for decades, and Ghost Ranch would lose additional acreage over the years as the Army Corps continued to enlarge its land claims behind the dam and impound more water. Eventually, the Abiquiú Reservoir became the designated permanent storage pool for Albuquerque's share of the San Juan/Chama Diversion project. Seeking to make the best of a frustrating situation, Ghost Ranch successfully negotiated with Albuquerque for water rights (to be used by neighbors downstream in Abiquiú) in exchange for the city being allowed to permanently flood more of the ranch's land.

Jim Hall was oft quoted as saying he did not want Ghost Ranch to be just for *Presbyterian* cows. Beginning in 1964, after years of reseeding and rotation programs on the ranch pastures, Ghost Ranch pastureland was opened to limited winter grazing. In 1967, local ranchers were actively recruited to the Winter Grazing Program, which gave them not only pastureland but also animal husbandry classes. Local ranchers without the adequate private land base to support their herds—or even just one cow—through a winter could do so at Ghost Ranch. The grazing program grew to become the New Mexico Producers and Marketing Coop, which was funded by both the Presbyterians and the Roman Catholics and boasted more than $1 million a year in sales among its participants.

The grazing program was a significant step toward what Hall hoped would be a better relationship between the "outsider Anglos" who had owned Ghost Ranch since the 1920s and the Hispanic community in Rio Arriba County. Hall did not want Ghost Ranch to function as an island for outsider Anglos. Within a year of his arrival, hoping to educate the ranch, and himself, about northern New Mexico community life, Hall invited various Hispanic and Native American scholars and social workers to give talks to Presbyterian board members. These men and women soon became Hall's advisors and personal friends, and he relied upon them to steer him and Ghost Ranch through the often-confusing cultural and political environment of northern New Mexican.

Tomás Atencio was a young social worker in Española when Hall first contacted him in 1962. Although raised a Presbyterian (his father was an ordained minister), Atencio shared the local Hispanic sentiment that Ghost Ranch was just another place for outsider Anglos to recreate: "Like many other large tracts of land in northern New Mexico, Ghost Ranch was alienated from the people of the region and their culture for many years: first because it was a dude ranch and later because it was for a Presbyterian Church institution perceived as 'only for outsiders.'"[18]

Atencio's initial suspicions about Hall's request to talk with him began to dissipate during his first interaction with the new ranch director:

> The Reverend James Hall walked into my office, tall and lanky, wearing slacks and a handsome pair of cowboy boots, a shirt open at the neck . . . and a cowboy hat in hand. [He] moved gradually but intentionally to the point of our meeting. . . . Would I present to that small group (the Board of Christian Education) on the subject of the needy and the neglected in northern New Mexico? Naturally, I jumped at it."[19]

Thus began what became a long and respectful relationship between Atencio and Hall that would involve numerous undertakings and projects. Ghost Ranch educational programs were soon giving outsiders an insider's look at local life. Atencio and additional Hispanic and Native American scholars and activists from all over New Mexico and the West led seminars on native life and culture, land and water issues.

The 1960s and early 1970s were a volatile time in northern New Mexico, especially in Rio Arriba County. Even Hall's and Ghost Ranch's sincere overtures to support and understand its neighbors through grazing programs and seminars taught by native scholars—and a sum given by the tax-exempt ranch annually to the county in lieu of, and greater than, land taxes—could not stem the tide of unrest and eventual violence that would challenge Ghost Ranch's role in northern New Mexico.

The lack of sufficient grazing land available for northern New Mexican ranchers began in the 1940s with the advent of the U.S. Forest Service's permit system. To the local cattle ranchers, who often owned only a few cows, the forest service's land-use policies seemed to favor large-scale ranchers. And because so much of the land claimed by the Forest Service had once belonged to community and individual land grants lost to the native people through fraud and legal shenanigans in the late 1800s, by the early 1960s there was a simmering sense of outrage toward Anglo property owners—and everyone and everything connected to the U.S. Forest Service.

The undercurrent of unrest became a frustration-driven activism by 1964, when a coalition of men from Rio Arriba villages began to cut fences, burn haystacks and barns, and vandalize irrigation ditches and homes of Anglo owners and even Hispanic owners who did not join in the violence and confrontation. Although the Piedra Lumbre had been a private grant (Ghost Ranch's northern third of the grant even obtained title insurance—a first in Rio Arriba County), miles of fences were cut in the Piedra Lumbre basin. Horses and cattle were shot, and cowboys out riding the range were fired upon. From Abiquiú to Coyote to Tierra Amarilla, tensions were mounting, and everyone who owned one was carrying a gun.

In October of 1966, just a half mile from Ghost Ranch's westernmost boundary, Reies Lopez Tijerina, the charismatic leader of the Alianza Federal de las Mercedes—the Federal Alliance of Land Grants (or Federal Alliance of Free City States), a Hispanic political group seeking to restore Spanish-American lands to their "rightful" owners—set up a tent village in the Echo Amphitheater campground. From their headquarters on seized national forest land, Tijerina announced to the invited press that la Alianza (also known as La Raza) was here to reclaim the San Joaquin de Rio Chama Grant—the lands west of the Piedra Lumbre Grant and Ghost Ranch. Forest Service rangers were arrested by Tijerina and the Alianza, and, after a mock trial, armed federal authorities moved into the canyon and ended the confrontation.

The armed takeover of Echo Amphitheater by the Alianza brought the unrest in northern New Mexico into the consciousness of the regional and even national press. The incident also heightened the state's focus on an investigation of Tijerina and the Alianza.

In the spring of 1967, the Alianza organized a rally of five hundred men and women at the Tierra Amarilla courthouse. Guided by Tijerina's provocative and colorful oration, they declared themselves the Pueblo Republica de San Joaquin, the Free State of Tierra Amarilla, elected a mayor and a town council, and announced their independence from the United States of America.

Local authorities managed to seize Alianza account books and membership roster and obtained a list of targeted sites for Alianza confrontation and seizure. Hall was informed that Ghost Ranch topped Tijerina's land seizure priority list. At the time, the staff at the ranch included numerous villagers from Canjilon, Abiquiú, and Coyote, all communities with Alianza followers. At staff meetings, ranch personnel spoke openly about the threats to Ghost Ranch; Hall expressed his sympathy with the Hispanic land struggles, but he also stressed that his first commitment was to protect Ghost Ranch's borders in a nonviolent manner.

In early June of 1967, the Alianza made plans to hold a village barbecue in Coyote, a community a few miles south of Ghost Ranch's borders on the Piedra Lumbre. State authorities learned of the event and the state police went in and arrested ten men for unlawful assembly before the picnic ever began. The ten were taken to the jail in Tierra Amarilla, where they awaited arraignment over the weekend. An outraged, and also publicity-seeking, Tijerina deputized twenty local farmers and ranchers and plotted a raid on the Rio Arriba courthouse, where their friends were incarcerated.

On Monday, June 5, the Alianza posse raided the Tierra Amarilla courthouse. With pistols and machine guns blazing, they freed their compadres, wounding a deputy sheriff and a state policeman before departing the premises. The Alianza raiders had hoped to arrest the district attorney, but took a sheriff's deputy and a UPI reporter hostage instead.

The men of La Raza fled into the mountains. They were pursued by two thousand lawmen—National Guardsmen, New Mexico Mounted Patrolmen, state policemen, sheriffs, even officers of the New Mexico Game and Fish Commission. The Canjilon Mountains that lift above the great Cliffs of Shining Stone were the focus of the manhunt, and Hall and the Ghost Ranch staff were told to be on high alert.

People were already on high alert: a drive to the Abiquiú post office meant passing through three police checkpoints; and from the ranch office, or from the patio of Casa del Sol, or from O'Keeffe's Rancho de los Burros, convoys of M-42 tanks and jeeps with mounted machine guns could be seen and heard as they rumbled across the Piedra Lumbre basin headed for the war zone to the north. Because Yeso Canyon offered at least one passable route down from the mountains for someone fleeing on foot or on horseback, a truckload of armed National Guardsmen were headquartered at Ghost Ranch. For added security the ranch's road grader was parked across the ranch entrance each night.

National television networks sent correspondents to cover the New Mexican manhunt. "It was very tense," John Dancy, NBC's reporter out of Los Angeles remembered. "There was a big search, with posses made up of men who looked like they had been taken right out of an Old West movie—guys in ten gallon hats, on horses, wearing six shooters. The courthouse raid was a very big story—NBC was there, and CBS . . . everyone."

Tijerina and his men were not found in the mountains. A week later, however, Tijerina was arrested near Albuquerque. He was sent to prison for a short time and then cleared of all charges.

Two years passed. The annual General Assembly of the United Presbyterian Church was held in San Antonio in the spring of 1969. The Hispanic coalition of the Presbyterian Church had asked for time to present key issues of their people to the national assembly. Jim Hall was in attendance and knew that La Raza would be making a statement.

To the chagrin of the Hispanic leadership at the assembly, a group of militant black activists led by James Forman chose that very week to occupy the headquarters of the Interchurch Center in New York City. Because the Presbyterians—along with the United Methodists, the United Church of Christ, and other Protestant denominations, plus the World Council of Churches—had their national headquarters in this building on Riverside Drive, all attention at the San Antonio assembly turned to the demands of the black coalition occupying their empty offices.

The Hispanic cause was completely upstaged. While most of the Presbyterian Church in San Antonio was talking about James Forman in New York, a small committee sought to appease the escalating anger of the Hispanic faction. Someone in the council meeting suggested that the way to make amends with the Hispanic Presbyterians was to give "them" Ghost Ranch.

Jim Hall was in the committee room when this suggestion was made. Unclear as to who "them" might be, but completely clear that Ghost Ranch was not going to be given away to anyone, Hall steered the committee to a more reasonable resolution. He suggested that the Presbyterians set aside funds in the amount of fifty thousand dollars to be used by Ghost Ranch to implement programs that would benefit the people and land in northern New Mexico.

Hall emerged from the committee room and learned that Albuquerque television stations had announced that Ghost Ranch was going to be given to Tijerina's La Raza. When he returned to New Mexico, Hall spent days "putting out fires"—explaining to friends and colleagues that Ghost Ranch was not being given to anyone. Most people understood that the misunderstanding was the result of misinformation. Most people, that is, except Reies Lopez Tijerina.

Ghost Ranch began to hear through friends in the local villages that Tijerina and his Alianza were planning their occupation of Ghost Ranch. In early June, at a barbeque in Coyote, the same village where ten Alianza members were arrested two years before, Tijerina announced that the seizure of Ghost Ranch would happen the following Sunday. Villagers were told to bring their chickens and pigs, dogs, cows, and children to occupy the ranch.

Hall received phone calls from several inside sources warning him of the impending siege: "The sources that I had were responsible. What were we going to do? Here was the Alianza, who at that time, put the fear of God into folks, a lot of folks, and they were going to move on Ghost Ranch."[20]

Hall contacted the state police and asked that they be standing by, but out of sight, on the upcoming Sunday. He also contacted a district attorney and judge in Española to obtain a court order to evict Tijerina if the visit became violent. And then Hall sat down and wrote out a position statement for his would-be occupiers that stated Ghost Ranch was interested in justice for all, had money to allocate for community betterment programs, and that the place was not up for grabs.

The staff at Ghost Ranch were told that they were welcome to attend Sunday's event, but that Hall understood if instead they chose, for personal or political reasons, to stay home.

Sunday, June 1, 1969: Hall and the ranch staff—all of the Ghost Ranch staff, men, women, and children, including Hispanic members of the local communities—dressed in their Sunday best, waited for their guests on the headquarters porch. There were tables set with coffee, punch, and cookies. Father Robert Kirsch of the Abiquiú parish heard from his parishioners of the upcoming confrontation and telephoned Hall and offered his support. Unbeknownst to Hall, Father Bob asked the folks at his morning masses in three separate villages to join him at Ghost Ranch that afternoon to support Hall and the Presbyterians: "I had masses that morning in Coyote, Youngsville and Gallina, and I told my people that we were going to have a special reception at Ghost Ranch and I wanted everybody to come and show their appreciation . . . because everybody loved Jim and Ruth. Jim Hall had reached out to everybody. Jim really had a *vision*."

Father Bob's thirty-car caravan of parishioners joined Tijerina's Alianza caravan on the highway several miles from the ranch and were assumed to be sympathetic to La Raza. Although Father Bob had openly criticized Tijerina's use of violent methods to address political inequities in northern New Mexico, the Irish priest and the Chicano activist had been friendly for years, and Tijerina was glad to see the priest. Father Bob recalled, "I was driving a little Volkswagen and I pulled up to Reyes and he said, '*Bueno* buddy! Why don't you lead us on to the ranch?' I said, 'Ah, *mejor que no* . . . it'd be better if I went up to the ranch and got them ready to receive you.'"

Father Bob and several of his followers arrived a few minutes ahead of Tijerina at Ghost Ranch, where they joined a second priest from Chama and the entire ranch staff on the headquarters portal. Everyone held copies of Hall's statement written in both English and Spanish. The group watched in silence and with no small amount of apprehension as a single line of what became more than one hundred pickup trucks and cars crested the hill and headed down the road to ranch headquarters. Thankfully, the pigs, chickens, and cows had been left in their home corrals.

Young Jon Hall stood with his father and mother. "We watched as the cars started coming over the hill, bumper to bumper, and parking in front of the office, and still coming over the far hill," he recalled. "It seemed like hundreds of cars were coming in. Tijerina was one of the first to get out with several people on either side of him. He came up

La Raza "march" on Ghost Ranch in June 1969. Reies Lopez Tijerina is at left, and Jim Hall is at right.

the steps. Dad went and met him and brought him up. Tijerina was surprised by the warm greeting."

Tijerina told Hall that he wanted to give some speeches and then talk alone with Hall. Hall said the speechifying would be fine, but there would be no private meeting. Whatever was to be said between them would be said in public. Tijerina and his lieutenants spoke a moment amongst themselves and then agreed to Hall's terms.

The priests handed everyone a copy of Hall's statement and then ushered the visitors into Convocation Hall. The large room was quickly packed to capacity, and an equal number of people stood outside, looking in through the windows and doors. Hall began, with Floyd Trujillo, Jim Shibley's ranchlands assistant from Abiquiú, translating. Hall restated and enlarged upon what he had said in his written statement, and then turned the podium over to Tijerina.

The audiotapes of this historic meeting in Convocation Hall were lost in a fire, but everyone remembers that Tijerina was spectacular. Trained as a Pentecostal minister, Tijerina, nicknamed *el Tigre*, the Tiger, was a great orator and a "stem-winder" in both Spanish and English. Tijerina spoke with eloquence about his people, about justice, about *la tierra*. He accused the Presbyterians of neglecting the local communities and of not caring about the plight of the poor in northern New Mexico. Finally, Tijerina demanded that Ghost Ranch be "returned" to his people.

"We received a good deal of hard language that day," Hall recalled later of Tijerina's speech.

Father Bob asked to speak after Tijerina sat down. The redheaded priest was an animated and emotional speaker and was fluent in Spanish. He piloted his own airplane into the rural corners of Rio Arriba, and he was well known and much respected among the mostly Hispanic Catholic community in northern New Mexico.

Father Bob took the podium and in Spanish and English gave a long and detailed speech about the Presbyterian Church in New Mexico.

> I told the people what the church had done by way of education, medical care, and so on. I kept saying "church" and every once in a while, I'd say "Presbyterian" so the people would understand that we all have a Church and the Church is the body of Christ, and our brothers and sisters at Ghost Ranch are of the Presbyterian tradition. I didn't have to sell them anything that day. They knew: the Spanish folks who worked on the ranch were treated with great love and care, with no condescension like at so many big ranches. At Ghost Ranch, everyone was treated with dignity. And Jim Hall was strong on that. And they knew this.

Hall was stunned by Father Bob's words to the crowd in Convocation Hall.

> [Father Bob] made a better speech than we could have made about ourselves. He pointed out that the Presbyterian Church had schools and hospitals up and down the Rio Grande Valley. . . . He said wherever Presbyterians had been, there were schools and hospitals. He said, "they do care about the poor and they do seek justice." . . . He said that Roman Catholic Churches were a lot bigger than the Presbyterian Churches, but they hadn't done what the Presbyterians had done in this area. Oh, man, that was a good speech from a Roman Catholic priest![21]

The meeting wound down. There was no citizen's arrest of the Reverend Hall, which had been at the top of Tijerina's agenda, and no one attempted to set up camp at Yeso Canyon. Coffee and cookies were served and accepted, and, after another half hour of conversation, the Alianza visitors returned to their cars and pickup trucks and drove off the ranch and home to their villages.

This June meeting with La Raza Unida, and the events that transpired at the General Assembly in San Antonio, served as a wake-up call for Hall and Ghost Ranch. Although the ranch had already embarked on several community programs such as the feedlot cooperative, Hall now placed community development at the top of his priorities. New staff positions were formed and local people, funded by the Presbyterians (sometimes in partnership with the Roman Catholics, and with the federal and state government), worked in and with the villages offering tax preparation assistance and community craft development classes. Ghost Ranch gave monies and lent expertise to the birth of the community economic initiative that became Tierra Wools in the village of Los Ojos. With Los Alamos National Labs, and state and federal funds, the ranch sponsored a multiyear passive solar adobe demonstration project, called the Sundwellings, which gave on-site training with pay to local men and women in the design and construction of passive solar housing. A High Desert Research Farm was implemented on the ranch, which, among other things, pursued the establishment of a native seed bank. And a Trailer Retrofit Project assisted local families seeking to make their trailer homes energy efficient—warmer in the winters and cooler in the summers.[22]

Following a fire that destroyed La Clinica, the only medical facility in Tierra Amarilla, Presbyterian money was offered to buy the clinic's mortgage from the local bank, which was distrustful of the "radical activists" managing the facility. With a no-interest loan from the Presbyterians, and an eventual insurance settlement, La Clinica was rebuilt and reopened.

Hall and the ranch's activism impressed even the local activists. Tomás Atencio wrote, "Ghost Ranch had gotten into the thick of it at the height of the Chicano Movement and did something great and unbelievable."[23]

The most dramatic and ultimately important contribution Ghost

Ranch made to northern New Mexico was to become known as the Great Land Trade. This historic land exchange took five years to complete and cleared more than one hundred private land titles disputed by the U.S. Forest Service. The land trade was orchestrated by Hall, but the foundation that enabled the complicated title and deed exchange to happen at all was laid by Arthur Pack.

After moving to Tucson in the late 1940s, Pack became as involved with that community's civic life and natural landscape as he had with the Piedra Lumbre and Rio Arriba County's. The people of Tucson had yet to take an active role in civic appreciation and protection of their surrounding desert environment. With the arrival of Pack and his friend, William Carr, this apathy about the natural world surrounding Tucson was going to undergo a dramatic change.

William Carr was a naturalist and conservationist who had come to Arizona in the 1940s to regain his health. Once an associate curator at the American Museum of Natural History, Carr's pioneering design of the Bear Mountain State Park Trailside Museum on the Hudson River in New York had brought him national recognition among conservation organizations. Pack and Carr had not seen each other in years and met by complete chance in Carr's secondhand bookshop in Tucson in 1950. They rekindled their friendship, which was based on their common belief that people in the modern world needed to be encouraged to interact with and understand the natural world around them.

Carr told Pack that he wanted to create a desert-side educational museum outside of Tucson. Carr had the skill and the experience to design a successful facility but needed financing and civic support to go forward. Pack liked everything about Carr's idea and soon secured the funding from the Charles Lathrop Pack Foundation. Pack also used his connections to gather community and political backing, and by 1952 Carr's idea of a Sonoran Desert outdoor museum became a reality.

The Arizona-Sonora Desert Museum opened on Labor Day to more than one thousand people who drove the fourteen miles from Tucson to the dusty, saguaro-studded site. In its first year, 200,000 visitors wandered the museum's outdoor trails and indoor exhibits. The Arizona-Sonoran Desert Museum was soon nationally recognized for its imaginative animal and nature exhibits, and for its ambitious and cutting-edge conservation education programs. Carr was the first di-

Moving the *Coelophysis* block from the quarry to the location of the Ruth Hall Museum of Paleontology in 1985.

rector, although poor health and exhaustion forced him to hand this position over to zoologist Bill Woodin within the year. Arthur Pack served as the first board president and was also named Tucson's first Man of the Year for his unwavering personal and financial commitment to the museum's evolution from dream into reality.

By the late 1950s, both Pack and Carr wanted to replicate what they had done on the edge of the Sonoran Desert on a much smaller scale on the Piedra Lumbre. With funding again from the Charles Lathrop Pack Foundation, and with Will Harris as architect, Carr and Pack created the Ghost Ranch Museum, an interactive, hands-on outdoor museum on a mesa across the badlands from the Cliffs of Shining Stone. Like its grander counterpart, the Ghost Ranch Museum had trails with displays that explained the local flora and fauna and an outdoor zoo of indigenous animals, including a large prairie dog village. The Ghost Ranch Museum was the first in the region to exhibit one of the original blocks of *Coelophysis* skeletons, excavated by Colbert in 1947. The museum charged no admission fee—Pack wanted local neighbors and schoolchildren to feel welcome.[24]

The operation of the new outdoor museum was overseen by Ghost Ranch Museum, Inc., a non-profit corporation controlled by a board of directors, which Pack served as president, with government grants and a private trust funding its annual budget. Pack's personal fortune, combined with funds from his father's forestry foundation, carried the museum through its first decade. In 1970, to better ensure its future, the board of directors agreed that the museum would run more efficiently and receive more and better funding if it belonged in its entirety to the Forest Service. The Forest Service was delighted to accept ownership of the highly successful trailside facility on the Piedra Lumbre. However, since the buildings and land belonged to the Presbyterians, the consent of the Church was needed before this transfer of ownership could transpire.

This proposed gift to the U.S. Forest Service coincided with Hall's and Ghost Ranch's efforts to alleviate regional tensions concerning land ownership past and present. The Ghost Ranch Museum, and its proven value to federal land personnel and their projects, gave Hall and the Presbyterians, as advocates for their frustrated neighbors seeking to reclaim disputed family lands held within national forest boundaries, something of value to take to the land title negotiation table with the Forest Service—clout.

Thinking that Hall wanted to ask for clear title for a piece of Ghost Ranch's campground that was mistakenly on Carson National Forest, USFS officials came to Hall's office to arrange the deal. Hall surprised them with a completely different proposal. Hall recalled that meeting.

> I understood that there were in the Santa Fe and Carson Forest approximately 125 problem tracts of land—owned legally by the Forest but historically claimed by residents of the area. . . . I said [to the Forest Service], You men know that even if you had ten "land men" working on those problems, some of them would not be resolved in your lifetime. Why don't you put together all of those claims possible against the appraised value of the museum land and buildings, and the land which we will give you in order to include the tract within the boundaries of the Carson Forest . . . and then we will give you the land and buildings, you give us

title to the disputed tracts, and we in turn will give them to the people.[25]

To Hall's relief and delight, the supervisor of the Carson Forest "bought into the dream," and thus began five years of meetings, miles of red tape, and an act of Congress. Guided by a panel made up of representatives from the Forest Service and the communities involved, with advisors and liaisons like Hall's friend Tomás Atencio, and with the nearly gratis services of sympathetic attorneys and patient surveyors, the dream became a reality on April 6, 1975. On that day at Ghost Ranch, the Ghost Ranch Museum was officially given to the U.S. Forest Service and 111 families received clear title to their homes and land. Clear title was also passed from the Forest Service through Ghost Ranch to half the village of Cañones, beneath Cerro Pedernal; a Roman Catholic church in Vallecitos; two penitent *Moradas* (meeting houses); and one *campo santo* (cemetery).

Nothing like this land trade had happened before nor has it happened since. Hall considered it Ghost Ranch's, and his own, greatest accomplishment: "In more than a hundred years of bitter history this remains as the only significant major effort to resolve problems of land ownership in Northern New Mexico. . . . In all Ghost Ranch's history of service and ministry, the Land Exchange still stands as a major accomplishment and contribution to the stability and security of life for our neighbors."[26]

One friend, John Purdy, later remarked to Hall that "it was a time when charity kissed justice."[27]

Reies Lopez Tijerina, out on parole and forbidden to engage in activist gatherings, returned to Ghost Ranch in 1972 to speak before a national conference of Chicano law students. Hall and Tijerina had become better acquainted since June of 1969, and the Alianza had used Ghost Ranch as a neutral ground upon which to meet in secrecy with state politicians, including the governor. Hall listened to Tijerina's speech to the young law students: "His speech to them was quite a different speech than the one [at Ghost Ranch] before. He made quite a good speech . . . saying, 'You can retain pride but you don't have to be filled with hatred in order to do it. You can have harmony even without unity, but let us seek unity.'"[28]

Throughout his tenure at Ghost Ranch, Hall remained active with

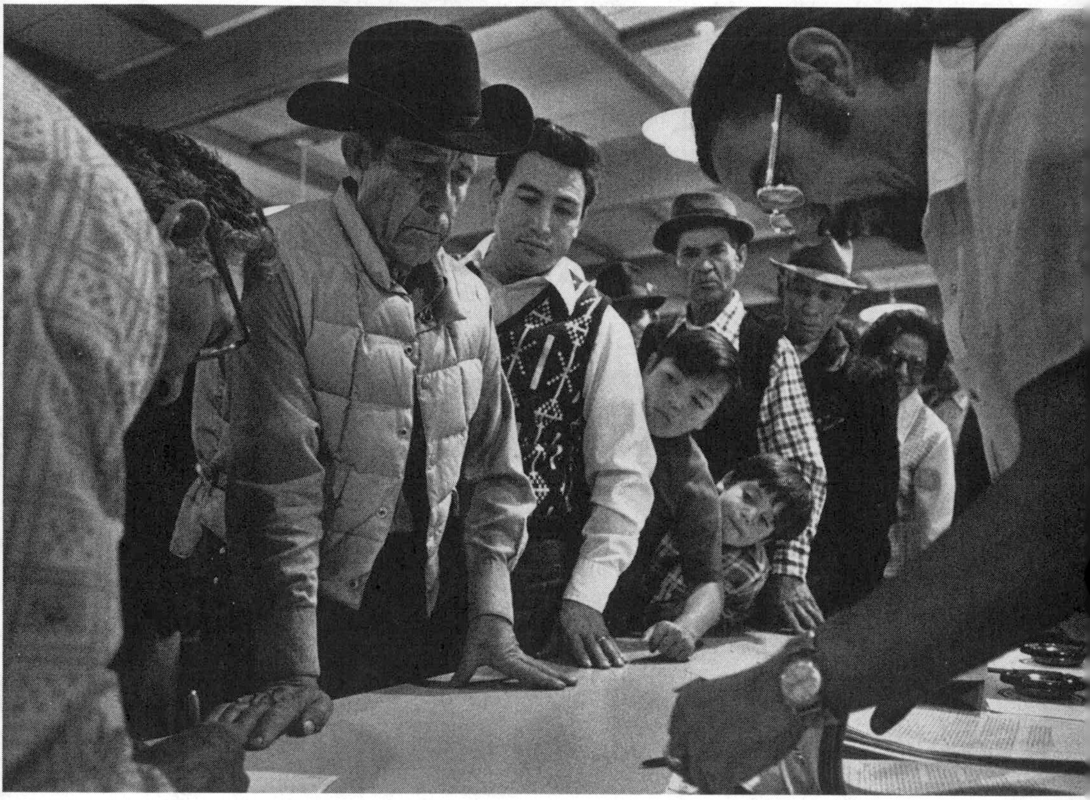

The Great Land Trade at Ghost Ranch in April 1976.

the board of Presbyterian Hospital, on which he had served since 1951. Hall became board chairman in 1971 and, for the next decade, never missed a meeting, although it involved a 250-mile round trip to Albuquerque. Under Hall's directorship, Presbyterian Hospital, later renamed Presbyterian Medical Services (PMS), grew from one Albuquerque-based hospital to a multihospital, statewide healthcare system with a $10 million foundation behind it. Hall's board championed small, locally operated medical facilities, and the eleven hospitals under PMS's umbrella (including Pack's Española Hospital) were directed by a board made up of the Hispanic, Native American, and Anglo people they served.

During the more than twenty-five years that Hall served as director of Ghost Ranch, the national Presbyterian Church was, for the most part, satisfied to let Hall hold the reins and steer the mission and educational programs at the ranch. But there were differences of opinion, and many questioned Hall's emphasis on what were seen as nonchurch programs and issues. And the ranch *was* owned by the national Church. Hall and his staff, and his many friends and advisors, many of whom formed the Chimney Rock Foundation (later the Ghost Ranch Foundation) to support Ghost Ranch financially in lean years, learned to straddle two worlds: that of a national educational organization with a high profile, and that of a patrón intimately linked with and responsible to a local, economically challenged rural community.

When asked exactly what theology was embraced and taught at Ghost Ranch, Hall responded, "Theology? Theology is what you *do*."[29]

Hall's theology of doing managed to undo the hard feelings and soften the stony silence between the Presbyterians and their famous neighbor, Georgia O'Keeffe. Hall did not make a point of making friends with Miss O'Keeffe. Jim Hall and his wife, Ruth, were simply good neighbors to their closest and only neighbor on the badlands under the cliffs. They respected her boundaries and made sure everyone who went out to that part of Ghost Ranch did the same.

O'Keeffe and Hall met for the first time out under the wide sky and hot sun of the landscape they both loved. She was on foot and he was on horseback when their trails across the Piedra Lumbre badlands crossed. Hall remembered, "We first actually met when one day I was coming up across the pasture horseback. She was walking back from the highway mailbox with a long, lithe, easy stride. I could see that if we held course our paths would cross. When they did, I said, 'Miss O'Keeffe, you walk like a 14 year old Indian girl.' She said, 'You must be Mr. Hall. I like your horse.'"[30]

O'Keeffe remembered her first meeting with Hall and his horse, Leather Britches. "One day, I was looking for a place in the shade to paint the cliffs—I turned—and saw Mr. Hall on horseback right behind me—I suppose we spoke—I don't remember. In time we became acquainted and he did many things to make my living there easier."[31]

Previous to O'Keeffe's desert meeting with Hall she had received a Christmas present of a burnished pueblo pot from his youngest son, Jon. It was 1961—the Hall family's first Christmas at Ghost Ranch—and Jon was ten at the time. He knew O'Keeffe was not very approachable: "I'd seen enough Shirley Temple movies about befriending the hermit, so I bought the little pot and sent it to O'Keeffe in the mail."

Young Jon did not hear anything from O'Keeffe about the gift until a month later. Jon was at the one-room Abiquiú post office with his mother when O'Keeffe pulled up in her pink Lincoln. "O'Keeffe asked my mom if I was the little boy who sent the pot? Then she invited me to come for lunch the next Saturday. So the following Saturday, mom dropped me at the gate of her house in Abiquiú. O'Keeffe had made some kind of weed soup, something green, and I worked my way through it halfhearted. She noticed and said, 'I bet a young boy doesn't like seaweed soup.' So we worked that out, and had lunch a couple more times."

O'Keeffe learned it was better to serve a ten-year-old boy a sandwich, and, after a few more visits, Jon Hall learned how to deal with O'Keeffe's unfriendly chow dogs. "Her dogs liked to bite. She was perfectly pleased when someone was bitten by them. When we would walk in the garden, she would coach me to not act afraid of them. They would come up and nuzzle my leg with their teeth. O'Keeffe would say 'don't act afraid!' I *was* afraid."

Young Jon's luncheons with O'Keeffe and her nippy chows broke the ice between the Hall family and O'Keeffe. By the late 1960s, O'Keeffe was routinely invited to share Christmas dinner with the Hall family at Casa del Sol. She usually accepted, and came with flowers and champagne and, one year, a stone pipe for Hall that he treasured for the rest of his life. "Georgia sat on a stool in the kitchen offering advice

Jim Hall on his horse Leather Britches at Ghost Ranch, c. 1979.

and help, picking up turkey carving fragments, easy and at home," Hall later wrote of one Christmas day. "She gave me a pipe, ordered from a Boston firm famed for outfitting expeditions. Luckily it has survived fire and theft and I still have it."[32]

O'Keeffe reminisced with the Halls about the early years at Ghost Ranch, about the Bennett family (she stayed in touch with Ted Bennett Jr.), and shared her memories of days past at the adobe house under the Puerto del Cielo. With a twinkle in her eye, O'Keeffe reminded the Halls of the adobe stairway that once led from the patio to the house roof, and of her unsanctioned visits to that roof when the Bennetts were not home. O'Keeffe's love of a night spent under the stars reminded Hall of his father, Ralph Hall. "O'Keeffe often mentioned spending the night there on the roof to take in the vastness of the sky, enjoying, as my father did, sleeping out in the 'Big Hotel.'"[33]

Hall came to know O'Keeffe as a good neighbor and generous friend. During the 1970s, when O'Keeffe's paintings were featured on the annual posters for the Santa Fe Chamber Music Festival, O'Keeffe arranged for the chamber orchestra to give a free, open-air concert for ranch guests each summer in the orchard. O'Keeffe herself attended the evening and listened from her chair under the apple trees near the old Garden House where she had begun her love affair with Ghost Ranch forty years before.

In 1971, O'Keeffe suggested to Hall that the ranch place the skull motif drawing given to Pack in the 1930s on the cover of the summer program brochure. Hall did, and that same year, with O'Keeffe's blessing, Hall declared the simple skull motif the official symbol of Ghost Ranch.

Once the bane of O'Keeffe's existence and the target of her belittlement and wrath, the United Presbyterian Church began to receive annual donations from O'Keeffe—often sizable sums—earmarked for Ghost Ranch operations. In 1983, when a fire completely destroyed the ranch headquarters, built in the 1930s by Stanley, O'Keeffe telephoned Hall and offered fifty thousand dollars and the use of her name in a fundraising campaign to rebuild the destroyed building.

In the early 1970s, the Halls asked O'Keeffe if they could buy the Burros House if and when she ever sold it. O'Keeffe suggested she leave a provision in her will offering the house to the Presbyterian Church for use by the Halls, as she would be glad to know who would

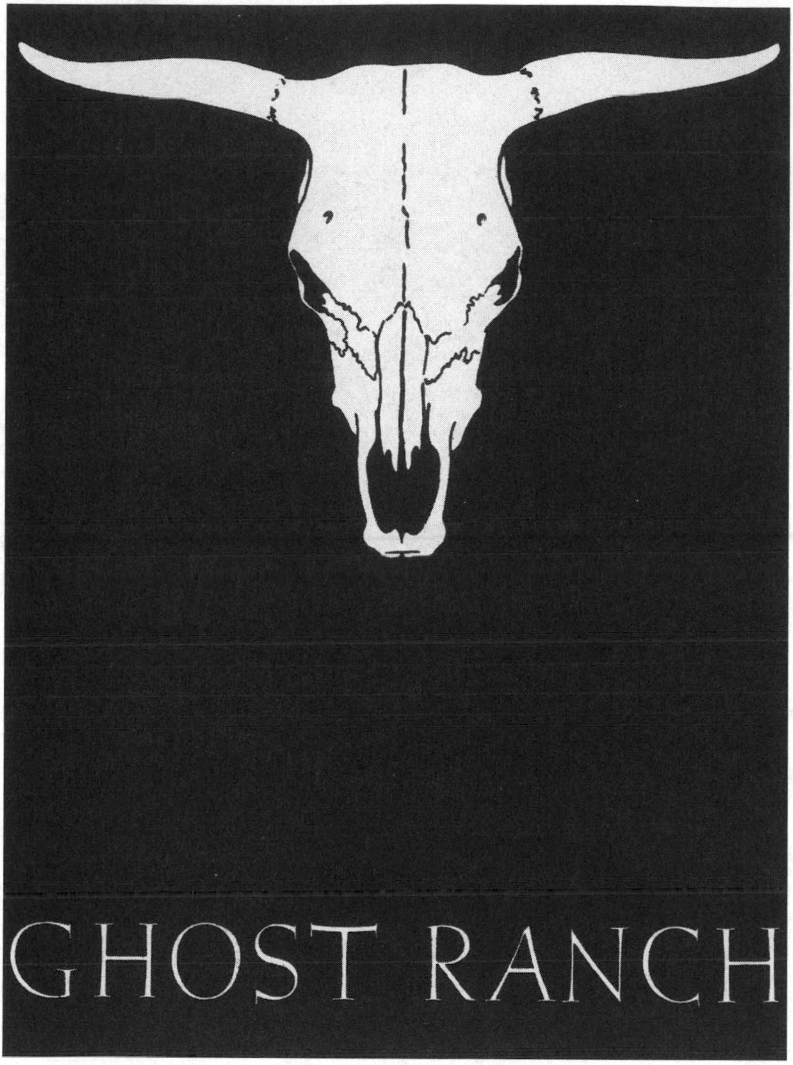

The cover of a 1936 Ghost Ranch brochure that incorporates the O'Keeffe skull drawing given to Arthur Pack.

A cattle roundup at Ghost Ranch in the winter of 2004.

live in the house after her. However, the eighty-four-year-old O'Keeffe reminded Jim and Ruth Hall that she planned to live to be one hundred, and that they could expect a long wait for the house. Several years later, O'Keeffe decided to give the house to her friend and manager, Juan Hamilton. But she did not forget her arrangement with the Halls; O'Keeffe donated the funds with which to build a new residence under the cliffs that was the designated home for her friends Jim and Ruth Hall for as long as they lived.

Afterword

Georgia O'Keeffe did not live to be one hundred but died at the age of ninety-eight in early March of 1986. Thc following fall, after twenty-five years, Jim Hall retired as director of Ghost Ranch. The house constructed for Jim and Ruth Hall with funds donated by O'Keeffe was ready for occupancy by 1986, but only Jim moved into the new adobe in the badlands under the cliffs. Ruth Hall's life at Ghost Ranch was prematurely ended by Alzheimer's disease, and by the mid-1980s she had moved into a convalescent center in Albuquerque.

Arthur and Phoebe Pack continued to return to the ranch until the late 1960s. Arthur died in 1975, and Phoebe's journeys home to the Piedra Lumbre ceased because the thin high-altitude air began to give her heart difficulties. Until her death, Phoebe continued to correspond with O'Keeffe, who in the last years wrote postcards asking—actually, demanding—that Phoebe come and see her when and if she returned to the ranch. The Packs' friendship with O'Keeffe outlasted the arguments and misunderstandings, and the last years of their lives brought a fondness between them.

After Arthur's death, O'Keeffe sat one afternoon in the living room of the Packs' former house behind the ranch headquarters. She was visiting with Jim Hall's assistant, Joan Boliek, who lived with her family in the residence now called Casa Loma. O'Keeffe sipped lemonade and looked out at the familiar landscape of red hills and mesas falling away to the far horizon. A pine tree, planted in the thirties, now stood as tall as the house and edged the east side of the scene framed by the windows of the former supper porch that had once served captains of industry, Hollywood royalty, dinosaur diggers, and atom splitters. The view from this room of windows is broad and spectacular—cottonwood trees mark the course of el Rito del Yeso through the sand hills beneath the red cliffs, and Pedernal marks the line between the earth and the sky—but that afternoon, O'Keeffe's aged but discerning eyes locked onto that towering nonnative spruce tree near the house. "Why, that doesn't belong there!" O'Keeffe said to Boliek. After a thoughtful pause, a gleam came into O'Keeffe's eyes. "Arthur did that, didn't he?"

Arthur did that, and a good deal more. His sweeping and singular gift of this place to the Presbyterians gave Ghost Ranch and its Intimate Immensity to thousands of people. In the fifty years since Pack's bequest, Ghost Ranch has become the destination for several generations of modern desert pilgrims who call the ranch the Magic Place —a pretentious pseudonym until one has come to Ghost Ranch and stumbled upon and perhaps been enveloped within the tangible, wondrous magic that lives here.

Jim Hall died of a heart attack in November of 1988. Hall was in his home under the cliffs that morning, and I like to believe that he died with his boots on, like all great cowboys and desert theologians. He had become, albeit reluctantly, a legend in his own time. And like all legends, when Hall retired as director of Ghost Ranch, his successors found it nigh impossible to fill his boots. Hall's directorial reach and grasp exceeded the bounds of any singular, certainly reasonable, job description, and so his "duties" at Ghost Ranch were divided up and reassigned to numerous positions in several departments.

Even distributed over an enlarged staff, overseeing the place of Ghost Ranch often proves baffling, if not overwhelming, to those who are its stewards. Ghost Ranch is a big place, physically and psychologically. More than ten thousand people visit the ranch annually, and for a large proportion of these visitors Ghost Ranch holds a rare and sacred position in their life story. For its staff, serving Ghost Ranch means serving the community of people who claim this place as their emotional and spiritual home.

Over the years names and faces change, but the landscape and people's experience of the land does not. Ghost Ranch is still and all a space occupied by a biblical emptiness. Ghost Ranch's programs will continue to evolve and respond to the society of humans and their temporal needs and issues, theological and otherwise. But the deep wild heart of Ghost Ranch is the main attraction and, like all Great Places, is valued because by its very nature the land exists beyond the arena of human society.

There are still plenty of ghost stories told around campfires under the cliffs near Yeso Canyon, and several times a year Ghost Ranch guests report sightings and soundings of what can only be described as spirits, apparitions, ghosts. Few visitors are afraid of the ghosts of Ghost Ranch, and many come hoping they will encounter one or two. O'Keeffe's spirit is the most popular, but, just as she was in life, O'Keeffe's is an elusive spirit in her afterlife.

With the departure of O'Keeffe, the Packs, and the Halls, the era that would become known as the Early Years came to an end, and a new era began. This new time will define itself with its own people and their stories. These people and their time here are the inheritors of the creation stories of Ghost Ranch, because they, we, are connected to and enlarged by the community that was birthed in the past and that continues to live alongside and underneath the present community as *presence*. And if the stories of the long-ago days teach us anything, it is to enjoy our moments upon this marvelous landscape, to tread lightly, responsibly, and carefully across this magic place and leave an unobtrusive but well-lit path for others to follow. Reflecting on his own time at Ghost Ranch, Jim Hall said, "How does one value a moment—or a year, or twenty-five years? It depends on the moment doesn't it—the content, the situation, the result. Some moments I've known spread a glow over all the years. The land trade alone validates twenty-five years of the ranch's efforts, and the changed-life stories from other happenings tug at our hearts, but better yet, send a gleam down the way of the years to come."[1]

Appendix

On the movie set of *And Now Miguel* in 1965.

The chapel built at Ghost Ranch for the *And Now Miguel* movie set. This location is now under the water of the Abiquiú Reservoir.

A cabin on the *City Slickers* movie set at Ghost Ranch. Pedernal Mountain is on the horizon.

A production scene from *The Missing*, shot at Ghost Ranch in 2003.

A production scene from *Wyatt Earp*, shot at Ghost Ranch in 1993.

Notes

Introduction

1. Sharon Butala, *The Perfection of the Morning*, 113.
2. O'Keeffe, quoted in Seiberling, "Stark Vision."
3. Stegner, *Where the Bluebird Sings*, 165.
4. Sibley, *High Country News*, March 18, 2002, 8.
5. Sheila Tryk, 25th Anniversary booklet, GRA.

CHAPTER 1. The Road to Ghost Ranch

1. Rinehart, *My Story*, 310.

2. All Tewa place-names from Harrington, *Ethnogeography of the Tewa Indians*, 119.

3. Jaramillo, *Shadows of the Past*, 110–11.

4. Curtis often traveled with her brother George, a writer, and with her patroness, Charlotte Osgood Mason. Mason devoted her life and substantial fortune to the enabling of gifted and creative young artists and writers. Mason's money and influence were pivotal to the Harlem Renaissance, and her hands-on and sometimes artistically controlling patronage of African American writers Zora Neale Hurston, Langston Hughes, Alain Locke, and Miguel Covarrubias, among others, is often the subject of criticism and controversy.

5. The physical and logistical difficulties Curtis faced while traveling and working in the inaccessible and largely unmapped territory of the Hopi Mesas in the early 1900s were enormous. But no less daunting were the political and social obstacles. Federal mandates ordered that all Native tribes adopt the English language and "live" like Anglo Americans. Curtis's work among the Native peoples was in direct defiance of the Assimilationist Act. In 1906, Curtis took her recordings of Native singers from Hopiland to the White House, where she insisted family friend President Theodore Roosevelt listen to them. Roosevelt was impressed by Curtis's recordings, and also by her lively, informed, and highly impassioned plea for the preservation and protection of Native art and culture. When Curtis departed Washington, she carried

a personal letter from the president that stated she was to proceed with her work among the Native Americans without interference from local authorities. Roosevelt did lift the ban on Native language and became an avid student of Indian life and culture. He visited Curtis's camp on the desert in Hopiland in 1913. Curtis's recordings of Native singers, as well as her prolific writings about the world of the American Indian published in magazines, contributed to the adoption of federal public policies that honored and protected Native American life and custom.

6. Wheelwright, "Journey towards Understanding," 13–14.

7. Ibid. The incident Wheelwright referred to concerned Hatch Polk, a Ute who had come to Louisa Wetherill for advice after an incident on the reservation. Although Wetherill told him to go directly to the authorities to clear up the matter, he went into hiding. Wetherill was later asked by U.S. Indian Service commissioner Cato Sells to convince the accused Ute, who was the son of Chief Polk, to give himself up for trial. The boy finally surrendered, was tried for murder, and found not guilty in April 1915.

8. Roy Chapin to Henry B. Joy, David Gray, Paul Gray, Lumen W. Goodenough, July 1916. This and all subsequently quoted letters between Chapin and Pfaffle, and Chapin and Curtis, from the Roy D. Chapin Collection, Michigan Historical Collections, Bentley Historical Library, University of Michigan. Copied by Peggy Pond Church, LAHM/PPC.

9. *Santa Fe New Mexican*, October 5, 1916.

10. Caroline Pfaffle to Mr. and Mrs. Roy Chapin, August 7, 1916, LAHM/PPC.

11. Ibid.

12. Jack Lambert to Peggy Pond Church, January 3, 1980, LAHM/PPC.

13. Wheelwright, "Journey towards Understanding," 42–43.

14. Caroline Pfaffle to Roy Chapin, December 13, 1917, LAHM/PPC.

15. Pfaffle to Chapin, February 26, 1918, LAHM/PPC.

16. Pfaffle to Chapin, March 6, 1918, LAHM/PPC.

17. Jim Thorpe to author, Feb. 20, 1991.

18. Cox, "Dude Ranches: New Mexico and Arizona."

19. Pfaffle, "Call of the Southwest."

20. Quoted in Love, "A Cowboy Recollects," 7.

21. Lewis, *Willa Cather Living*, 141–42.

22. Quoted in Love, "A Cowboy Recollects," 7.

23. Notebook of Carol Bishop Stanley.

24. Pfaffle to Eldridge L. Adams, December 13, 1921; collection of Al Bredenburg.

25. Pfaffle to Adams, December 16, 1921; letter copied by Augusta Curtis; collection of Al Bredenberg.

26. Wheelwright, "Journey towards Understanding," 8.

27. Ibid., 18.

28. The recorded deed trail is convoluted and contradictory and sheds little light onto the shadowy poker game: the warranty deed from Miguel A. Gonzales to Alfredo Salazar, Toribio Salazar and wife, Emilia S. Salazar, is dated March 5, 1928. The deed sat unrecorded in the Salazar home for almost another year and was filed in Tierra Amarilla in February 1929. Why did the Salazars wait so long? It was a long, hard ride by horseback or wagon to the Rio Arriba county seat. It was not unusual for New Mexicans to delay filing until there was legal reason to necessitate the arduous journey. Such a reason—perhaps a poker game—may have prompted the Salazars' 1929 appearance before the T. A. county clerk; they may have been filing a deed to land they no longer owned. A quick three months later, the newly filed deed to HES 127 was signed over to and recorded by Caroline S. Pfaffle. This would suggest that the fateful poker game happened in the spring of 1929. But Caroline Stanley's meticulously detailed account book states that the place called Ghost Ranch—valued at six thousand dollars—was *acquired* in 1928.

29. Quoted in Love, "A Cowboy Recollects," 7. Lambert met the wealthy White sisters that winter and was soon employed to help manage and build their new Santa Fe property, *El Delirio*. Lambert remained with the White sisters, whose compound eventually became the School of American Research, until he retired.

30. Information about the summer of 1931 from correspondence between Francis Wilson, Esq., and Mary Cabot Wheelwright, NMSRA.

CHAPTER 2. The Experience of Simplicity

1. Kittredge, *Who Owns the West?* 35.

2. Seals, "Joy Filled Reflections."

3. The Night Riders were a notorious ring of sheep, cattle, and horse rustlers who terrorized Rio Arriba County in the late 1920s and early 1930s. They were led by Ghost Ranch cowboy Jack McKinley's older brother, Bill. The gang of some fifteen Hispanic bandits led by the "big Anglo" McKinley were finally caught and sent to prison for the robbery of thousands of dollars' worth of Indian blankets and jewelry taken from the Los Luceros home of Mary Wheelwright. Seals, "Joy Filled Reflections."

4. Pack, *We Called It Ghost Ranch*, 31.

5. This quotation, and all subsequently uncited quotations, is from a conversation between the author and the named speaker during interviews for the Ghost Ranch History Project. Transcripts from these interviews are held at the Ghost Ranch Archive (GRA), Poling-Kempes Collection.

6. Pack, *We Called It Ghost Ranch*, 21.

7. Ibid., 23.

8. Ibid., 24.

9. Pack, *From This Seed*, 62.

10. Ibid., 60.

11. Ibid., 56.

12. Arthur and Brownie adopted Vernon in 1928, when he was almost three years old. The identities of Vernon's biological parents were, per his request, never revealed to him, although Vernon did know that his birth father had worked at *Nature Magazine*.

13. Parker, "Hank Weiscamp Story."

14. Pack, "Conservation."

15. Pack, "Southwestern Conservation League," 25.

16. Ethan Carr, "Park, Forest, and Wilderness," 21. The Park Service did employ master plans that designated wilderness areas, road corridors, and developed areas. But the controversy did not end in the 1930s: it intensified as conflicting definitions of wilderness continued to drive a wedge between recreational developers and low-use wilderness advocates. In 1964, the Wilderness Act finally separated wilderness—pristine lands that were left inaccessible to the public—from front land park—land made accessible to the general public.

17. Pack, quoted in "Southwestern Bookshelf," 29.

18. Pack, *Challenge of Leisure*, 81.

19. Bennett Jr., "Reminiscences from the Thirties," 1–2.

20. Bennett Sr., daily diary, September 9, 1933, Art Institute of Chicago.

21. Bennett Jr., "Reminiscences from the Thirties."

22. Pack, *From This Seed*, 84.

23. Pack, *We Called It Ghost Ranch*, 18.

24. Ibid., 18.

25. Ibid.

26. *New York Times*, "Robert Wood Johnson, 74, Dies."

27. Ibid.

28. Abstract of title, *El Rito del Yeso*, vol. 2, Board of Christian Education, PCUSA, GRA.

29. Bennett Jr. to James W. Hall, September 19, 1988, GRA.

30. Bennett Jr., "Reminiscences from the Thirties," 6.

31. Pack, *We Called It Ghost Ranch*, 59.

32. Bennett Jr., "Reminiscences from the Thirties," 4.

33. Ibid.

34. Pack, *From This Seed*, 91.

35. Preston, "Mystery of Sandia Cave," 70.

36. Pack, *We Called It Ghost Ranch*, 42.

37. Ibid.

38. Ibid., 43.

39. Frank and Brownie Hibben returned to New Mexico in 1937. Hibben was a popular and vibrant professor of archaeology at the University of New Mexico for the next three decades and, in 1961, cofounded and served as director for the university's Maxwell Museum of Anthropology. Hibben authored many books on archaeology and became an internationally known big game hunter, his exploits in the wild featured in a twenty-eight-part ABC television series, *On Safari with Frank Hibben*.

Hibben's professional career became the center of national controversy after several colleagues challenged his claims that he had found evidence in Sandia Cave, New Mexico, that proved humans had lived there twenty-five thousand years ago. Hibben was accused of faking his research at Sandia Cave and at several other sites. Although he was never publicly accused of scientific misconduct, several of Hibben's claims—including Sandia Cave—have been discredited, and archaeologists often refer to field research distortions as "hibbenisms." Through astute investments of Brownie's money, Hibben amassed a sizable fortune. Before his death, in 2002 (Brownie died in 1992), he gave $3.5 million for the construction of the Hibben Center for Archaeological Research at UNM and left the university a $10 million endowment called the Hibben Trust to support student field research.

40. Pack, *We Called It Ghost Ranch*, 44, 46.

41. Pack, quoted in Mathewson, *William L. Finley*, 16.

42. Ibid.

43. "Recipes from the Ghost Ranch," booklet, c. 1941, GRA

44. Ghost Ranch guest brochure, 1936, author's collection.

45. La Farge, "They All Ride."

46. La Farge to Arthur N. Pack, October 30, 1935, GRA.

47. Leach, "Abroad at Home," 258.

48. La Farge to Arthur N. Pack, October 30, 1935, GRA.

49. Leach, "Abroad at Home."

CHAPTER 3. Georgia O'Keeffe and Ghost Ranch

1. O'Keeffe, Quoted in Janos, "Georgia O'Keeffe," 117.

2. O'Keeffe to Rebecca Strand [James], August 24, 1929, quoted in Cowart, Hamilton, and Greenough, *Georgia O'Keeffe*, 194.

3. O'Keeffe to Russell Vernon Hunter, spring 1932, quoted in ibid., 207.

4. Ibid.

5. O'Keeffe to Rebecca Strand [James], April 26, 1934, quoted in Cowart, Hamilton, and Greenough, *Georgia O'Keeffe*, 221.

6. O'Keeffe to Dorothy Brett, October 12[?], 1930, quoted in Cowart, Hamilton, and Greenough, *Georgia O'Keeffe*, 201.

7. O'Keeffe, quoted in Tryk, "O'Keeffe," 20.

8. O'Keeffe to Alfred Stieglitz, September 20, 1937, in *Catalogue of the 14th Annual Exhibition*, 10.

9. O'Keeffe, quoted in Tomkins, "Rose in the Eye," 40.

10. O'Keeffe, quoted in Tryk, "O'Keeffe," 25.

11. Ibid., 20.

12. Ibid.

13. Dorothy Brett, quoted in Lisle, *Portrait of an Artist*, 277.

14. O'Keeffe to Stieglitz, July 29, 1937, in *Catalogue of the 14th Annual Exhibition*, 4.

15. O'Keeffe to Stieglitz, September 20, 1937, in ibid., 10.

16. O'Keeffe, quoted in Rose, "Visiting Georgia O'Keeffe," 60–61.

17. O'Keeffe, "About Myself," in *Catalogue of the 14th Annual Exhibition*.

18. Bennett Jr., "Reminiscences from the Thirties."

19. O'Keeffe, quoted in Bry, *Some Memories of Drawings*, unpaginated.

20. Ibid.

21. Pack, *We Called It Ghost Ranch*, 44. Phoebe Pack claims that the skull drawing was given as a wedding present to the Packs in 1936. In 1971, at O'Keeffe's suggestion, the skull motif she sketched for Pack, and that he used for the symbol for his Ghost Ranch, became the official insignia for the Ghost Ranch Conference Center.

22. O'Keeffe to Cady Wells, n.d., quoted in Robinson, *Georgia O'Keeffe*, 431.

23. Phoebe Pack to Isabel Ziegler, Tucson, May 1988, quoted in Ziegler and Ziegler, *Soul Is Dead That Slumbers*, 315.

24. Pack, *We Called It Ghost Ranch*, 63.

25. Ibid.

26. O'Keeffe to Stieglitz, August 26, 1937, in *Catalogue of the 14th Annual Exhibition*, 8.

27. O'Keeffe to Stieglitz, July 29, 1937, in *Catalogue of the 14th Annual Exhibition*, 3.

28. O'Keeffe to Cady Wells, n.d., quoted in Robinson, *Georgia O'Keeffe*, 431.

29. O'Keefe, quoted in Janos, "Georgia O'Keeffe," 116.

30. O'Keeffe, quoted in Seiberling, "Stark Vision."

31. Ziegler and Ziegler, *Soul Is Dead That Slumbers*, 313.

32. O'Keeffe, quoted in Taylor, "Lady Dynamo," 9.

33. O'Keeffe to Stieglitz, August 26, 1937, in *Catalogue of the 14th Annual Exhibition*, 8.

34. O'Keeffe, quoted in Wallach, "Georgia O'Keeffe."

35. O'Keeffe, quoted in Zito, "Georgia O'Keeffe," 1.

36. Wilnuet Roland-Holst to author, September 17, 1993.

37. Ibid.

38. Heard was a Cambridge-educated theologian whose monthly journal, *The Realist*, was sponsored by H. G. Wells, among others. In 1929, Heard had published a prize-winning book of essays, *The Ascent of Humanity*, and in the following four decades would write thirty-seven more books before his death in 1971. In the 1930s, Heard had his own BBC program, which discussed scientific and current affairs, and he was a widely respected lecturer on comparative religion and the evolution of consciousness.

39. O'Keeffe to Stieglitz, August 22, 1937, in *Catalogue of the 14th Annual Exhibition*, 6.

40. Ibid.

41. Heard poem quoted by O'Keeffe to Stieglitz, ibid.

42. Ansel Adams to Stieglitz, September 21, 1937, quoted in Alinder and Stillman, *Ansel Adams*, 98.

43. Ibid.

44. Wallace Stegner, foreword to Alinder and Stillman, *Ansel Adams: Letters and Images*, v.

45. O'Keeffe to Stieglitz, September 20, 1937, in *Catalogue of the 14th Annual Exhibition*, 11.

46. Adams to Stieglitz, September 21, 1937, in Alinder and Stillman, *Ansel Adams*, 98.

47. O'Keeffe to Stieglitz, September 29, 1937, in *Catalogue of the 14th Annual Exhibition*, 10–11.

48. O'Keeffe to Maria Chabot, November 1941, quoted in Cowart, Hamilton, and Greenough, *Georgia O'Keeffe*, 232.

49. O'Keeffe to Ettie Stettheimer, August 15, 1940, quoted in ibid., 230–31.

50. O'Keeffe to Chabot, December 9, 1944, Maria Chabot Archive, GOKMRC.

51. O'Keeffe to Chabot, May 13, 1947, Maria Chabot Archive, GOKMRC.

52. Stieglitz to O'Keeffe, June 3, 1946, quoted in Pollitzer, *Woman on Paper*, 249.

53. O'Keeffe, quoted in Seldis, "Georgia O'Keeffe at 78," 14.

CHAPTER 4. War Nearby and Faraway

1. Oppenheimer, quoted in Lamont, *Day of Trinity*, 226.

2. Pack, *We Called It Ghost Ranch*, 91.

3. Packs' Christmas letter, Ghost Ranch, 1939, GRA.

4. Ibid., 1940.

5. Pack, *We Called It Ghost Ranch*, 77.

6. Ibid.

7. Ibid., 78.

8. Chabot to O'Keeffe, December 10, 1941, Maria Chabot Archive, GOKMRC.

9. O'Keeffe to Chabot, April 8, 1943, Maria Chabot Archive, GOKMRC.

10. Chabot to O'Keeffe, April 20, 1943, Maria Chabot Archive, GOKMRC.

11. O'Keeffe in Janos, "Georgia O'Keeffe," 114–17.

12. Chabot to O'Keeffe, October 15, 1944, Maria Chabot Archive, GOKMRC.

13. Ibid., March 13, 1948, Maria Chabot Archive, GOKMRC.

14. Ibid., November 15, 1943, Maria Chabot Archive, GOKMRC.

15. Pack, *We Called It Ghost Ranch*, 80.

16. Oppenheimer, quoted in Lamont, *Day of Trinity*, 46.

17. Pack, *We Called It Ghost Ranch*, 79.

18. Lamont, *Day of Trinity*, 241.

19. Pack, *We Called It Ghost Ranch*, 82.

20. Ibid.

21. Phoebe Pack to Sam Ziegler, Tucson, February 1988, quoted in Ziegler and Ziegler, *Soul Is Dead That Slumbers*, 160.

22. O'Keeffe, quoted in Seiberling, "A Flowering," 50–53.

CHAPTER 5. Bones of Serendipity

The author thanks Edwin and Margaret Colbert, Alex Downs, Dave Gillette, Adrian Hunt, Bob Hunt, and Sam Welles for their patient and informative assistance.

1. Colbert, *Digging into the Past*, 430.

2. Colbert, *Little Dinosaurs of Ghost Ranch*, 10.

3. Ibid., 14.

4. *Oxford English Dictionary*, quoted in ibid., 21.

5. Colbert, *Little Dinosaurs of Ghost Ranch*, 91.

6. All details of the 1933 Canjilon Quarry campsite are from Camp, "Field Notes."

7. Camp, ibid., June 22, 1933.

8. Camp, ibid., July 22, 1933.

9. Welles, "Canjilon Quarry Field Notebook," August 4, 1934.

10. Welles, ibid., June 22, 1934.

11. Pack, *We Called It Ghost Ranch*, 92.

12. Ibid.

13. Colbert, *Digging into the Past*, 285.
14. Colbert, "Little Dinosaurs of Ghost Ranch," 392.
15. Ibid., 393.
16. Ibid., 394.
17. Colbert, *Little Dinosaurs of Ghost Ranch*, 20.
18. Ibid., 24–25.
19. Colbert, "Arthur and Phoebe Pack," 13.
20. Colbert, *Little Dinosaurs of Ghost Ranch*, 51.
21. Pack, *We Called It Ghost Ranch*, 93.
22. LeViness, "Digging for Dinosaurs," 45.
23. Colbert, "Arthur and Phoebe Pack," 13.
24. Colbert, "Little Dinosaurs of Ghost Ranch," 396.
25. Colbert, *Little Dinosaurs of Ghost Ranch*, 214.
26. Ibid., 220. Colbert's wife, Margaret Mathew Colbert, the daughter of William Diller Mathew, became one of the world's leading restoration artists. Her paintbrush and ink served as the "eyes of paleontologists" through her paintings, drawings, and murals of the dinosaurs and their ancient world reproduced in books, in museums, and on film. Margaret Colbert gave form and color to dinosaurs like *Coelophysis* in her restoration work. Margaret Colbert and several other artists were acknowledged by *Jurassic Park* author Michael Crichton for their inspiring and scientifically accurate renderings of the ancient reptiles and dinosaurs. Her murals are at the Petrified Forest National Park, the Rainbow Forest Museum, Big Bend National Park, and the New Mexico Museum of Natural History.

CHAPTER 6. A Theology of Place

1. Pack, *We Called It Ghost Ranch*, 136.
2. Payne, "Ghost Ranch."
3. O'Keeffe to Jim Hall; Jim Hall to author, author's collection, GRA.
4. The house was almost renamed *Casa del Gloria* (House of the Glory) after local workers told Payne that this piece of the desert between the two chimneys was known locally as *La Puerta del Gloria* (Door of the Glory), through which the souls of the blessed passed on their way to heaven.
5. Payne, quoted in Jameson, "Ghost Ranch," 15–16.
6. Harris, "Man Does Well."
7. James W. Hall, "Where It Is with Ghost Ranch."
8. Driscoll's will stipulated that should her two sons not choose to keep her home in Santa Fe, the proceeds from the sale of the property were to be placed in a trust for unrestricted use by Ghost Ranch. In 1982 the sale of the Driscoll home gave the ranch a trust worth more than $2 million.

9. Ralph J. Hall, *Main Trail*, 28.

10. Grant Sutherland King, "Missionary to the Cowboys."

11. Ralph J. Hall, *Main Trail*, 189.

12. Hessel, "Jim Hall," 4.

13. Colbert, *Little Dinosaurs of Ghost Ranch*, dedication page.

14. Ellis, "Ghost Ranch Archaeologists," 2.

15. Ellis pioneered the technique that used statistical analysis and tree-ring dating at archaeology sites—she studied with and assisted A. E. Douglas, "father" of dendrochronology—that helped to transform archaeology from a "soft" social science into a "hard" science. Ellis did not simply study the Native Americans of the Southwest, but became close friends with the Pueblo people, who were her subjects. Beginning in the 1950s, she tirelessly lent her expertise to help various New Mexican Pueblos establish land and water claims, and she often served as a rebuttal witness. In the realm of Spanish New Mexican history, Ellis received international recognition when she discovered the site of San Gabriel del Yungue, the first capital of Spanish New Mexico, at the confluence of the Chama and Rio Grande rivers, in 1962. She was a prodigious writer and published over three hundred scholarly articles and authored many books.

16. Wermuth, "Jim Hall," *Ghost Ranch Journal* 2, no. 1 (Winter 1987).

17. James W. Hall, "Where It Is with Ghost Ranch."

18. Atencio, "Ghost Ranch."

19. Ibid., "Letter to Jim Hall."

20. James W. Hall to Joshua Keesecker, May 8, 1988, author's collection.

21. Ibid.

22. Hall received the Peter Van Dresser Award from the New Mexico Solar Energy Association in 1986 for "exemplary contribution to the field of solar energy and related arts, sciences and technologies, local and community self-reliance and sustainable growth and development."

23. Atencio, "Letter to Jim Hall."

24. The Ghost Ranch Museum eventually became the Forest Service and the Soil Conservation Service's regional teaching headquarters. After it opened in 1959, the Ghost Ranch Museum (later renamed the Ghost Ranch Living Museum) counted more than one thousand visitors a day on summer weekends.

25. James W. Hall, "Great Land Trade," 16–17.

26. Ibid.

27. John C. Purdy, quoted by Jim Hall in *Ghost Ranch Journal* 1, no. 1 (Winter 1986).

28. James W. Hall, "Where It Is with Ghost Ranch."

29. Ibid., quoted in Tryk, "Ghost Ranch."

30. James W. Hall, "Memories of Georgia O'Keeffe."
31. Copyright Georgia O'Keeffe, in "Ghost Ranch: The First 25 Years," GRA.
32. James W. Hall, "Memories of Georgia O'Keeffe."
33. Ibid.

Afterword

1. James W. Hall, 1980, quoted in "Service of Celebration" (memorial service program), November 26, 1988.

Selected Bibliography

Abbreviations

GOKMRC	Georgia O'Keeffe Museum Research Center
GRA	Ghost Ranch Archives
LAHM/PPC	Los Alamos Historical Museum/Peggy Pond Church Collection
MNM	Museum of New Mexico History Library
NMSRA	New Mexico State Records and Archives
PCUSA	Presbyterian Church (USA)

Archival Sources

Arizona Historical Society, Tucson: Arthur Newton Pack Collection.

Art Institute of Chicago: Edward H. Bennett Sr. Collection. Ryerson and Burnham Libraries, reels 10 and 11, series 3: boxes 31, 34, 35, 38.

Georgia O'Keeffe Museum Research Center. Maria Chabot Archive. Georgia O'Keeffe clipping file.

Ghost Ranch Archives: Collections and papers of Edward H. Bennett Jr.; James Wallace Hall; Arthur and Phoebe Pack; Lesley Poling-Kempes; Presbyterian Church (USA) and Ghost Ranch Conference Center, deeds and abstract of title, Ghost Ranch; files pertaining to development of conference center; *Ghost Ranch Journal*; "Ghost Ranch: The First 25 Years"; Twenty-fifth anniversary booklet.

Ghost Ranch Library: Special Collection, Southwest Room. Maps, periodicals, and pamphlets about Ghost Ranch, including *Nature Magazine*.

Los Alamos Historical Museum: Peggy Pond Church Collection. Files and papers pertaining to Natalie Curtis Burlin, Roy Chapin, Jack Lambert, Roy and Carol Pfaffle, and Ramon Vigil Ranch.

Museum of New Mexico: Jack Lambert files, including Richard L. Pfaffle, "The Call of the Southwest" (Santa Fe: Santa Fe New Mexican Publishing Corp., n.d.).

New Mexico State Records and Archives. Papers of Francis Wilson, Esq. Santa Fe.

Published and Unpublished Sources

Adams, Ansel. *An Autobiography*. Boston: Little, Brown, 1985.

Alinder, Mary Street. *Ansel Adams: An Autobiography*. Boston: Little, Brown, 1985.

Alinder, Mary Street, and Andrea Gray Stillman, eds. *Ansel Adams: Letters and Images, 1916–1984*. Boston: Little, Brown, 1985.

Atencio, Tomás. "Ghost Ranch: An Illusion or a Reality?" in "Ghost Ranch: The First 25 Years" (May 8, 1980). GRA.

———. "Letter to Jim Hall," August 31, 1990. *Ghost Ranch Journal* 5, no. 3 (Fall 1990); and *Ghost Ranch Journal* 6, no. 1 (Winter 1991).

Babcock, Barbara A., and Nancy J. Parezo. *Daughters of the Desert: Women Anthropologists and the Native American Southwest, 1880–1980*. Albuquerque: University of New Mexico Press, 1988.

Bachelard, Gaston. *The Poetics of Space*. Boston: Beacon Press, translation 1969.

Bennett, Edward H., Jr. "Reminiscences from the Thirties." Unpublished memoir, author's collection; also held in GRA collection.

Borne, Lawrence R. *Dude Ranching: A Complete History*. Albuquerque: University of New Mexico Press, 1983.

Bry, Doris, ed. *Some Memories of Drawings*. Albuquerque: University of New Mexico Press, 1974.

Burlin, Natalie Curtis. Papers and correspondence. Personal collection of Alfred Bredenberg. See also nataliecurtisburlin.org.

Butala, Sharon. *The Perfection of the Morning*. Toronto: HarperCollins, 1994.

Camp, C. L. "Field Notes, C. L. Camp, Berkeley to Canjilon and Tucumcari, New Mexico, 1933." Collection of University of California, Berkeley.

Carr, Ethan. "Park, Forest, and Wilderness." *George Wright Forum*, 17, no. 2 (2000).

Carr, William H. *Pebbles in Your Shoes*. Tucson: Arizona-Sonora Desert Museum, 1982.

Catalogue of the 14th Annual Exhibition of Paintings. New York: An American Place, December 27–February 11, 1938.

Chauvenet, Beatrice. *Hewett and Friends: A Biography of Santa Fe's Vibrant Era*. Santa Fe: Museum of New Mexico Press, 1983.

Colbert, Edwin H. "Arthur and Phoebe Pack and the Dinosaurs of Ghost Ranch." *Ghost Ranch Journal* 2, no. 2 (Spring 1987): 13.

———. *Digging into the Past*. New York: Dembner Books, 1989.

———. "Little Dinosaurs of Ghost Ranch." *Natural History*, November 1947.

———. *The Little Dinosaurs of Ghost Ranch*. New York: Columbia University Press, 1995.

———. *Men and Dinosaurs*. New York: E. P. Dutton, 1968.

———. *The Triassic Dinosaur Coelophysis*. Bulletin Series 57. Flagstaff: Museum of Northern Arizona, 1984.

Comfort, Mary Apolline. *Rainbow to Yesterday: The John and Louisa Wetherill Story*. New York: Vantage Press, 1980.

Cowart, Jack, Juan Hamilton, and Sarah Greenough. *Georgia O'Keeffe: Art and Letters*. Washington, D.C.: National Gallery of Art, 1987.

Cox, Orville. Papers, including "Dude Ranches: New Mexico and Arizona," c. 1925. Personal collection of Martha Cox Boyle.

Ellis, Florence H. "Ghost Ranch Archaeologists—Digging and Delving." *Ghost Ranch Journal* 1, no. 3 (Fall 1986): 2.

Eyle, Alexandra. *Charles Lathrop Pack: Timberman, Forest Conservationist and Pioneer in Forest Education*. Syracuse: SUNY, 1992.

Foster, Lawrence G. *Robert Wood Johnson: The Gentleman Rebel*. State College, Pa.: Lillian Press, 1999.

Gibson, Arrell Morgan. *The Santa Fe and Taos Colonies*. Norman: University of Oklahoma Press, 1983.

Gillmor, Frances, and Louisa Wade Wetherill. *Traders to the Navajos: The Story of the Wetherills of Kayenta*. Albuquerque: University of New Mexico Press, 1952.

Grand Canyon MacLeans. Issue 3 (July 1996). Champaign, Ill.: Leonard and Millan, 1996.

Hall, James W. "The Great Land Trade—Ten Years After," *Ghost Ranch Journal* 1, no. 1 (Winter 1986): 16–17.

———. "Memories of Georgia O'Keeffe." *Ghost Ranch Journal* 1, no. 2 (Spring 1986).

———. "Where It Is with Ghost Ranch: Remarks by the Director." June 1972. GRA.

Hall, Ralph J. *The Main Trail*. Abiquiú, N.Mex.: Ghost Ranch Conference Center, n.d.

Harrington, John Peabody. *The Ethnogeography of the Tewa Indians*. 29th Annual Report of the Bureau of American Ethnology. Washington, D.C.: GPO, 1916.

Harris, Will T. "Man Does Well to Take a Low Profile." *Ghost Ranch, 1955–1975: Those Early Years*. GRA.

Hessel, Dieter T. "Jim Hall—Artisan of Ghost Ranch." *Ghost Ranch Journal* 2, no. 1 (Winter 1987): 4.

Hibben, Frank C. *Indian Hunts and Indian Hunters of the Old West*. Long Beach, Calif: Safari Press, 1989.

Jameson, Vic. "Ghost Ranch." *Presbyterian Life*, March 2, 1957.

Janos, Leo. "Georgia O'Keeffe at Eighty-Four." *Atlantic Monthly*, December 1971.

Jaramillo, Cleofas. *Shadows of the Past*. Santa Fe: Ancient City Press, 1972.

King, Grant Sutherland. "Missionary to the Cowboys." *Christian Herald*, August 1948.

King, Mary Scott. "Jack Lambert: The Last of His Kind." *Santa Fe New Mexican*, February 17, 1974, 5.

Kittredge, William. *Who Owns the West?* San Francisco: Mercury House, 1996.

La Farge, Oliver. "They All Ride." *Vogue Magazine*, May 1, 1936.

Lamont, Lansing. *Day of Trinity*. New York: Atheneum, 1965.

Leach, Henry Goddard. "Abroad at Home." *Forum and Century*, November 1935.

LeViness, W. Thetford. "Digging for Dinosaurs 175 Million Years Old." *New Mexico Magazine*, January 1948, 45.

Lewis, Edith. *Willa Cather Living: A Personal Record*. Lincoln: University of Nebraska Press / Bison Books, 2000.

Lisle, Laurie. *Portrait of an Artist: A Biography of Georgia O'Keeffe*. 1980. Reprint, New York: Washington Square Press, 1986.

Love, Marian F. "A Cowboy Recollects." *Santa Fean*, December 1981.

Luhan, Mabel Dodge. *Edge of Taos Desert: An Escape to Reality*. 1937. Reprint, Albuquerque: University of New Mexico Press, 1987.

Margoliek, David. *Undue Influence: Epic Battle for the Johnson and Johnson Fortune*. New York: William Morrow, 1993.

Mathewson, Worth. *William L. Finley: Pioneer Wildlife Photographer*. Corvallis: Oregon State University, 1986.

New York Times, "Robert Wood Johnson, 74, Dies, Chairman of Johnson & Johnson," January 31, 1968.

O'Brien, Sharon. *Willa Cather: The Emerging Voice*. New York: Oxford University Press 1987.

O'Keeffe, Georgia. *Georgia O'Keeffe*. New York: Viking Press, 1976.

Pack, Arthur Newton. *The Challenge of Leisure*. New York: Macmillan, 1934.

———. "Conservation." Editor's Column. *Nature Magazine*, March 1936.

———. *From This Seed*. Unpublished autobiography. GRA.

———. "Southwestern Bookshelf." *New Mexico Magazine*, January 1935.

———. "The Southwestern Conservation League." *New Mexico Magazine*, October 1934.

———. *We Called It Ghost Ranch*. Abiquiú, N.Mex.: Ghost Ranch Conference Center, 1979.

Parker, Earl. "The Hank Weiscamp Story." In "End of an Era: Hank Wiescamp Estate Dispersal," *NFQHA Foundation Quarter Horse Journal*, July 1998.

Payne, Paul Calvin. "Ghost Ranch and the Board of Christian Education." *Ghost Ranch, 1955–1975: Those Early Years*. GRA.

Pfaffle, Richard L. "The Call of the Southwest." Santa Fe: Santa Fe New Mexican Publishing Corp., n.d. MNM.

Pollitzer, Anita. *Woman on Paper*. New York: Simon and Schuster, 1988.

Preston, Douglas. "The Mystery of Sandia Cave." *New Yorker*, June 12, 1995.

Rinehart, Mary Roberts. *My Story*. New York: Farrar and Rinehart, 1931.

Robertson, Edna, and Sarah Nestor. *Artists of the Canyons and Caminos*. Santa Fe: Ancient City Press, 1976.

Robinson, Roxana. *Georgia O'Keeffe: A Life*. New York: Harper and Row, 1989.

Rose, Barbara. "Visiting Georgia O'Keeffe." *New York Magazine*, November 9, 1970, 60–61.

Rothman, Hal K. *On Rims and Ridges: The Los Alamos Area Since 1880*. Lincoln: University of Nebraska Press, 1997.

Rudnick, Lois Palken. *Intimate Memories: The Autobiography of Mabel Dodge Luhan*. Albuquerque: University of New Mexico Press, 1999.

Seals, Elizabeth Bartlett. "Joy Filled Reflections of the Ghost Ranch." GRA.

Seiberling, Dorothy. "A Flowering in the Stieglitz Years." *Life*, March 1, 1968, 50–53.

———. "Stark Vision of a Pioneer Painter." *Life*, March 1, 1968, 40–53.

Seldis, Henry. "Georgia O'Keeffe at 78." *Los Angeles Times "West" Magazine*, January 22, 1967.

Sibley, George. *High Country News*, March 18, 2002.

Stanley, Carol Bishop. New England Conservatory of Music: Alumni records.

Stegner, Wallace. *Where the Bluebird Sings to the Lemonade Springs*. New York: Random House, 1992.

Taylor, Carol. "Lady Dynamo—Miss O'Keeffe, Noted Artist, Is a Feminist." *New York World Telegram*, March 31, 1945.

Ternes, Alan, ed. *Ants, Indians, and Little Dinosaurs*. New York: Charles Scribner's Sons, 1975.

Tobias, Henry J., and Charles E. Woodhouse. *Santa Fe: A Modern History, 1880–1990*. Albuquerque: University of New Mexico Press, 2001.

Tomkins, Calvin. "The Rose in the Eye Looked Pretty Fine." *New Yorker*, March 4, 1974.

Tryk, Sheila. "Ghost Ranch: It's Not Your Average Parish." *Santa Fe New Mexican*, May 14, 1972.

———. "O'Keeffe." *New Mexico Magazine*, January/February 1973.

———. Twenty-fifth anniversary booklet. GRA.

Wallach, Amei. "Georgia O'Keeffe." *Newsday*, October 30, 1977.

———. "Under a Western Sky." *Horizon* 20 (December 1977): 26.

Weigle, Marta, and Kyle Fiore. *Santa Fe and Taos: The Writer's Era*. Santa Fe: Ancient City Press, 1982.

Welles, Samuel. "Canjilon Quarry Field Notebook," 1934. Author's collection.

Wermuth, Lora Morgan. "Jim Hall." *Ghost Ranch Journal* 2, no. 1 (Winter 1987).

Wheelwright, Mary Cabot. Papers, including "Journey towards Understanding," unpublished autobiography, 1957. Wheelwright Museum of the American Indian.

Whitaker, George, and Joan Meyers. *Dinosaur Hunt*. New York: Harcourt, Brace and World, 1965.

Ziegler, Samuel R., and Isabel H. Ziegler. *For the Soul Is Dead That Slumbers: A Memoir*. Private publication, © Norman P. Ziegler. GRA.

Zito, Tom. "Georgia O'Keeffe." *Washington Post*, November 9, 1977.

Illustration Credits

Amon Carter Museum

A Plymouth advertisement shot at Ghost Ranch. Photograph by Laura Gilpin. © 1979 Amon Carter Museum, Fort Worth, Texas, Bequest of the artist.

Lance Reventlow. Photograph by Laura Gilpin. © 1979 Amon Carter Museum, Fort Worth, Texas, Bequest of the artist.

Ansel Adams Publishing Rights Trust

Georgia O'Keeffe and bones found on the desert. Photograph by Ansel Adams. Collection Center for Creative Photography, University of Arizona. © Trustees of The Ansel Adams Publishing Rights Trust. All Rights Reserved.

The Ghost Ranch ox skull and sign. Photograph by Ansel Adams. Collection Center for Creative Photography, University of Arizona. © Trustees of The Ansel Adams Publishing Rights Trust. All Rights Reserved.

Orville Cox and Georgia O'Keeffe. Photograph by Ansel Adams. Collection Center for Creative Photography, University of Arizona. © Trustees of The Ansel Adams Publishing Rights Trust. All Rights Reserved.

O'Keeffe painting *Gerald's Tree*. Photograph by Ansel Adams. Collection Center for Creative Photography, University of Arizona. © Trustees of The Ansel Adams Publishing Rights Trust. All Rights Reserved.

Janet Biddle

Tim Pfeiffer and Georgia O'Keeffe. Collection of Janet Biddle, Ghost Ranch Archives.

Kent Bowser

The restored Ghost House interior. © Kent Bowser, 2004.

Orphan Mesa and the badlands. © Kent Bowser, 2004.

The red Triassic badlands at Ghost Ranch. © Kent Bowser, 2004.
A cattle roundup in 2004. © Kent Bowser, 2004.
A cabin on the *City Slickers* movie set.© Kent Bowser, 2004.

Margaret Colbert

Edwin H. Colbert and crew. Edwin H. Colbert Collection, Ghost Ranch Archives.
Georgia O'Keeffe and nuns visiting the fossil quarry. Edwin H. Colbert Collection, Ghost Ranch Archives.
Ghost Ranch foreman Herman Hall removing blocks of fossils. Edwin H. Colbert Collection, Ghost Ranch Archives.
Plastering *Coelophysis* bones at the quarry. Edwin H. Colbert Collection, Ghost Ranch Archives.

Ghost Ranch Archives

Ghost Ranch cliffs. Bennett Collection.
Orville Cox's touring car in the Rio Grande. Martha Cox Boyle Collection.
Construction foreman Ted Peabody. Bennett Collection.
Ghost Ranch headquarters. Pack Collection
Interior of a Ghost Ranch guest cottage. Photograph by T. Harmon Parkhurst, Pack Collection.
Ghost Ranch foreman Lloyd Miller. Betty Bartlett Seals Collection.
Head wrangler Jack McKinley. Bennett Collection.
Arthur N. Pack with a baby antelope. McKinley/Pack Collection.
A touring car in Monument Valley. Pack Collection.
The newly completed Rancho de los Burros. McKinley/Pack Collection.
Eleanor "Brownie" Pack photographing antelope. McKinley/Pack Collection.
Norrie, Vernon, and Peggy Pack on burros. McKinley/Pack Collection.
Frank Hibben tutoring Norrie and Vernon Pack. McKinley/Pack Collection.
Edward H. Bennett Sr. Bennett Collection.
The Edward H. Bennett House. Bennett Collection.
Seward and Robert Wood Johnson's house. Photograph by T. Harmon Parkhurst, Pack Collection.
Maggie Johnson and her daughter Sheila. Photograph by T. Harmon Parkhurst, Pack Collection.
The dining room at the Ghost Ranch headquarters. Photograph by T. Harmon Parkhurst, Pack Collection.
Mary Duncan feeding baby antelope. McKinley/Pack Collection.
Ghost House and the ranch garden. Pack Collection.

Phoebe Pack. Photograph by T. Harmon Parkhurst, Pack Collection.
Garden House at Ghost Ranch. Photograph by T. Harmon Parkhurst, Pack Collection.
David McAlpin and William Thurber leaving for a pack trip. Pack Collection.
Arthur and Phoebe Pack with Charlie and Pipper. Pack Collection.
Dale Brubaker and George Carson. Collection of Dale Brubaker.
Cowboy preacher Ralph Hall. Photographer unidentified.
A Ranchman's Cowboy Camp Meeting. Photograph by Bill Muldrow.
Jim Hall and Hobbs volunteers completing the Padre Jim bridge.
The La Raza "march" on Ghost Ranch.
Moving the *Coelophysis* block. Photograph by Lawrence P. Byers.
The Great Land Trade.
Jim Hall on his horse Leather Britches. Photograph by Grantland Groves.
A brochure cover with the O'Keeffe skull drawing. Pack Collection.

James W. Hall

Jim Hall. Collection of the Hall Family, Ghost Ranch Archives.

Jon Hall

On the movie set of *And Now Miguel*. Photograph by Jon Hall, Ghost Ranch Archives.
The chapel built for *And Now Miguel*. Photograph by Jon Hall, Ghost Ranch Archives.

Fred Lyon

Georgia O'Keeffe with Rosie and Louisa Trujillo. Photograph © Fred Lyon.
Cary Grant and his wife, Betsy Drake. Photograph © Fred Lyon.

David Manzanares

A production scene from *The Missing*. Photograph: www.shootnewmexico.com.
A production scene from *Wyatt Earp*. Photograph: www.shootnewmexico.com.

Henry P. McKinley and Margaret P. McKinley

Carol Stanley at a desert campsite. McKinley/Pack Collection, Ghost Ranch Archives.

Rancho de los Burros under construction. McKinley/Pack Collection, Ghost Ranch Archives.

A view of Chimney Rock. McKinley/Pack Collection, Ghost Ranch Archives.

New England Conservatory of Music

Carol Bishop Stanley and *The Neume* staff.

Lesley Poling-Kempes

Ruth Hall showing children dinosaur fossil sites.

University of California Museum of Paleontology

Dr. Charles Camp at the Canjilon Quarry.

Index

Note: Page numbers in italics refer to illustrations.

About the Author

Lesley Poling-Kempes has lived in Abiquiu, New Mexico, and has been affiliated with Ghost Ranch since the 1970s. Poling-Kempes is the author of *The Harvey Girls: Women Who Opened the West* and *Valley of Shining Stone: The Story of Abiquiu* and co-author of *Georgia O'Keeffe and New Mexico: A Sense of Place.* Her first novel, *Canyon of Remembering*, was a Spur Award finalist. She has completed a second novel, *The Bone Horses*.

Ghost Ranch

Lesley Poling-Kempes

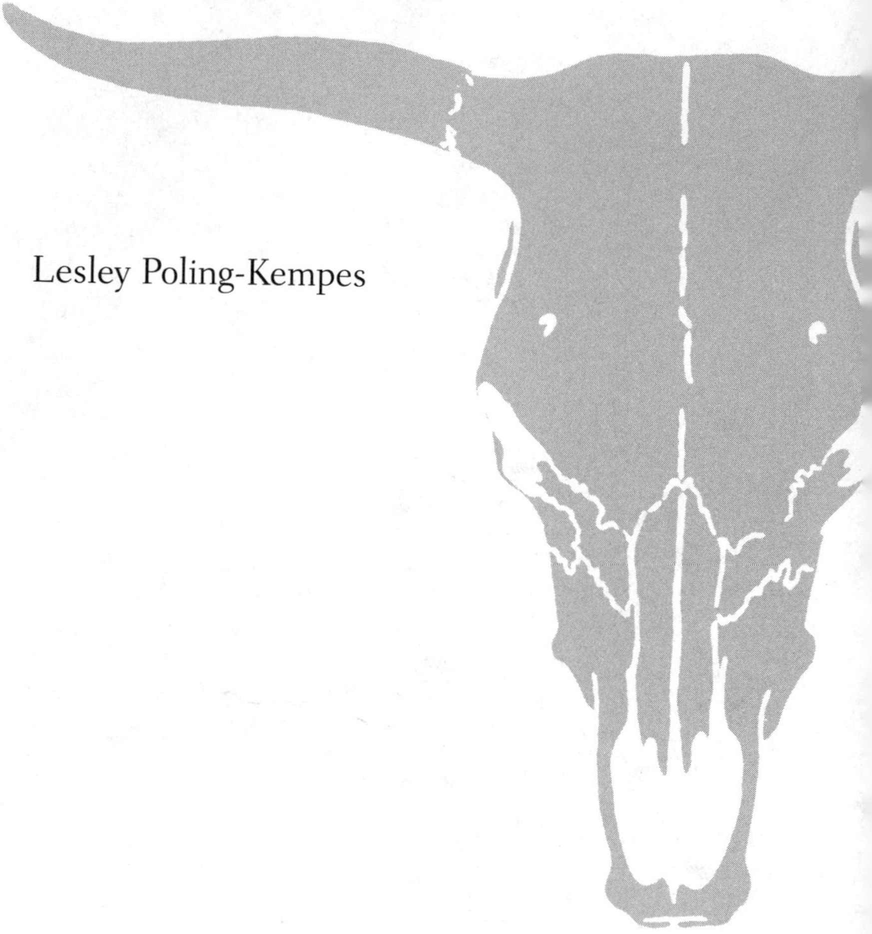